"Multilateral co-operation is in peril, yet as the Covid-19 emergency has demonstrated it is needed more than ever. This book, drawing on the expertise and perspectives of scholars from many different countries and cultures, notably from China, East-Asia, Europe and the Americas, explores the current threat to multilateral institutions from the rise of nationalism and the re-emergence of great power politics, and sets out the practical reforms and changes in discourse which are needed to renew the multilateral ideal. It makes a valuable contribution to a crucial debate."

Andrew Gamble, *University of Sheffield and University of Cambridge, UK*

"Multilateralism is under threat: this timely and balanced volume considers how obstacles to its renewal can be overcome, and new regimes of collaboration born to reflect fast-changing international realities."

Louise Fawcett, *University of Oxford, UK*

TOWARDS A NEW MULTILATERALISM

This edited book focuses on the dynamic balance between global cultural diversity and multilateral convergence in relevant policy areas that involve actual and potential policy convergences (and divergences): the environment, trade, peace and security, and human rights.

It offers theoretical reflections about the impact of the concept of multiple modernities on new ideas, cultural backgrounds, and/or national or regional particularities. An interdisciplinary team of authors combines comparative policy analysis with theoretical dialogue about the conceptual, institutional, normative, and political dimensions of a new kind of multilateral cooperation. Finally, the book concludes that by stimulating an intercultural dialogue which goes beyond a mere "rational choice" approach, we can foster progress through a better understanding of the opportunities and limitations offered by a pluralist, varied, post-hegemonic, and multilayered form of multilateral cooperation.

This book will be of key interest to scholars and students of European/EU studies, economics, human rights, climate change, history, cultural studies, international relations, international political economy, security studies, and international law.

Thomas Meyer is Professor Emeritus of Political Science at the Technical University of Dortmund, Germany, and Editor in Chief of the monthly political magazine *Neue Gesellschaft/Frankfurter Hefte*.

José Luís de Sales Marques is President of the Institute of European Studies of Macau (IEEM), Macau.

Mario Telò is Jean Monnet Chair of International Relations at the Université Libre de Bruxelles, Belgium, and Rome's LUISS, and a member of the Royal Academy of Sciences, Brussels.

This edited volume on *Towards a New Multilateralism: Cultural Divergence and Political Convergence?* is the fourth publication in an ongoing joint research and dialogue project spearheaded by the Institute of European Studies of Macau.

Published within the Routledge Globalisation, Europe, and Multilateralism series, each entry associated with the project brings together outstanding international scholars seeking to explore the new forms of multilateral cooperation that have emerged or may emerge in response to the multiple modernities that have taken shape across the world, be it in Europe, Asia, Africa, or the Americas.

Previous entries in this ongoing project include:

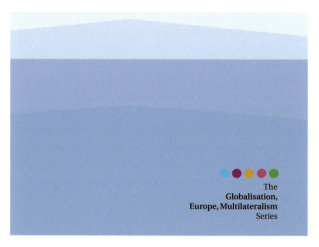

Meyer, Thomas, José Luis de Sales Marques, (eds.)
Multiple Modernities and Good Governance. Routledge, 2018.

With contributions by Acharya, Al-Nasser, Castells, Hall, Kaul, Kocka, Meyer, Nida-Rümelin, Ngo, Sales Marques, Snyder, Tao, and Telò.

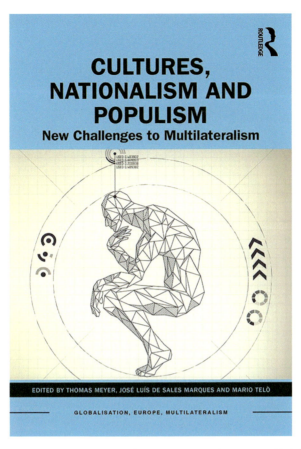

Meyer, Thomas, and José Luis de Sales Marques, and Mario Telò (eds.) *Cultures, Nationalism and Populism: New Challenges to Multilateralism.* Routledge, 2019.

With contributions by Cerutti, Chung, Flôres, Gamble, Hinchman, Latif, Meyer, Qin, Sales Marques, Song, Telò.

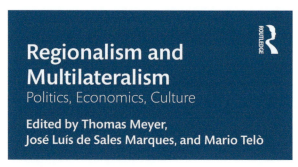

de Sales Marques, José Luís, Thomas Meyer, and Mario Telò, (eds.) *Regionalism and Multilateralism: Politics, Economics, Culture*. Routledge, 2020.

With contributions by Ummu Salma Bava, Antonio de Aguiar Patriota, Louise Fawcett, Evi Fitriani, Andrew Gamble, Moonsung Kang, Peter J. Katzenstein, Alexander Libman, Thomas Meyer, Qin Yaqing, Weiqing Song, Mario Telò, and Jianwei Wang.

TOWARDS A NEW MULTILATERALISM

Cultural Divergence and Political Convergence?

Edited by Thomas Meyer, José Luís de Sales Marques, and Mario Telò

First published 2021
by Routledge
2 Park Square, Milton Park, Abingdon, Oxon OX14 4RN

and by Routledge
52 Vanderbilt Avenue, New York, NY 10017

Routledge is an imprint of the Taylor & Francis Group, an informa business

© 2021 selection and editorial matter, Thomas Meyer, José Luís de Sales Marques, and Mario Telò; individual chapters, the contributors

The right of Thomas Meyer, José Luís de Sales Marques, and Mario Telò to be identified as the authors of the editorial material, and of the authors for their individual chapters, has been asserted in accordance with sections 77 and 78 of the Copyright, Designs and Patents Act 1988.

All rights reserved. No part of this book may be reprinted or reproduced or utilised in any form or by any electronic, mechanical, or other means, now known or hereafter invented, including photocopying and recording, or in any information storage or retrieval system, without permission in writing from the publishers.

Trademark notice: Product or corporate names may be trademarks or registered trademarks, and are used only for identification and explanation without intent to infringe.

British Library Cataloguing-in-Publication Data
A catalogue record for this book is available from the British Library

Library of Congress Cataloging-in-Publication Data
Names: Meyer, Thomas, 1943– editor. | Sales Marques, Jose Luis de, editor. | Telò, Mario, editor.
Title: Towards a new multilateralism : cultural divergence and political convergence? / edited by Thomas Meyer, José Luís de Sales Marques, and Mario Telò.
Description: Abingdon, Oxon ; New York, NY : Routledge, 2020. | Includes bibliographical references and index.
Identifiers: LCCN 2020045716 (print) | LCCN 2020045717 (ebook) | ISBN 9780367632946 (hardback) | ISBN 9780367632915 (paperback) | ISBN 9781003118671 (ebook)
Subjects: LCSH: International cooperation. | International relations and culture.
Classification: LCC JZ1318 .T696 2020 (print) | LCC JZ1318 (ebook) | DDC 303.48/2—dc23
LC record available at https://lccn.loc.gov/2020045716
LC ebook record available at https://lccn.loc.gov/2020045717

ISBN: 978-0-367-63294-6 (hbk)
ISBN: 978-0-367-63291-5 (pbk)
ISBN: 978-1-003-11867-1 (ebk)

Typeset in Bembo
by Apex CoVantage, LLC

CONTENTS

List of illustrations *xii*
List of contributors *xiv*
Acknowledgments *xx*
Foreword *xxii*

Introduction 1
Thomas Meyer and Mario Telò

PART I
Environmental policy, climate change, and ecological civilization **15**

1 Meeting Sustainable Development Goals through a paradigm shift in the newly emerging world pattern 17
   Pan Jiahua and Yang Xinran

2 China's global ecological civilization and multilateral environmental governance 32
   Coraline Goron

3 Chinese power sector regulation: key lessons for developing nations 56
   Deborah Seligsohn

PART II
Trade wars, economic cooperation, and social justice 69

4 The crisis of international trade and its cultural and political implications: is the EU's approach contributing to a renewal of multilateralism? 71
   Mario Telò

5 EU–China economic and trade relations in the hard times of the world economy 95
   Ding Chun and Zhang Xiaotong

6 Towards a comprehensive approach to trade and social justice 107
   Renato G. Flôres Jr.

PART III
Which global governance and multilateral peacekeeping? 117

7 Multilateralism in crisis: a European perspective 119
   Michael Zürn

8 Human security, climate change, and migration: a European perspective 132
   Nuno Severiano Teixeira, Joana Castro Pereira, and Susana Ferreira

PART IV
Universalism versus relativism in protecting human rights 151

9 Multiple modernities and universal human rights 153
   Thomas Meyer

10 Human rights and a "garden" of human community in the post-globalization era 170
    Eun-Jeung Lee

11 The crisis of multilateralism and the future of human rights 183
    André W. M. Gerrits

PART V
Towards a new multilateralism: deepening the conceptual dimension   197

12 Multilateralism via inter-practicality: institutions and relations   199
    Qin Yaqing

Index   *217*

ILLUSTRATIONS

Figures

1.1	A new world pattern emerging	18
1.2	Population estimates in selected countries (1950–2100)	20
1.3	Primary energy consumption in selected countries (1965–2018)	22
1.4	CO_2 emissions per capita in selected countries (1971–2017)	23
1.5	A comparison of essentials between industrial and ecological civilizations	27
2.1	The institutionalization of the concept of sustainable development	36
2.2	Chinese academic (2000–19) and newspaper (2007–19) references to the concepts of "ecological civilization" (EC) and "community of common destiny" (CCD)	40
2.3	Logo of the Kunming CBD COP15, with the COP's theme "Ecological Civilization – Building a Shared Future for All Life on Earth"	50
3.1	The self-enforcement payment feedback system	63
5.1	Slowdown in global trade growth	96
5.2	World trade growth	97
5.3	FDI inflows, global and by economic group, 2007–18 (billions of dollars)	97
5.4	Global economic policy uncertainty	98
5.5	Foreign investment restrictions and regulations are on the rise	98
5.6	Impact of 2019 US-China trade restrictions	98
5.7	The EU's top five partners in trade of goods, 2018	99
5.8	Chinese FDI in the EU	100
5.9	EU outward foreign direct investment (OFDI) to China	100
7.1	Rise of international authority	123

7.2 Global Human Development Index   124
7.3 Global Gini Index   125
7.4 Annual deaths in military combat, globally   125

Tables

1.1 Human Development Index in selected countries (1990–2018)   24
3.1 Comparison of Indian and Chinese power plant air quality
     standards   60
4.1 Shares of the world market for export of goods (2017)   76
4.2 Shares in the world market for import of goods (2016)   76
4.3 EU trade with its main partners (2018)   83

CONTRIBUTORS

Ding Chun is Professor of Economics and Director of the Center for European Studies at Fudan University and serves as Vice President of the Chinese Association of European Studies. Ding was awarded a Jean Monnet Chair by the EU. A past president of the European Union Studies Association Asia-Pacific (2018–19), he held the Robert-Schumann Professorship at the University of Luxembourg. He was senior fellow of ZEI at the University of Bonn, a member of the International Academic Board at the Center for European Research at the University of Gothenburg, and a member of the (Davos) World Economic Forum's GAC on Europe. His academic specialties include European integration, European economy, China-EU relations, and social welfare issues. He has over 140 published works in Chinese, English, and German.

Susana Ferreira is Associate Professor of International Relations and Director of the Master's Program in Risk Management in Conflicts at the Antonio de Nebrija University. A researcher at the Portuguese Institute of International Relations, NOVA University of Lisbon, she is also affiliated with both the Research Group on Public Policies, International Security and Global Governance at the European University of Madrid, and the Research Center on Security and Defense from the Portuguese Military University Institute. She holds a PhD in international relations and international security from the NOVA University of Lisbon and the UNED, and she received the Extraordinary Doctoral Award of the UNED (2016–17) for her dissertation. Her main fields of interest include international migration, border management, international security, the Mediterranean region, and the European Union.

Renato G. Flôres Jr. is Director of the International Intelligence Unit of the Fundação Getulio Vargas (FGV) think tank and Professor in the FGV Graduate

School of Economics in Rio de Janeiro, Brazil. Trained as a mathematician and economist, he worked for a few decades in economic modeling before moving to a broader view of international political economy, one that incorporates contributions from geopolitical and international relations theory. He is a specialist on Asia (particularly India and Indochina) and the BRICS. He also studies future trends in global governance, peace and the nuclear game, sustainability, and the distribution of opportunities. An internationally recognized teacher and scholar, he has lectured at universities in Europe, Latin America, and Asia and has published more than 100 papers in books and in peer-reviewed journals. With his former PhD student, Gustavo de Athayde, he co-authored an original extension of portfolio choice theory that opened up a booming line of research in that field. He also has expertise in the economics of art, having acted as a UNESCO consultant on cultural diversity issues.

André W. M. Gerrits, a historian, is Professor of International Studies and Global Politics at the Institute for History, and Chair of the BA Urban Studies, at Leiden University. Previously, he held the chair in Russian History and Politics at Leiden University and the Jean Monnet Chair in European Studies at the University of Amsterdam. He was also a senior research fellow at the Netherlands Institute of International Studies Clingendael. He has published widely on Russian foreign policy, the history and politics of Eastern Europe, and the topic of nationalism.

Coraline Goron is Assistant Professor of Environmental Policy at Duke Kunshan University. In 2017, she obtained a double PhD in politics from the University of Warwick (UK) and the Université Libre de Bruxelles (Belgium) under the European Erasmus Mundus Program on globalization, the EU, and multilateralism. In 2018, her dissertation *Climate Revolution or Long March, The Politics of Low-Carbon Transformation in China, The Case of the Power Sector* was awarded the Marthe Engelborghs-Bertels Prize for Sinology. In 2018–19, she held a postdoctorate at the Oxford University China Center. Her research centers around China's domestic politics of environment, climate change, and energy, as well as the country's increasing role in the global governance of environmental issues. She recently published "Ecological Civilization and the Political Limits of a Chinese Concept of Sustainability" in the journal *China Perspective*.

Eun-Jeung Lee is Professor at the FU Berlin, where she serves as Director of the Institute of Korean Studies and Vice Director of Graduate School of East Asian Studies. She is a member of both the Academy of Science and Humanity in Berlin-Brandenburg and Academia Europea. In 2014 she was nominated to membership in the German-Korean Advisory Body for Foreign Policy Aspects of Unification. She received the Mirok Lee Prize in 2013 and has studied at the Ewha University, Korea, and the University of Göttingen. She finished her habilitation in 2001 at the University of Halle, Germany, and has taught at universities in Korea, Japan, and Germany. The editor of several books, she also has published more than 100 papers and nine monographs, including *Sŏwŏn, die konfuzianischen Privatakademien in Korea; Ostasien denken; Korea im demokratischen Aufschwung; "Anti-Europa": Die Geschichte der Rezeption des Konfuzianismus und der konfuzianischen Gesellschaft seit der frühen Aufklärung*; and *Konfuzianismus und Kapitalismus*.

Thomas Meyer is Emeritus Professor of Political Science at the Technical University of Dortmund and Editor in Chief of the monthly political magazine *Neue Gesellschaft/Frankfurter Hefte*. He has held visiting professor and guest lecturer positions at numerous universities, particularly in East and Southeast Asia, including Todai University, Tokyo; Beida University, Beijing; and the Indian Institute of Management, Bangalore. He directed projects for the well-respected German Research Foundation on such topics as political communication in the media (1995–2001) and the theory and practice of social democracy (2002–06). From 2000 to 2007 he served as academic advisor to the European Commission for the Social Sciences and Humanities, and from 2004 to 2008 he was a member of the GARNET Network of Excellence, funded by the European Commission. His research focuses on comparative social democracy, European studies, mass media and politics, religious and political fundamentalism, and the cultural foundations of politics. Among his many books are *The Theory of Social Democracy* (2007), *Identity Mania* (2001), and *Media Democracy* (2002).

Pan Jiahua is Director-General of the Institute for Urban and Environmental Studies and Professor of Economics at CASS University. He serves as Editor in Chief of the *Chinese Journal of Urban & Environmental Studies*. He received his PhD at Cambridge University in 1992. His areas of academic specialization include the economics of sustainable development, energy and climate policy, the global economy, and environmental and natural resource economics. He worked for the UNDP Beijing Office as an adviser on environment and development and was the lead author of the IPCC Working Group III 3rd, 4th and 5th Assessment Report on Mitigation. A member of both the China National Expert Panel on Climate Change and the National Foreign Policy Advisory Group, he is Advisor to the Ministry of Ecology and the Environment as well as President of the Chinese Association for Urban Economy. He has authored over 300 papers, articles, and books in both English and Chinese. Selected as China Green Person of the Year for 2010–11, he is also a past winner of the Sun Yefang Award of Economic Sciences (2011) and the China Environment Prize (2016).

Joana Castro Pereira is a postdoctoral researcher at the Portuguese Institute of International Relations of NOVA University of Lisbon. Between January 2017 and April 2018, she was a postdoctoral fellow at the Institute of International Relations of the University of Brasília. Her current research focuses on the governance of climate change and biodiversity in the Amazon. She is co-editor (with André Saramago) of *Non-human Nature in World Politics: Theory and practice* (forthcoming from Springer International Publishing). She has published in prestigious journals such as *Global Policy, Water Alternatives, Global Environmental Politics*, and *Journal of Latin American Studies*. She also has collaborated with international governmental institutions such as the European Union and the EU-LAC Foundation.

Qin Yaqing is Professor of International Studies at China Foreign Affairs University (CFAU), Executive Vice-President of China National Association for International Studies (CNAIS), and Associate Member of the Royal Academy of Belgium and Global Fellow at the Peace Research Institute, Oslo. Previously, he served on the Resource Group for the UN High-Level Panel for Threats, Challenges, and Change (2003–04), organized by then UN Secretary-General Kofi Annan, and worked as Special Assistant to the Chinese Eminent Person, China-ASEAN Eminent Persons Group (2005). He has served on numerous national and international editorial boards including, *Global Governance, East-West Policy Studies Series*, and *Chinese Journal of International Politics*. His academic interests include international relations theory, global governance, and regionalism. He has written for numerous journals, including *International Studies Review, Chinese Journal of International Politics*, and *International Relations of the Asia-Pacific*. His most recent publication is *A Relational Theory of World Politics* (Cambridge University Press, 2018).

José Luís de Sales Marques has been President of the Board of Directors of the Institute of European Studies of Macau (IEEM) since January 2002. From 1993 to 2001, he served as the mayor of Macau. His research, teaching, and writing focus on Asia–Europe relations, EU–China dialogue, regional integration, and urban studies.

Deborah Seligsohn is Assistant Professor of Political Science at Villanova University. Her research focuses on Chinese politics, US-China relations, and energy and environmental politics in China and India. Prior to receiving her PhD in political science and international affairs in 2018 from the University of California, San Diego, she worked in both the non-governmental organization and government sectors on energy, climate, and the environment. From 2007 to 2012, she was based in Beijing as the principal advisor to the World Resources Institute's China Energy and Climate Program. She also had over 20 years' experience in the US Department of State, working on energy and environment issues in China, India, Nepal, and New Zealand. Her most recent position was as environment, science, technology, and health counselor in Beijing from 2003 to 2007. Her work has appeared in political science journals and through the World Resources Institute, as well as in the *Washington Post, South China Morning Post, Financial Times*, and other publications.

Nuno Severiano Teixeira is Professor of International Relations at NOVA University of Lisbon and the Director of the Portuguese Institute of International Relations. Previously, he served in the Portuguese government as minister of defense (2006–09) and minister of interior (2000–02). Teixeira was visiting professor at

Georgetown University (2017–19); senior visiting scholar at the Robert Schuman Centre for Advanced Studies European University Institute–Florence (2010); and visiting scholar at the Institute for European Studies, University of California, Berkeley (2004). He holds a PhD in the history of international relations from the European University Institute–Florence (1994). He has published extensively on the history of international relations and European integration as well as in the fields of military history and security and defense studies.

Mario Telò is the Jean Monnet Chair of International Relations at the Université Libre de Bruxelles, where he is the coordinator of the Globalisation, Europe, Multilateralism (GEM) international doctoral program and the past president of the Institute for European Studies. He also teaches at the LUISS University and School of Government in Rome and has been a visiting professor at numerous universities worldwide. He has served as a consultant to the European Council, European Parliament, and European Commission. He is the author of 32 books and over 100 articles published in seven languages. His recent works include *Europe: A Civilian Power?* (2006); *European Union and the New Regionalism* (2014); *International Relations: A European Perspective* (2016); and *Regionalism in Hard Times* (2016). He participates regularly in public debates concerning international relations and the future of the European Union.

Yang Xinran, a graduate of Huazhong University of Sciences and Technology, is the research assistant in the Research Institute for Eco-civilization, Chinese Academy of Social Sciences. Her academic interests include sustainable development, climate change economics, and environmental economics.

Zhang Xiaotong is Professor of the School of Political Science and Public Administration, Wuhan University, a Member of the Advisory Committee for Economic and Trade Policy (Economic Diplomacy Subcommittee) of the Chinese Ministry of Commerce, and Executive Director of Wuhan University Center for Economic Diplomacy. Formerly, he worked at the US desk of the Chinese Ministry of Commerce and served as trade attaché at the Chinese Mission to the European Union in Brussels (2004–10). He obtained his PhD in political science at the Université Libre de Bruxelles (ULB) in Belgium. He published *Brussels Diary*, a biography about his working experiences as a trade diplomat, and edited an anthology on *China's Economic Diplomacy in the 21st Century*. He was a visiting scholar at the Johns Hopkins University's SAIS in 2014–15. His major research interests include economic diplomacy, geopolitics, and European studies.

Michael Zürn is Director of the research unit Global Governance at WZB Berlin Social Science Center and Professor of International Relations at the Free University of Berlin. Since 2019, he has been the spokesperson of the Cluster of Excellence Contestations of the Liberal Script (SCRIPTS), funded by the German Research Foundation. He was the founding rector of the Hertie School of Governance and director of the Special Research Center on "Transformations of Statehood" at the University of Bremen. He is a member of the Academia Europeana and the Berlin-Brandenburg Academy of Sciences as well as of numerous editorial and advisory boards, and he has been a guest lecturer at several prominent universities including Harvard and the London School of Economics. His main research focus is the emergence and functioning of inter- and supranational institutions and the normative tensions and political conflicts that these developments occasion.

ACKNOWLEDGMENTS

This edited volume, like the international Macau Forum that inspired it, would have not come to light without the generous support of both the Brussels-based Foundation for European Progressive Studies (FEPS) and the Macau Foundation, the leading funding mechanism for culture, science, and education of the government of the Macau Special Administrative Region. It operates under the direction of the Institute of European Studies of Macau (IEEM), which seeks to heighten Macau's role as a bridge between cultures.

The conference from which the papers selected for publication here were drawn was jointly chaired by Dr. José Luís de Sales Marques, the president of IEEM; Professor Maria João Rodrigues, President of the FEPS; and Thomas Meyer and Mario Telò, European scholars who serve as visiting professors at IEEM. Professor Zhou Hong of the Chinese Academy of Social Sciences and Professor Qin Yaqing, the former president of China Foreign Affairs University, provided the conference with academic support, which the editors deeply appreciate.

We also would like to express our gratitude to the GEM (Globalisation, Europe, Multilateralism) program, the tricontinental academic network coordinated by Mario Telò on behalf of the Institut d'Etudes Européenes at the Université Libre de Bruxelles. Funded by Horizon 2020 under the auspices of the EU Commission's Research Directorate General, GEM provided support for the scholarship of several contributors to this book as well as for the book itself.

The Regional Center for Political Education Baden-Württemberg graciously granted permission to reprint material contained in the chapter by Michael Zürn, which originally appeared in 2019 under the title "Der Multilateralismus in der Krise: Legitimationsprobleme im globalen politischen System," in issue 78 of *Deutschland & Europa: Zeitschrift für Gemeinschaftskunde, Geschichte und Wirtschaft Friedens- und Sicherheitspolitik in der Europäischen Union.*

Acknowledgments

The editors are indebted to a long list of individuals and institutions who, in one way or another, made this book possible, particularly Beatrice Lam for her indispensable work at every stage in the process of bringing the project to fruition. We thank Andrew Taylor and Sophie Iddamalgoda at Routledge Press and the anonymous reviewers chosen to review the manuscript for their helpful suggestions. We thank also the students and academicians of IEEM, the University of Macau, and the informed participants at our conferences for their invaluable contributions, as well as the staff who help us to complete the project.

Finally, a special word of appreciation goes to Professors Lew and Sandy Hinchman of the United States, who assisted the editors and the authors in preparing this volume for publication.

FOREWORD

Towards a New Multilateralism: Cultural Divergence and Political Convergence? is the collective effort of an international panel of leading scholars engaged in open dialogue in search of answers to the core political issues and challenges facing the present world. The contributors assembled in Macau on November 3, 2019 under the aegis of the Macau Forum on Multiple Modernities and Multilateral Convergence, which has been convened yearly since 2016 by the Institute of European Studies of Macau (IEEM). This latest iteration was co-organized with the Foundation for European Progressive Studies (FEPS), chaired by Professor Maria João Rodrigues, a distinguished academic with a brilliant political career as a minister in the Portuguese government, an adviser to the European Council and EU Commission, and a member of the European Parliament. The cooperation with FEPS was an important indication of how far our forum has progressed since its inception. During that time, four books of collected papers (including the present volume) have been published by Routledge Press. It is also a clear signal that progressive and forward-looking scholars and institutions acknowledge the importance of platforms like ours in stimulating dialogue concerning different concepts of modernity. They likewise value our effort to bring to the same table experts from different cultures and cultural milieus who are hoping to renew multilateral cooperation. It is indeed noteworthy that this most recent forum coincided with the 75th anniversary of the foundation of the United Nations.

The last conference took place slightly less than a year before the anthology's publication; however, political instability worldwide has dramatically increased in a short period of time for several reasons. First, of course, we note the effects of the global COVID-19 pandemic that has practically stopped the world and disrupted normal life for months, thereby jeopardizing the well-being of billions of people. But we must not overlook the simultaneous outbreak of intense competition among great powers, which has led to the continuing erosion of international cooperation and the fragility of multilateral institutions. Considering that international conditions have become so fraught and that they pose a threat to peace itself, the need for more cross-cultural dialogue, multilateral cooperation, and political convergence is setting the tone for progressive thought and human action. The world cries out for encounters conducted in the spirit of multiple modernities, openness, solidarity, and respect for humanity in the quest for peace, development, and security.

The chapters contained in this volume are innovative social-scientific contributions written by distinguish academics, all of whom edited their original papers in order to take into account the discussions that took place at the conference as well as recent developments on the world stage. The quality of these carefully revised papers reflects the erudition and acumen of their authors as well as the coherence and focus of the program that has brought them together over the last four years. Thus, it is only fair that I should salute my colleagues, Professors Mario Telò and Thomas Meyer. The two have worked around the clock to make sure that we would come up with a solid program – even unique – that would generate a collection of distinguished articles. They also deserve credit for having jointly authored an illuminating introduction. We at the IEEM are most grateful for their contributions.

The Macau Special Administrative Region (MSAR) is living through an unprecedented and exciting era. On the one hand, we are celebrating the 20th anniversary of the return of Macau to the motherland. On the other hand, together with ten other cities of the Pearl River Delta, we have embarked on the process of creating the Guangdong–Hong Kong–Macau Greater Bay Area. This move reflects a national strategy to develop a world-class cluster of cities the size of Croatia yet with a combined population of over 70 million and an estimated GDP (at the time of writing) of USD 1.5 trillion, or 12% of China's total GDP.

Macau's role is to act as a base for cultural cooperation and interchange, promoting dialogue between Chinese culture and diverse other cultures. Hence, the forum on multiple modernities and multilateral convergence embodies the spirit of global cultural exchange. We hope that, as soon as conditions permit, it will open a much wider window for progressive dialogue in search of new forms of multilateralism, bringing together different and even divergent cultures in search of political convergence and international cooperation.

Last but not least, a word of appreciation to the Macau Foundation, the support of which has been crucial in bringing this book to fruition, and to Routledge Press for its continuing openness to our project.

José Luís de Sales Marques
President, Institute of European Studies of Macau

INTRODUCTION

Thomas Meyer and Mario Telò

At the beginning of the twenty-first century, peaceful multilateral cooperation among diverse states, regions, and cultures has been put at risk. We are witnessing a paradox. Natural and social scientists agree that the COVID-19 pandemic and the socio-economic crisis that followed in its wake are of a global and transnational nature, that they constitute a threat to the whole of humankind, and that they can only be addressed by enhancing international cooperation. Nevertheless, not only have national governments reacted in a fragmented manner to date, but they also have emphasized that the nation-state is making a comeback as a vital institution, both at the level of nationalist demands for protection and of the inward-looking, exclusionary policies that many states have adopted. Few would dispute that the past 75 years have been the longest period of global peace in recorded history, partly thanks to the establishment of the United Nations and multilateral networks. However, recent evidence shows a decline both in multilateral institutions in general and in those concerned with public health policy in particular. The latter has emerged as the weakest link in the chain of international cooperation.

The topic of this book is timely, because it highlights the fate of a great and indispensable political ideal that is in danger of failing as it runs up against the reality of power politics, fragmentation, and competition. Even before the COVID-19 outbreak, the international scene had been evolving increasingly into a multipolar order in which instability and uncertainty were intensified despite the emergence of common problems. Neither of the pro-multilateralism factors frequently cited today – close economic interdependence and cooperation on the one hand and the multiplication of multilateral regimes, forums, and organization on the other – seems sufficient to moderate power politics and nationalist fragmentation (Gamble 2014). Even prior to the global health emergency, the contemporary world order already had been weakened by several factors: the controversies about globalization, the defection of the former hegemonic power (the US) from its political and moral responsibilities, the rise of new global and regional powers, and the emergence of various types of "hard" nationalism combined with widespread mistrust towards supranational organizations. Long-established international rules, regimes, and institutions currently are being contested and delegitimized.

The impact of the coronavirus pandemic will intensify and accelerate these trends and their magnitude, and most likely will modify the interactions among the main global actors. An unprecedented economic recession, dramatically increasing inequalities, and discrepancies both between and within countries and regions risk making nationalistic attitudes and demands for authoritarian government the prevailing mood of the time. In this context, the tensions among great powers – most notably between the US and China – on trade, new technologies, and security have deepened, and they are tending to spill over into more and more policy fields, as witnessed by the reciprocal charges of responsibility for mishandling (or even triggering) the pandemic.

This climate of radical mistrust and mutual recriminations multiplies the obstacles to international cooperation. We have here the very opposite of a win-win situation. No new hegemonic power is likely to emerge from today's unprecedented crisis. Growing competition between the US and China is likely to characterize the world order in the foreseeable future. That competition may complicate efforts to create more effective instruments of global governance.

Nevertheless, in such a challenging environment it seems evident that the principal contemporary issues selected for study in this volume – climate change, trade protectionism, the advancement of human rights, and peace and security (not to mention issues such as energy diversification, digitalization, massive migration flows, international terrorism, poverty, and inequalities in wealth distribution) – cry out for a new multilateralism. In short, what is needed here is more than merely a managerial updating of the already existing instruments for a better functioning multilateral governance. Nothing short of radical renewal is required, with a focus on improving our collective instruments to ensure peace and stability through global cooperation on environmental, public health, trade, security, and human rights policies. The World Health Organization (WHO) has proven itself still to be too weak an instrument to safeguard the very public common good that it was created to ensure. However, in opposition to those who advocate defection from and boycott of multilateral cooperation in health, this book supports arguments for a stronger WHO. We would like to give the organization a more binding coordinating role at both the regional and global levels. It should assume a variety of tasks: peer review of best practices, the establishment of common guidelines, regular monitoring of the follow-up by independent authorities, and recommendations for action in case of implementation failure.

Thus, the overall purpose of this book is to present new and updated arguments demonstrating that it is both necessary and feasible for states and social actors to address the paradox detailed above and jointly enter a new era of global multilateralism. What is this new multilateralism? Three-quarters of a century after the San Francisco Conference founding the UN and the subsequent Bretton Woods conference in which the International Monetary Fund and World Bank were established, multilateralism has arrived at a crossroads: will it collapse, or will it undergo a profound overhaul? Most scholars and observers have concluded that the hegemonic era that characterized the last few decades has come to an end not only because of its deficits in regard to legitimacy, representation, and efficiency but also because crucial actors openly have chosen to boycott it, thereby disturbing its smooth operation. However, in spite of defections and attacks, the institutionalization of international life shows resilience and sometimes progress. Although the EU's 27 member states took a historic step forward towards deeper internal integration in July of 2020, the EU needs to build convergences with other regional and national actors in order to establish a new multilateralism at the global level. Our book offers evidence that new forms of cultural dialogue and pluralistic, many-layered multilateral cooperation are emerging at the global, regional, and inter-regional levels, focused on traditional challenges and humanity's newly recognized collective goods. Cultural backgrounds and cognitive priors matter a great deal in establishing the framework for intercultural dialogues and convergence.

A variety of paths towards modernization

Some people argue that a new clash of civilizations increasingly motivates and exacerbates both long-standing and more recent conflicts between today's superpowers, rendering them insurmountable and impeding the emergence of a genuine new multilateralism. True, we live in a time in which the claims to superiority made by "the West" increasingly are being questioned by emergent actors not only economically and politically but also at the deeper cultural level. In recent decades, it has become obvious that modernization does not follow a single trajectory, that of its Western forerunners, but rather allows for a variety of different pathways. The century-long global supremacy of the West, especially that of its political and cultural leader, the US, is now up in the air, together with the global regime that it established and supported: the more or less peaceful multilateral cooperation among diverse states and regions. This work seeks to identify the causes of the decline of Western hegemonic order along with the myriad ramifications of that decline for the future.

Our overall research program, of which this volume is but the latest expression, has been carried out under the auspices of the Institute of European Studies of Macau. That program is designed to clarify the impact of civilizational diversity on multidimensional multilateralism by incorporating the analytical approach fostered by the concept of multiple modernities. We began our project by focusing on new analytical concepts that – much like the literature on multiple modernities itself – claim to represent a non-Western political perspective on modernization. Nevertheless, that approach presupposes that there is, in fact, a common core within all forms of modernity that includes at least the following elements: good society, good governance, human security, and the existence of different varieties of capitalism. Our efforts to explore this topic resulted in an anthology on *Multiple Modernities and Good Governance*. Subsequently we invited papers on related issues, which also bore fruit in edited collections published by Routledge. *Cultures, Nationalism and Populism* focused on the problems posed by recent nationalist fragmentation, while *Regionalism and Multilateralism* took a comparative approach to regional, interregional, and multilateral attempts to counter that very trend. The main objective of the present work is to determine whether and to what degree such concepts enable us to bring to light both the differences and the common features or policy convergences among the multiple modernities of our time in crucial policy fields, especially with respect to their political implications and consequences.

So far, most of the political and academic debates aimed at understanding the emergent international scene described above have been carried on within the framework of two alternate paradigms: Samuel Huntington's theory (Huntington 1996) of the clash of civilizations and Francis Fukuyama's thesis concerning the "end of history" (Fukuyama 1992). The former rests on the claim that cultural identities now have shunted aside ideology as the basis for foreign relations. For Huntington, both the quest for national power and the world's major cultures are caught up in a fundamental conflict over ultimately irreconcilable cognitive premises, ethical-political values, and lifestyles. Fukuyama, by contrast, postulates the final, historic triumph of Western political culture and its economic model over its erstwhile rivals, the fate of which has been irremediably sealed by the collapse of the Soviet empire and its ideology of domination. Hence, according to this view, in the future the typical 1990s combination of liberalism and neoliberalism, both in the realm of domestic politics and with respect to the international political and economic order, will be the only game in town, which all entities will have to accept sooner or later.

More recently, a new analytic paradigm has emerged that is intended to overcome the shortcomings of those outlined above: namely, the multiple modernities approach, first articulated by Israeli sociologist Shmuel Eisenstadt. It explores the terrain between these two alternatives and recognizes that almost every society, no matter which civilization it happens to exemplify, will modernize in its own way – at least in some politically relevant respects. But precisely because its process of modernization finds expression within quite different cultural contexts, it may turn out that modern societies will never converge on a single model. Instead, they will remain culturally distinct as far ahead as the eye can see. The premises on which the social, ontological, and political order are based, and their legitimation, no longer can be taken for granted as objective or given. As Eisenstadt remarks in his now classic essay:

> One of the most important implications of the term "multiple modernities" is that modernity and Westernization are not identical; Western patterns of modernity are not the only authentic modernities, though they enjoy historical precedence and continue to be a basic reference point for others.
> *(Eisenstadt 2000: 2–3)*

What makes Eisenstadt's approach so promising, in our view, is that it does not stipulate anything close to Huntingtonian relativism. Instead, it presupposes a common core of all the different types of modernity. Eisenstadt's proposal for the definition of such a core has been the target of recent academic controversies. He sees the key difference between modernism and traditionalism in "the conception of *human agency*, and of its place in the flow of time" (Eisenstadt 2000: 3). In his view, modernism embraces an idea of the future that is characterized by a number of alternatives realizable through autonomous human agency, or the principle of subjectivism.

The Fukuyama-Huntington controversy has found echoes in wide-ranging philosophical debates over multiculturalism and the degree to which other cultures (whether within Western societies or in other countries) should be treated as monolithic, and thereby "essentialized," or whether they should be understood as dialectical processes of renewal and reinterpretation of their traditions, open to innovation and the adoption of patterns, practices, and ideas, such as human rights, from their interaction with other cultures.

The present anthology sheds light on these questions as well. It may turn out that different forms of modernity converge on certain aspects of honest, effective global governance via distinct political and cultural traditions. As Amartya Sen (2000: 231–34) has pointed out, so-called Asian values are not inherently authoritarian. After all, it is clear that allegedly Western values such as toleration and dissent have long lineages in Asian thought as well. Therefore, at least in principle, convergence upon certain basic orientations is possible when it comes to enacting and enforcing certain modern values such as responsible, honest governance and basic rights. The latter, for example, claim universal validity; they are not merely Western inventions and may be conceived and formulated in various ways in different cultures. For that reason, Western countries ought to take a self-critical look at what concepts like basic rights or good governance and multilateral cooperation might mean in the cultural traditions of their non-Western counterparts.

In preparing this collection, we opted for a bottom-up approach, one that analyzes the basic features of selected policies in fields of undoubted relevance for all countries in all civilizations in today's world. The point is to determine the extent to which they are built on converging values and principles. Obviously, climate change/environmental protection, fair trade, and security policy all belong in this category. Human rights belong there, too, when we take the relevant UN declarations and pacts as definitive. Yet, the crucial point here is whether this common ground is still sustainable given all the disputes, hostilities, and quarrels of recent decades, when some of the key actors in the global arena such as China have complained that the concept of human rights regularly has become "weaponized" in ideological feuds.

At any rate, in the present phase of global reorientation the cultural factor (i.e., differing cultural worldviews, identities, practices, and their use by political actors) plays a highly ambivalent – even contradictory – role in politics, ideological debate, and intellectual discourse. Two different tendencies that must not be confused stand out in our current context: first, the trend to question institutionalized, universalistic norms and values in the name of cultural nationalism; and second, the drift towards aggressive religious fundamentalism in the form of identity politics that attacks the very foundations of civilization. Both trends have become louder and more truculent. Some economically successful authoritarian models of development in East Asia have emerged as serious rivals to Western modernity. Meanwhile, Islamic State activities in Syria, Iraq, and beyond continue to attract young people who are alienated from their own societies in Europe and parts of Asia and Africa. Finally, the Western model has been put on the defensive by populist and fundamentalist movements even within countries that had been bastions of Western modernity until quite recently.

Convergences and divergences in four intertwined policy fields

The four topics of common global concern that we have chosen for analysis in this volume seem to be the most promising for finding answers to our research questions. Far exceeding the powers of any single national Leviathan to resolve, each of these challenges to human survival demands continuing multilateral cooperation built on mutual trust. Furthermore, all are multi-actor issues in which regions and participatory transnational networks matter as driving forces. This is self-evident for ecological and security policies. It is likewise obvious in regard to trade, which often in the past has functioned as the driver of interdependence, mutual advantage, and peaceful cooperation but now is jeopardized by trade wars and assailed by demands for enhanced environmental, social, and living standards. There is an evident link between the upgrading of trade regimes and conflict prevention as well as between trade wars and security complications. The organization immediately involved in resolving such difficulties is the World Trade Organization (WTO), but these challenges far exceed its remit.

Our last dimension of multilateral cooperation concerns human rights. We propose to discuss them as a particularly sensitive field at the crossroads between institutionalized universalism (UN Declarations) and de facto cultural relativism. The conceptual and philosophical aspect must be combined here with the analysis of the diverse "background cultures and cognitive priors" (cf. Qin 2018; Acharya 2018; Katzenstein 2019) and practices, legal definitions, and alternative ways of governance at the regional and global multilateral levels. But first, in the wake of the fierce feuds of recent decades, we must clarify whether the concepts and the relevant terms used in these debates have the same meaning for all interlocutors or whether a fresh look is needed to reestablish a common understanding of their significance.

The rationale of the process that eventually led to the present volume was to bring together internationally renowned academic experts on our various topics who simultaneously represent, as far as possible, diverse civilizational backgrounds. As mentioned above, this book, like its predecessors, is based on the series of open conferences held in the context of the Macau Forum. The papers have been revised thoroughly in light of discussions held during the fourth such forum, held in 2019. The collective research project gradually has advanced from verification of the multiple modernity thesis towards the study of concrete policy fields. The chapters included here are arranged according to the topics and debates aired during the conference.

Climate change/environmental protection

Under this category of multilateralism, the evolution of sustainable development goals and the Conference of Parties or COP regime (Treaty of Paris, 2015) are examined. The contributions by Pan Jiahua and Yang Xinran, Coraline Goron, and Deborah Seligsohn investigate these matters of top priority for our collective future by tracing out three diverging perspectives: the Chinese, European, and American. However, while taking into account the civilizational implications of environmental policies and the related sustainable economic models, they look for possible compromises that might lead to a multilateral form of environmentalism. Combating climate change is also a way to protect new civic rights and foster sustainable growth.

The chapters by Pan and Yang and by Goron are tightly linked to the main aim of the book, because both consider the challenges posed by a potential "paradigm shift." Both begin by recognizing the significance of the differences between developed and developing counties over environmental policy. To bring about convergence on approaches to sustainable development, a new framework is urgently needed. The United Nations 2030 Agenda (approved in 2015) pledges to value rights-based justice among the world's peoples by emphasizing the centrality of the concept of human development with harmony between man and nature. Unfortunately, this formula may conflict with the imperatives of industrial civilization. To achieve convergence upon the goal of an ecological civilization, according to Pan and Yang, efforts must be made to accelerate the shifting process through transformative thinking and new approaches to forms of cooperation and institutional design. Like Pan and Yang, Goron wonders whether the Chinese concept of "ecological civilization" (EC) might help to foster multilateral convergence. After analyzing the political and cultural values of China's EC concept, its policy discourse and institutional practice in the field of climate change and biodiversity, and its reception by the international community, she concludes that prospects for EC to provide an alternative paradigm for multilateral cooperation are limited at best. She points out that it does not always dovetail well with China's authoritarian political culture and suffers from the limitations on dialogue within multilateral institutions, especially because so far the environmental communities outside China have not paid much attention to it. However, the EC concept already contributes to the diversification of environmental discourses and may impact global environmental governance by enabling China to become more actively involved in that project. Deborah Seligsohn, in her chapter, offers a positive assessment of the Chinese government's policies since 2003. The People's Republic raised its air pollution standards for power plants three times, moving them from the status of "quite weak" to among the toughest in the world. The progressive tightening of regulations in China shows how multilateral cooperation – here the effort to reduce air pollution – might converge on a common set of standards, regulations, and industrial policies.

International trade

International trade has provided the historical background for multilateralism since the seventeenth century, although by the advent of the new millennium it had come to include explicit references to matters of the environment, social life, peace, and culture. While trade once served as the driver of interdependence and growth, it is now threatened by trade wars and has become the target of demands by popular for higher environmental, social, and living standards. According to the chapters written by Mario Telò and by Ding Chun and Zhang Xiaotong, there is an evident issue linkage between the upgrading of trade regimes and the prevention of conflict and between trade wars and threats to international security. These chapters present the alternative options facing the world's main trade powers in the aftermath of the deadlock that hobbled the WTO's Doha Development Round. Both explore the hypothesis that a major convergence may be underway, one that promotes an innovative combination of regional, interregional, and global efforts to usher in a new era of multilateral trade arrangements, keep protectionism in check, deter trade wars, and discourage isolationism. Telò underpins this strategy by canvassing the empirical research being done on a wide array of second-generation regulatory interregional trade arrangements (Fawcett et al. 2015) initiated by the EU, including the Southern Common Market (MERCOSUR), the Canada-EU Trade Agreement, and negotiations for a Comprehensive Agreement on Investment between the EU and China. Meanwhile, Ding and Zhang examine the controversial triangular relations between China, the EU, and the US ("triplexity"). The authors regard this trend as a way to keep protectionism within limits and to revive multilateralism by introducing new, upgraded trading ties. The authors point out that two major economic powers, China and the EU, both of nearly continental size, continue to adhere to multilateralism and resist trade protectionism, and they also display a commitment to combat COVID-19. Although they pursue diverse policy paths (the Belt and Road Initiative in China's case and multilateralism plus interregionalism in the case of the EU), the projects they have chosen are both crucial in the struggle to contain the isolationist and protectionist zeitgeist. However, the future of EU-China relations will play out against the backdrop of the "triplexity" outlined by the authors and of course the hard times that the world economy and global politics are now enduring. Triplex negotiations will need to put considerable emphasis on the linkages between trade and peaceful conflict resolution. The multidimensionality and cultural aspects of trade are an innovative avenue for further study and essential for our research agenda, a point that has been confirmed by many scholars in Europe, Asia, and the Americas (including the eminent Brazilian intellectual and former minister Celso Lafer 1999). Of course the debate has not yet been concluded, as reflected in the present book's internal pluralism.

A critical vision of trade is presented in the chapter by Renato G. Flôres Jr, who rejects efforts to link trade to other issues such as environmental protection or improved labor conditions. The author is skeptical about the assumption that trade fosters peaceful relations, reminding the reader that it has been associated with violence, exploitation, and conquest for centuries, especially in the British Empire. Indeed, trade could be considered just one more way to accumulate power (e.g., in the so-called US-China trade war, the conflict is really about "technological supremacy"). Despite his skepticism about trade's benefits, Flôres has not abandoned hope that multilateralism remains the best way to resolve global problems. He offers a series of suggestions that can be boiled down to two consistent messages: first, we need to strengthen the best multilateral institutions, the WTO and the UN; second, trade should be treated, and negotiated as trade, and nothing else.

Global governance and multilateral peacekeeping

For organizational reasons, two European scholars contributed to the subject matter for this section. Nevertheless, several Chinese scholars (Professors Song Xinning and Zhou Hong) and students also took part in the subsequent discussion about the papers. Michael Zürn of Germany is a leading European expert on international politics in the age of ongoing globalization. The main concern of his chapter is the scheme of transnational governance that enables (or hampers) sustainable security and arms control policies, because the latter cannot be considered as an isolated field of political action. Although Zürn's take on that topic is rather critical, he offers a clear starting point for a renewal of the endangered and moribund institutions of global multilateralism. There can be no doubt that multilateralism is in a state of crisis not only in terms of decreasing trust in its institutions and arrangements but also, on a deeper level, with respect to the norms, rules, and practices of the international realm as such. We are witnessing a pervasive crisis of the very foundations of global governance. Zürn presents an endogenous explanation for this development, laying blame on procedural weaknesses within the system. In his view, the crisis of global governance is a crisis of legitimacy. Its roots lie in the lack of persuasive narratives of legitimation, a failing that is generated by both the inherent structure and the procedural practices of the system itself. The institutionalization of inequality and a technocratic bias in the justification of authority are responsible for this failure. An examination of the arguments marshaled by the most prominent critics of the global governance system reveals that they all more or less explicitly focus on these systematic legitimacy deficits. As a consequence, the reform of the institutions and practices of global governance, with the aim of bestowing effective equality on all the actors and participants in that entire system, appears to be the indispensable precondition for global confidence-building. Furthermore, it will be the principal condition for preserving exiting treaties, security institutions, and arms control agreements while enabling new ones to be crafted.

The ideas presented by Nuno Severiano Teixeira, Joana Castro Pereira, and Susana Ferreira are drawn largely from Teixeira's experience as an international scholar and as a former minister of defense in Portugal. At bottom, their chapter offers a thoroughgoing critique of the foreign policies of the present US government, which seeks to dismantle transnational institutions and restore the principle of bilateralism in all policy fields of global relevance. Security and arms control in particular are beyond doubt issues of existential concern for humanity. Adopting a European perspective, Teixeira, Pereira, and Ferreira argue that this kind of threat requires a comprehensive and transnational response if it is to be defused successfully. Moreover, security will involve not only international cooperation among states but also the engagement of international and non-governmental organizations and even the empowerment of people themselves. In short, to live in a more secure world, we will have to invent a new kind of multilateralism. The chapter starts on a theoretical note by tracing the genealogy of the concept of security and seeking to identify the understanding of it that prevails today. The authors then present two cases studies of issues that take top priority on the European policy agenda: climate change and international migration. In this respect, the chapter amounts to an extended argument with the positions on security policy taken by the Trump administration. We note in passing that the participants from Asia, including the vice president of the Chinese Academy for Social Sciences in Beijing, Zhou Hong, gave an oral presentation that resonated with the line of argument espoused by the Portuguese authors.

Human rights

Human rights, the final dimension of multilateral cooperation that we address in this book, is a particularly sensitive issue. It can hardly be denied that the US has adopted a twofold strategy in recent decades: on the one hand, to downplay its own deficiencies and, on the other, to weaponize the concept of human rights to attack China while underestimating the progress made there on the social and economic fronts. These are the aspects that Thomas Meyer stresses in his chapter. He reminds us that, according to the UN Covenants on Basic Rights (which represent binding law, not mere suggestions), basic social and economic rights are as much preconditions for human freedom as are liberal and political rights. This is one area in which the deficits in parts of the US, especially, are serious. If we wish to tell the honest, complete story of human rights protections in today's world, we need to shine a light on many of these failures of the US federal government and some of its individual states. More generally, Meyer tackles some of the delicate issues involving the meaning and scope of the universality of basic rights under conditions of multiple modernities. If there are many paths to modernity, do human rights possess no more than a relative validity? Meyer argues that even if we take full account of both the conceptual and philosophical sides of basic rights and provide a thorough analysis of various background cultures and cognitive priors, legal definitions, and alternative modes of governance at the regional and multilateral levels, there still will be an unambiguous claim in favor of the validity of rights that protect the space of action of the individual subject as the ultimate source of legitimacy for the structures and actions of government. A fresh dialogue among all civilizations on this point could establish a new and universally respected balance between broad-based claims and cultural rights. It is important to understand that the mere existence of a set of institutions neither constitutes nor guarantees the realization of human rights. The dawning awareness of multiple modernities suggests the possibility of a dialogue that might bridge the widening gap between rhetoric and reality, offering all involved parties the chance to account for the cultural connotations of their actual understanding and handling of human rights. Even if such conversations might not result in changes in the texts of valid UN documents, they most probably would build trust by allowing each interlocutor to understand everyone else's real viewpoint.

South Korean scholar Eun-Jeung Lee, who teaches in Berlin, is an expert on the history of political philosophy in both Europe and East Asia. Her chapter reconstructs the ideas of Johann Gottfried Herder, the eminent late eighteenth-century thinker who tried to understand the roles and relationships of different historical cultures, particularly with respect to contacts between Europe and East Asia. Lee contends that the majority of regimes facing criticism in the international community for their human rights violations have, at some point, cast themselves as advocates of cultural relativism. To such regimes, arguing in favor of the universality of human rights looks like an act of subservience to Western-centricity. The gulf between cultural relativism and universalism in the conception of human rights shows no signs of closing. Lee proposes an approach that upholds the universalist nature of human rights while reconciling it with the historical and cultural particularities of divergent cultural contexts. Herder's metaphor of human civilization as a community in the form of a "garden" provides us with a useful tool. To Herder, the beauty of this garden of human community lies in the fact that the flowers of cultures growing in its midst achieve a state of mutual harmony. The protection of specific human rights in full awareness of their somewhat relative character and the protection of human rights in the human community as a whole, as a matter of universal principle, ultimately cannot be viewed as distinct undertakings.

André W. M. Gerrits starts his chapter with a discussion of two key interrelated aspects of the post–Cold War global liberal order: multilateralism and the international human rights regime. He concedes that the dominant notion of human rights was inspired by Western liberal values. Its global reach and institutionalization reflect the material and immaterial dominance of the West, especially during the first two decades after the Cold War. However, he goes on to point out that the global marketplace of ideas is changing under the influence of the major power shifts that we are currently witnessing. Accordingly, Gerrits asks whether this means that the end times of human rights have arrived or whether human rights will survive as international norms, albeit perhaps in a mitigated form. He discusses three issues that are crucial to the future of human rights: the role of the state in the global human rights effort, the ambition to "regionalize" human rights, and the need to bring human rights closer to the lives of ordinary people. He also addresses the challenges facing states, organizations, and individuals that remain committed to liberal human rights. Their future strategies will involve a complex combination of competition and compromise. Human rights discourse is not an eternal, universal language; it is a product of its time. Liberal powers need to develop a future human rights regime that simultaneously configures authority and organizes diversity. This requires a pragmatic approach, both with respect to the ideational and to the practical aspects of human rights, but the core of human rights as we know them should not be at stake.

In place of a conclusion

The final, highly original chapter was contributed by one of the leading Chinese experts on international relations, Qin Yaqing, who thematizes multilateralism via the "inter-practicality" of institutions and relations. In a sense, Qin's text combines a commentary on most of the ideas figuring in the other chapters with some sage advice, from an East Asian point of view, to all readers. It also touches upon some of the discourse-changing insights of the French sociologist and philosopher Michel Foucault. Qin highlights the epistemic role of diverse practices (whether as instruments of domination or cooperation) that contain tacit knowledge and a kind of wisdom that theoretical concepts and arguments cannot easily capture. Practices are the vehicles of accumulated experiences and knowledge that, under appropriate circumstances, can facilitate cooperation and build trust within any conceptual framework. Often they belong to the very features that help to constitute the particular identity of a given culture or civilization and regulate the actions of individuals, groups, and institutions within it, both tacitly and effectively, even though they are never made explicit in any discourse or account. Thus, Qin offers a useful tip: we should be modest in our claims to have understood even our own culture, let alone other ones. He also reminds us that embarking on practical cooperation typically does not require a complete prior consensus at the conceptual level. That is a valuable insight in view of the conceptual endeavors made in previous chapters of this book. Combined with the input of our other authors, it lays the intellectual foundations for the concept of a "new" multilateralism that can avoid both the inertia of hegemonic multilateralism and the dangers of inward-looking nationalism and cultural relativism.

References

Acharya, A. 2018. "Multiple Modernities in a Multiplex World." In T. Meyer & J. de Sales Marques (eds.), *Multiple Modernities and Good Governance*. Abingdon, UK & New York: Routledge, pp. 73–82

Eisenstadt, S. 2000. "Multiple Modernities." *Daedalus* 129(1): 1–29

Fawcett, L., F. Ponjaert, & M. Telò (eds.). 2015. *Interregionalism and the EU*. Abingdon, UK & New York: Routledge
Fukuyama, F. 1992. *The End of History and the Last Man*. New York: Free Press
Gamble, A. 2014. *Crisis Without End? The Unravelling of Western Prosperity*. London: Palgrave Macmillan
Huntington, S. 1996. *The Clash of Civilizations and the Remaking of World Order*. New York: Simon & Schuster
Katzenstein, P. 2019. "Constrained Diversity: Modernities, Regionalism, and Polyvalent Globalism in World Politics." In T. Meyer, J. de Sales Marques, & M. Telò (eds.), *Regionalism and Multilateralism: Politics, Economics, Culture*. London & New York: Routledge, pp. 17–35
Lafer, C. 1999. *Comercio, Desarmamento, Direitos Humanos* [Trade, Disarmament, and Human Rights]. Sao Paolo, Brazil: Paz e Terra
Qin, Y. 2018. *A Relational Theory of World Politics*. Cambridge, UK: Cambridge University Press
Sen, A. 2000. *Development as Freedom*. New York: Alfred A. Knopf
Treaty of Paris. 2015. Treaty of Paris. Available at: https://unfccc.int/process-and-meetings/the-paris-agreement/the-paris-agreement

PART I
Environmental policy, climate change, and ecological civilization

1
MEETING SUSTAINABLE DEVELOPMENT GOALS THROUGH A PARADIGM SHIFT IN THE NEWLY EMERGING WORLD PATTERN

Pan Jiahua and Yang Xinran

The emerging world pattern and its implications for sustainable development

National circumstances differ, and each country must decide how best to implement the UN's Sustainable Development Goals (SDGs), based primarily on its social, economic, and environmental conditions as well as its natural resource endowment (Pan & Chen 2016). Since the late 1980s, the world has initiated a shift away from ideological competition between the East (led by the former communist Soviet Union) and the West (headed by the US and its allies) towards global integration of the world economy. During the early stages of that process, the world was reshaped from a bipolar (capitalist vs. communist) divide into a tripartite structure comprising rich developed countries, countries in transition (Russia and Eastern Europe), and other developing countries. With the Eastern Bloc completing the transition from centrally planned to market economies and China accelerating its market-oriented reform process, the world now divides neatly into two groups: the rich developed and the poor developing countries, or in geopolitical terms, the North and the South.

While some formerly transitional countries such as Hungary and Poland and a few formerly developing countries like South Korea and Singapore have upgraded their level of development and been accepted as members of the rich countries' club, the Organization for Economic Co-operation and Development (OECD), the South-North divide remained largely unchanged in the 1990s and the early 2000s. However, late in the 2000s and early in the 2010s, when a few large developing economies – China and India in particular – experienced a sustained period of high growth, a new group began to take shape, which we may call "emerging economies." By contrast, most other less developed countries have maintained essentially the same status that they previously had with respect to their levels of economic development, population growth, energy consumption, and greenhouse gas emissions.

Now, as we enter the 2020s, a new world pattern is beginning to develop, the contours of which are becoming ever more strongly apparent (see Figure 1.1). In general, the incipient world pattern shows a shift from a simple South-North divide into three categories: the rich North, the newly emerging countries, and other developing countries. Although the less developed states share somewhat similar features, in particular a low level of economic attainment, the other two groups are not exactly the same. Within each of them, different prospects of and roads to development are readily apparent. In brief, the developed North displays two types of economies: one characterized by physical saturation and the other in a state of actual or potential physical expansion. The emerging economies group also contains two different types: those approaching physical saturation and those with the potential for large-scale expansion. These five types of economies will have highly different capabilities for meeting their SDGs.

To be specific, developed countries – also referred to as high-consumption countries – share comparable levels of economic development and high levels of consumption. Their per capita income may continue to grow, but as far as the basic necessities are concerned, their consumption level is largely saturated. However, in terms of both physical space for economic expansion and demographic trend lines, there are clearly two categories here. Europe and Japan represent one typical category, with limited or no physical space for economic expansion and stable or even declining population levels. It is easily understandable that a mature economy like that of an EU country or Japan would need to build more miles of highways or

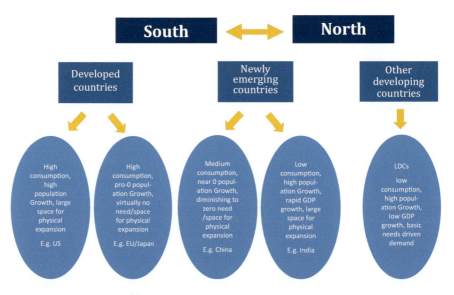

FIGURE 1.1 A new world pattern emerging

high-speed rail lines, because almost all of their land area has been utilized. As the population has stopped growing or even entered into a steady decline, there will be no need to construct many more new houses or manufacture greater quantities of other durable capital goods such as cars, although replacement or upgrading will take place. According to Japanese statistics, Japan's population has been shrinking at an annual rate of between a quarter of a million and half a million people since 2016.[1] It is unlikely that such a trend will be reversed. In the European cases, immigration from outside the EU – especially from Muslim countries – may stabilize or even increase their populations, but the consequences will be more complicated. The other category of rich economies such as the US, Canada, and Australia have lower population densities and relatively higher levels (above zero) of population growth. That combination of factors would mean that a country like the US has plenty of space for physical expansion and will see an increasing demand for housing and durable capital goods like automobiles as its population continues to grow. The UN's population statistics show that the US population increased from about 250 million in the 1950s to 320 million in the 2010s and is projected to reach 450 million by the end of this century. This suggests that the US economy is mature but not saturated.

After decades of high rates of economic growth, newly emerging economies have reached a level of higher middle income, larger than many other developing countries and with a prospect of continued increase, yet even their economies will remain at a substantially lower level of affluence than those of the developed world. China provides an example. In 2019, its per capita GDP reached USD 10,000, which is still less than 30% of the world average or the threshold of high-income countries.[2] However, the projection is that China will continue its rapid growth and surpass the lower limit of the high-income economies by 2025 or thereabouts (Li et al. 2020). In China, the level of consumption remains low, relative to developed rich countries. According to the World Bank, in terms of automobile ownership per thousand persons, the number for China is less than 300 while the figure for the EU and Japan is over 550, with over 800 for the US. Due to the scarcity of land suitable for dwelling, most Chinese reside in multi-story, high-rise apartment buildings with per capita living space averaging around 40 square meters, similar to the size that prevails in Japan but quite a bit lower than the European average and substantially lower than that of the US. As in Europe and Japan, space for physical expansion in China is limited, and population growth is peaking and will decline in the longer run. But over 600 million Chinese in rural areas remain at a very low level of consumption, and upgrading their living standards to match those of their urban counterparts would mean a substantial increase in demand for housing, automobiles, and other essentials, because the average rural income still amounts to only about a third of that enjoyed by urbanites.[3] Like China, India is an emerging economy, though it is relatively less affluent and much less saturated in regard to physical infrastructure and levels of consumption. In 2019 China produced 996.3 million tons of raw steel while India produced only about 111.2 million tons.[4] One can imagine that further increases

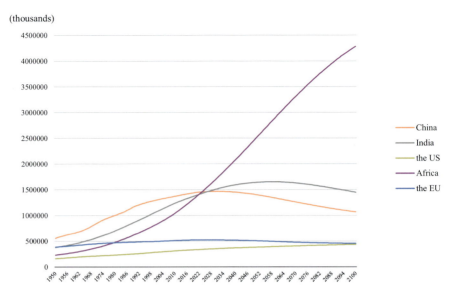

FIGURE 1.2 Population estimates in selected countries (1950–2100)

Source: United Nations, Department of Economic and Social Affairs, Population Division (2019). World Population Prospects 2019, Online Edition. Rev. 1.

in steel production may be minimal or even negative in China, whereas India will be expected to produce more in order to meet the demand required by its ongoing processes of urbanization and industrialization. In contrast to the stabilization of population taking place in China, high rates of population growth are expected for India; in fact, that country will surpass China to become the world's most populous country in two or three more years and continue to increase until it reaches the 1.7 billion mark after the middle of this century. Clearly, all those additional people will need more housing and consumer goods. In general, the category of "other developing countries" includes many at a lower level of income and development but still with high rates of population growth (see Figure 1.2). That would mean that although these economies will be far from mature and saturated, their continued growth will be problematic. Indeed, they still will have to struggle to meet the basic needs of their citizens.

A change in the global landscape for development

Apart from the overall features of physical space for economic expansion and demographic trends, the world pattern also can be portrayed in terms of percentage share of the global total by individual economies or groups of economies, using indicators such as GDP, energy consumption, and greenhouse gas emissions, in addition to somewhat more comprehensive ones like the Human Development Index (HDI) and energy mix.

The weight of an economy over the world total is a simple and direct indicator that reveals the relative importance of an individual country's economy (Wang 2015). Mature or developed economies take a huge share of the world's total product, and as a result these economies dominate the operation of the global economy, including rule-making and rule enforcement. With the rise of the developing countries, especially the newly emerging economies, their share of total product declines, and consequently their power to make and enforce rules for their own benefit will be challenged by those who are increasingly big players. As calculated from World Bank data, the US and the EU are the world's two largest economies. Their combined share of the global total amounted to 60% in the early 1990s but diminished steadily to around or below 45% in the late 2010s. Emerging economies, on the other hand, have been increasing their share of the world's total output. Take China as an example. The Chinese economy's percentage share of the world total was only 1.6% in 1990, but it continued to grow year by year, reaching 16% in 2018. Interestingly, the least developed countries' proportion has remained roughly the same at less than 1%, even though their share of the global population has risen a great deal. Despite the substantial changes going on in the international economic landscape, the rich developed economies would like to keep existing global economic institutions as they are. The latter, after all, were established under their rules, which may not be fair to poor developing countries. The trade dispute between developed countries and many of the rest may well illustrate the fact that rich countries are unwilling to assume responsibilities for supporting the implementation of SDGs in the least developed countries. And while rich countries resist changing the rules, they nevertheless call for action on sustainability and other issues from emerging economies. In the meantime, the newly emerging economies have made use of existing rules in their process of development but would like to make changes to reflect and protect their interests in the global economic regime. Self-interest among the industrialized civilizations is probably not enough to motivate them to provide the amount of financial support that poor countries would need to achieve the SDGs. The newly emerging economies wish to make a deal for cooperation between the developed and more advanced developing economies; however, without a true paradigm shift, such collaboration probably will prove difficult.

With respect to energy consumption, the overall logic indicates that higher levels of economic development will increase demand but that, over time, the increase will fall to zero and even turn negative. Figure 1.3 shows that energy use by the US and the EU already peaked by 2007 and 2006, respectively; still, the decrease from that point has been minimal as both economies have maintained a relatively high level of consumption. Energy demand in developing economies has been growing and has yet to peak. Considering demographic trends, future energy demand in the US is likely to increase in order to keep up with the demand for a high quality of life. However, any such augmentation will be offset by improvements in energy efficiency, so the actual increase will be minimal or even negative. If we look at energy demand in the EU and Japan, decreases in energy consumption would be

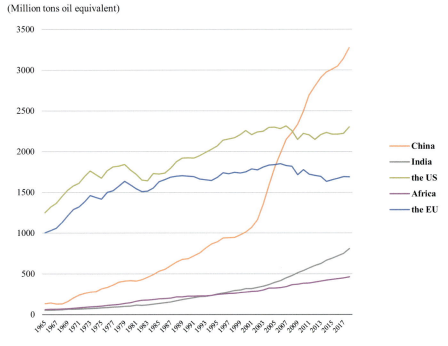

FIGURE 1.3 Primary energy consumption in selected countries (1965–2018)

Source: BP Statistical Review of World Energy, June 2019.

expected as the population in these saturated economies falls. Because the quality of life in China is still low compared to the developed rich countries, Chinese energy consumption exhibits an upward trend, but the increase will not be substantial and is expected to peak in the near future. Low-income countries, under the double pressure of rapidly growing population and citizens' expectations for improvement in their quality of life, will see increases in energy demand intended to support their economic development. Because sustainable energy is central to economic growth, social progress, and environmental sustainability, sustainable energy supplies are indispensable in developing countries to facilitate their action for SDGs.

Carbon emissions come mainly from fossil fuel combustion. Industrialization and urbanization require low-cost energy consumption, and for that fossil fuels are a good choice compared to zero-carbon renewables and nuclear. Developed countries have reached peak emission levels both in the aggregate and in per capita terms along with their total consumption of energy, but per capita emission levels have remained high. For example, CO_2 emissions per capita (see Figure 1.4) in the US declined from more than 22 tons in the 1970s to 14 tons in 2017 – twice as much as in the EU and China – and the rate of decline is slow. In fact, projections show that if no additional efforts are made, the numbers still will be over 10 and 5 tons in 2050 and 2100, respectively. The EU has done a better job than the US in terms

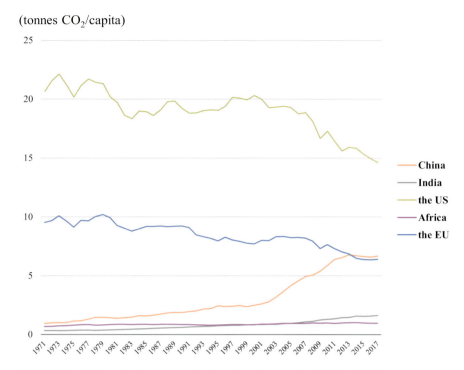

FIGURE 1.4 CO_2 emissions per capita in selected countries (1971–2017)
Source: International Energy Agency (2019), CO_2 Emissions from Fossil Fuel Combustion.

of promoting a low-carbon lifestyle, but the rate of emissions still lags far behind the target set by the Paris Agreement. Newly emerging economies like India are in the process of rapid industrialization and urbanization, hence they will witness per capita increases in emissions. If India were to follow a development path similar to that of China, where emissions per capita have increased from 0.9 to 7 tons in the last 50 years, CO_2 emissions in India eventually would surpass the total of those in China and the US. Africa, the continent with the highest rate of population growth in the world, will emit more CO_2 in 2100 than the EU did in 2017 even without any increase in the per capita level of emissions.

The HDI is calculated based on several factors: life expectancy, to represent a long and healthy life; the number of years of education to indicate the level of knowledge attained; and per capita national income to capture the extent to which purchasing power matches consumer demand. In general, such an index provides a supplementary metric for evaluating a country's overall level of development. It is thought to be a better measure than GDP using a national system of accounting. As the statistics show in Table 1.1, the US consistently achieves a very high human development level and positions itself among the top 15 countries as judged by this standard. The numbers for the EU also reveal a very high overall level of human development but still lower than the level of the US, because some EU member

TABLE 1.1 Human Development Index in selected countries (1990–2018)

	1990	*2000*	*2005*	*2010*	*2015*	*2018*
Very high human development	0.779	0.823	0.846	0.866	0.886	0.892
High human development	0.568	0.63	0.665	0.706	0.738	0.75
Medium human development	0.437	0.497	0.536	0.575	0.616	0.634
Low human development	0.352	0.386	0.435	0.473	0.499	0.507
World	0.598	0.641	0.669	0.697	0.722	0.731
China	0.501	0.591	0.643	0.702	0.742	0.758
EU	0.755	0.810	0.842	0.862	0.879	0.888
US	0.86	0.881	0.896	0.911	0.917	0.92
India	0.431	0.497	0.539	0.581	0.627	0.647

Source: Human Development Report (1990–2018); data available at http://hdr.undp.org/en/data.

states have achieved a very high level while others remain at a relatively moderate level; for example, Ireland is ranked fourth but Bulgaria is ranked 58th. China has made steady progress over the past three decades, from medium to high human development levels; still it ranks only 85th among some 170 countries. Although India's level of human development has been classified as medium, it remains far below the world average, with a ranking of 130. Most developing countries exhibit only a low or medium level of human development, and while progress certainly has been made in these countries, the achievements are inadequate to narrow the gap with the developed world.

A sustainable energy supply requires a large and increasing share of zero-carbon renewable sources in the energy mix in order to mitigate climate change and reduce emissions of conventional air pollutants such as NO_x and SO_2. Dirty coal is normally deemed cheaper in the energy market because its negative environmental costs often are not taken into account. Therefore, the share of coal in the energy mix is higher in developing than in developed countries. The share of coal in the energy consumed in China and India remains much higher than the world average, and zero-carbon renewables are far behind the level attained by developed countries. However, newly emerging economies are making more efforts to decarbonize their economy than even the highly developed economies. Some EU countries like the UK and Germany will have gotten rid of coal by 2040. It does not look possible for China to cut coal consumption to zero by 2050, but the share of coal consumption in the energy mix in China has been falling at an impressive rate, from 66% in 2015 to 57.7% in 2019[5] – an average annual rate of reduction of 1.6 percentage points. Wind and solar power capacity installed in China is first in the world now, while 20 years earlier that number was nearly zero. By contrast, both the US and India have much lower levels of renewable energy utilization, below the average world number of 7% or so. To reduce fossil fuels in the energy mix, a country's resource endowment obviously matters, but financial and technological capabilities also are of great importance for making progress in that endeavor.

The global landscape has changed substantially and is evolving continuously. The US economy will retain its economic power in the years to come, while the other developed economies with a high rate of saturation of development will remain mature and rich, but their share of the world's total economy will continue to decline. As an emerging economy, China will enlarge its share of the global economic pie, but increases in its energy consumption will be minimal in the future. India will differ from China in terms of the growth of its economy and the projected increases in its energy consumption. As their populations grow at a relatively high rate, many other less developed countries will have difficulty making their transition to a lower carbon-use future. The developed rich countries will need to take the lead and demonstrate how low-carbon development can succeed, while the less developed countries will have to try to avoid taking a high-carbon development path to achieve their sustainable development goals. The Chinese project of moving away from a heavy-industrial approach to development towards an ecologically responsible transformation has shown that such policies can work as a means of achieving SDGs. China's transformative policy can be of great value to the global community as an example of how SDGs can be attained by a turn towards a low-carbon economy.

A new vision for a sustainable future

The taken-for-granted goals of development and the foundations of policy orientation since the Industrial Revolution have been to accumulate wealth and spur economic growth. Because most countries have followed this logic, serious problems, such as widening income disparities, environmental degradation, resource depletion, and biodiversity loss, have worsened over the same period. Sustainable development has been recognized as the solution to such problems, yet policymaking in the industrial age has failed to clarify the relationship between humanity and nature. Fast-changing world patterns require a new approach that will allow for sustainable development.

The launch of the 2030 Agenda for Sustainable Development (also referred to as the 2030 Agenda) represents a new start of the transformative process at the global level, as the title of the document indicates: "Transforming Our World."[6] The plan of action as detailed in the Agenda goes beyond the conventional three pillars approach to sustainable development (economy, society, and the environment). That approach did not work well in the past because it still adhered to the model of industrial civilization, calling for economic efficiency, environmental protection, and equity among people and generations. The problem is that although people assumed that all these individual pillars would be consistent with each other, they actually were not. Given the assumptions of the industrialization model, each pillar functioned independently of the others and, in fact, on the whole they offset one another. As a result, it is hard to see how any sort of harmony between man and nature ever could emerge. The new UN agenda adds two new dimensions: peace and partnership. Evidently these two elements are supposed to promote harmony among nations, among people, and between man and nature. Peace is the condition for economic prosperity, environmental protection, and social equity. For the achievement of peace, mutual understanding and cooperation are indispensable; otherwise people will seek to maximize their own advantages without taking into account the needs of others. In fact, they might try to prosper at the expenses of others. In short, we may now have a transformative structure for implementing SDGs, namely, the integration of the so-called five Ps: people-centeredness, economic prosperity, the planetary boundary, peace, and partnerships (Pan & Chen 2016).

The purpose of development is to serve people's needs, and no one should be left behind in the process. Eradication of absolute poverty, hunger, and gender discrimination and access to basic education and health care, clean water, and energy are the key elements behind the human rights to survival and subsistence living. People-centered development requires that the basic necessities of life must be secured. The satisfaction of people's basic needs can be achieved only through the creation of decent jobs, the improvement of both physical and social infrastructure, fair income distribution, the construction of livable and resilient settlements, and producing and consuming in a sustainable manner. Economic prosperity must be green so as not to endanger our living environment in the longer run. Climate security, biodiversity, and healthy oceans are vitally important for the sustainability of planet Earth. Human beings are highly constructive but at the same time can be very destructive. Misconduct and crime can disrupt harmony at local levels, while the clash of civilizations and warfare can destroy trust, social order, and the accumulated wealth of humankind. Loss of biodiversity damages our living community. Without harmony between man and nature, our environment will be degraded. Harmony is the precondition for human well-being, economic development, and environmental protection. And we must work together to build partnerships for strengthening global solidarity. All human beings inhabit the same global village. For both short-term challenges and longer-term concerns, all the stakeholders should stand together, hand in hand, to find "win-win" solutions.

The new vision of 5-P integration has certain advantages for achieving sustainable development goals in a mutually supportive and reinforcing manner. Harmony and partnership are the keys to operationalizing and enhancing people-centered economic development and environmental protection. Peace and partnership must be built into the process of human and economic development and planetary preservation. This 5-P integration represents a new approach, a transformative model for sustainable development. In other words, the UN Agenda provides a vision and elements for a new development paradigm, although it does not show that – or how – we must shift away from industrial civilization.

A shift towards a new paradigm of ecological civilization

A paradigm shift is implied in the UN Agenda for Sustainable Development, and some key elements such as harmony, sustainability, transformation, justice, and inclusiveness do not fit well with the characteristic language of industrial civilization. China has followed the industrial approach towards development following its reforms and opening up in the late 1970s. But adopting the Western model of industrialization inflicted tremendous harm on nature and society. However, by the turn of the century the cultural heritage and Oriental philosophical understanding of the relationship between man and nature already had launched the revival and reframing of the practice of ecological civilization. Moreover, the "ecological civilization" approach to development has been further enhanced, summarized, and promoted in the process of urbanization and industrialization. The outcome shows that China has acted as a pioneer in building an ecological civilization and has mitigated the harmful impact of the industrial approach to nature and society, with positive implications for global efforts to tackle the challenge of transformation.

Industrial and ecological civilization are two different paradigms for development and we need to understand and compare the differences between them such that a transformation can be directed and accelerated. From Figure 1.5, we can see that some differences are fundamental while others are somewhat technical. Under industrial civilization, the ethical foundation is utilitarian and measurement of value is based on human labor, with limited or no attention to nature. To measure the success of an individual or of a group/country, the key indicator is utility: if something is useful, then it possesses value; otherwise there is no value to be measured. This mode of reasoning explains why self-interest dominates a company's or a nation's decision-making processes. In contrast to the characteristic utilitarianism of industrial societies, ecological civilization pursues harmony between man and nature.

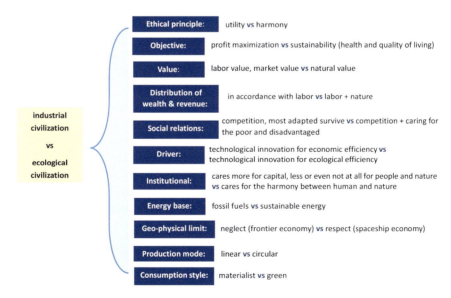

FIGURE 1.5 A comparison of essentials between industrial and ecological civilizations

Source: Pan (2015).

Moreover, ecological civilization seeks ecological justice and social justice: equitable sharing of gains from natural resources, combined with respect for human rights.

In industrial civilizations, the overarching objective is to maximize profits and accumulate wealth. As a result, entire societies come to worship GDP as the indisputable measure of success while staking everything on competition and the quest for immediate financial gains. However, in ecological civilization objectives are more broadly conceived. They include both the preservation of natural assets and the production of material wealth. Natural assets can be maintained by allowing natural processes to work on their own, without extra investment. And in fact, the value of such natural assets actually may appreciate, in contrast to the declining value of human-generated assets over time. The accumulation of material wealth requires a huge amount of costly maintenance and upkeep, which will eventually evaporate through depreciation.

Furthermore, the supply of energy services in industrial civilization relies heavily on fossil fuels. By contrast, ecological civilizations seek to bring about a transition towards sustainable sources. In addition, economic operations under ecological civilization clearly acknowledge the existence of natural limits and are made compatible with the rigidity of resource constraints.

As the dominant paradigm begins to shift, production and consumption patterns also will begin to adapt to changed realities. Under industrial civilization, the mode of production is linear, moving from the extraction and use of raw materials through the production process to culminate in products and waste. Under ecological civilization, on the other hand, the mode will be circular, from raw materials through the production process to products and raw materials. Moreover, lifestyles will be transformed from wasteful and luxurious consumption under industrial civilization into low-carbon, quality-conscious, healthy, and rational consumption in the era of ecological civilization.

Of course, shifting from industrial to ecological civilization does not mean that the merits of industrial civilization must be shunted aside completely. Indeed, all the positive features of industrial civilization should not only be retained but further developed. The technological innovation that can contribute to sustainability and efficiency improvements should be encouraged, but such innovations can inflict damage on nature. The wasting of resources must be restricted or even forbidden. Moreover, institutional systems based on utilitarian principles (e.g., democracy, the rule of law, and market mechanisms) can be incorporated directly into the new era of ecological civilization. However, the paradigm of ecological civilization has features that are unique to it, such as ecological compensation and ecological red lines, as well as the appraisal and evaluation of natural resource inventories and changes.

Accelerating the transformative process

As an agenda for social and economic transformation, the vision and the implications of ecological civilization are clear. However, there are 17 Sustainable Development Goals and 169 targets. Consequently, there is a long way to go before we can implement and achieve them all. Moving ahead one step at a time is the only reasonable way to undertake that transformative process. In addition, transformation literally and fundamentally is different from either revolution or transition. Revolution destroys the old without considering how it is to be replaced. Transition moves from start to finish without looking at how structures undergo intrinsic change (Pan 2016). Transformation is a process that builds upon what already exists, creating a new system that differs from the old one. A new era of ecological civilization must be different from what preceded it, even though some fundamental principles will carry over. One implication is that we should learn some lessons from ecological practices employed in agrarian societies. Also, the process of transformation should be made more inclusive in several respects: in ways of thinking, forms of cooperation, and the reform of institutional systems.

Transformative thinking is crucial for the shift from industrial to ecological civilization. It aims at rethinking or reconsidering the real source of our problems. In the past, poverty alleviation was regarded as burdensome, and it was not seen as the responsibility of the rich. If the issue is examined further, people trapped in poverty can be productive laborers and attractive targets for market expansion. And there is no guarantee that anybody will be exempt from falling into a poverty trap, no matter what the reason may be. Zero-sum thinking overlooks the potential demand for consumption and economic growth when poverty is alleviated. Besides, environmental fragility is often the root cause of extreme poverty. Ecological rehabilitation and restoration are very much in line with the improvement of primary productivity. Wastewater treatment and air pollution control help to secure a high-quality environment, and that, in turn, is an important part of human well-being. Moreover, improving environmental conditions may help enhance productivity. For example, high-quality natural assets bring ecological dividends. Ecologically sustainable products often can be sold, while a healthy environment attracts ecotourism. Investment in renewables certainly will create jobs, generate income, and lead to zero-carbon electricity for energy services.

The importance of cooperation is highlighted in the transformative process through two new pillars: peace and partnerships. Developed countries provide financial and technical support for their developing counterparts to alleviate poverty. This is the good side of the wealthy countries' efforts in the Global South, but we have to make sure that support from the rich world should be environmentally friendly and ecologically sustainable. For instance, climate change and environmental risks are in many cases the root cause of poverty, hence cooperation should meet the criteria of low-carbon energy and affordability.

Partnership-building as specified in the 2030 Agenda must be mutually beneficial and complementary. The developed rich countries such as the US have the economic capability and advanced technology, but support for SDG implementation in developing countries should avoid high-carbon lock-in technologies and demonstrate low-carbon lifestyles. As most developing countries lack the funds and technologies to accomplish sustainable transformation, cooperation between them and wealthier countries will ensure a win-win partnership not only from the perspective of economic prosperity but also for global environmental sustainability.

Institutional innovation will promote effective implementation of cooperative transformation. The Paris Agreement under the UN Framework Convention on Climate Change initiates another international transformative agenda. The Paris Agreement adopts a bottom-up approach to climate actions, calling for individual parties to make nationally determined contributions. What the parties have committed to, however, falls short of meeting the Paris Agreement temperature targets of keeping temperature rise below 2°C by 2100 as compared to pre-industrial levels. Most experts believe that aiming at a target of 1.5°C would be preferable. The negotiations among the parties have been painfully slow and difficult. In addition, protecting and maximizing national interests under the industrial civilization model prevents the delegates from taking more ambitious actions. This is another area of global transformation that has to be accelerated.

Climate targets are somewhat more distant: for instance, the 2°C limit on global temperatures by the end of the century and net zero emissions by the middle of the century. Yet all these longer-term targets will require action right now; otherwise there will be not be enough time to get climate change under control. The SDGs set in the 2030 Agenda have a clear timeline: achievement of the goals within the next decade. This would mean that the SDGs are shorter-term targets than those pertaining to climate change. However, all the targets can be and should be translated into immediate actions. We have no time to wait, let alone to waste. In order to accelerate the transformative process, we need to make fundamental changes. As argued here, that means initiating a shift of the development paradigm from the pursuit and preservation of one's own self-interest under industrial civilization to a win-win scenario in which man and nature are brought into harmony under ecological civilization. Heading in the right direction is indispensable to transformation. The practices adopted by China in its ongoing effort to build an ecological civilization may serve as a model. A low-carbon consumption policy encourages the use of renewable forms of energy and promotes their development. More importantly, there is an urgent need to follow and enforce the principles and institutions implied and specified in the process. That is, we must push forward the shift towards ecological civilization in ways that are green, creative, and sharing. In this regard, the Chinese experience – setting forth all the relevant targets in five-year plans – secures the step-by-step process of transformation.

Notes

1 United Nations, Department of Economic and Social Affairs, Population Division (2019). World Population Prospects 2019, Online Edition. Rev. 1.
2 According to World Bank thresholds for income classification, high-income economies are those with a gross national income per capita of USD 12,376 or more.
3 According to the National Bureau of Statistics, average income is RMB 16,021 (rural) and RMB 42,359 (urban).
4 According to data from the World Steel Association; www.worldsteel.org/steel-by-topic/statistics.html.
5 BP Statistical Review of World Energy, 2019.
6 United Nations (2015).

References

International Energy Agency. 2019. "CO$_2$ Emissions from Fossil Fuel Combustion." IEA, Paris. Available at http://webstore.iea.org/co2-emission-from-fuel-combustion-2019

Li, P., G. Chen, C. Wang, W. Li. Feng, & Y. Zou. 2020. *Society of China: Analysis and Forecast*. Beijing: Social Sciences Academic Press

Pan, J. 2015. *China's Environmental Governing and Ecological Civilization*. Beijing: Springer/China Social Sciences Press

Pan, J. 2016. "Implementation of the Targets Set in the Paris Agreement through Transformative Development." *Journal of Environmental Economics* 1(1): 1–9

Pan, J. 2018. "Building an Ecological Civilization in the New Era: Cognition, Development Paradigm, and Strategic Measures." *Chinese Journal of Urban and Environmental Studies* 6(2). doi:10.1142/S2345748118500094

Pan, J. & Z. Chen. 2016. *A Transformative Agenda. Sustainable Development Goals for 2030: Global Vision and Chinese Experience*. Beijing: Social Sciences Academic Press

United Nations. 2015. "Transforming Our World: 2030 Agenda for Sustainable Development." United Nations, New York. Available at https://sustainabledevelopment.un.org/content/documents/21252030%20Agenda%20for%20Sustainable%20Development%20web.pdf

United Nations, Department of Economic and Social Affairs, Population Division. 2019. "World Population Prospects 2019." Online Edition. Rev. 1. Available at https://population.un.org/wpp/Download/Probabilistic/Population/

Wang, M. 2015. "Road to Paris: The Changed and Unchanged in International Responsibility System." In W. Wang & G. Zheng (eds.), *Annual Report on Actions to Address Climate Change: A New Start and Hope to Paris*. Beijing: Social Sciences Academic Press, pp. 1–16

2
CHINA'S GLOBAL ECOLOGICAL CIVILIZATION AND MULTILATERAL ENVIRONMENTAL GOVERNANCE

Coraline Goron

If not for the COVID-19 pandemic, 2020 should have been the year to launch a crucial decade for global environmental governance. On the one hand, the 26th Conference of the Parties (COP26) to the UN Framework Convention on Climate Change (UNFCCC), to be hosted by the UK in Glasgow in partnership with Italy, was set to reckon with the ability of the 2015 Paris Agreement to ramp up countries' commitments and thereby narrow the emissions gap and secure a chance of keeping global temperature rise below the agreed-upon 2°C. The Intergovernmental Panel on Climate Change (IPCC) had concluded in 2018 that because global temperatures have already increased by 0.8–1.2°C above pre-industrial levels, current policies were insufficient and would lead to a dramatic 3–6°C warming by 2100 (IPCC 2018). On the other hand, the 15th Conference of the Parties (COP15) to the United Nations Convention on Biodiversity (CBD), to be hosted by China in the city of Kunming, was expected to conclude a Paris-like agreement and a new global governance framework to halt the accelerating decline of biodiversity worldwide, which some have characterized as the sixth mass extinction (e.g., Laurence & Ehrlich 2016). In this case as well, the ineffectiveness of current actions was confirmed in 2019 by the Intergovernmental Science-Policy Platform on Biodiversity and Ecosystem Services (IPBES 2019). Yet, both conferences have been postponed until 2021, and the looming global economic crisis caused by the measures adopted to tame the pandemic cast doubts on the capacity and willingness of governments to increase their environmental ambitions.

These scientific warnings and the high expectations initially set for COP26 and COP15 underscore the failure of the global governance frameworks established under the UNFCCC and the CBD since their adoption in 1992 to achieve their environmental goals. The ineffectiveness of multilateral environmental governance in the face of accelerated economic globalization is, according to some, not only a problem of international cooperation and institutions but also and more fundamentally a problem of global values, and more precisely the priority that has been given to economic growth and trade globalization over the environment under the mantra of development in the current world order. This subjection, critics argue, has been embedded in the practice of sustainable development as promoted by the UN since the early 1990s (Bernstein 2002).

From that perspective, the shortcomings of international cooperation practices in the field of environment, defined as "socially meaningful patterns of action which, in being performed competently, simultaneously embody, act out, and possibly reify background knowledge and discourse in and on the material world" (Adler & Pouliot 2011; see also Qin 2019, 2020), stem from the underlying belief, embodied in the principle of sustainable development and theorized by ecological modernization theorists (Mol & Spaargaren 2000), that economic growth and environmental protection are mutually compatible and that therefore the objective of achieving global development and modernization through growth and trade can be pursued (Clapp & Dauvergner 2016).

In other words, if there is an environmental problem with the dominant global culture of development and modernization, then the question arises of whether a shift away from the paradigm of sustainable development at the global level is necessary to achieve more ambitious and effective global environmental governance. A well-documented plurality of environmental discourses has emerged and shaped environmental politics in developed countries since the 1990s (Dryzek 1997). Indeed, as Weale argued in one of the first volumes on environmental politics, environmental politics always have confronted different societal and political programs upholding different understandings of what the environment is, what its protection entails, and what role the economy and the state should play in it (Weale 1992: 30–32).

Since then, "deep greens" (eco-centrists), "red greens" (eco-socialists), and "blue greens" (liberal environmentalists) have proposed widely divergent politico-economic programs to achieve sustainability, even though the deep greens and red greens arguably have remained marginalized in most countries. More recently, new kinds of environmental discourses rooted in traditional cultures and religions have emerged, notably in developing countries. While they do not always take a political form, in some cases they have succeeded in bringing about significant changes. For instance, the promotion of the traditional Quechuan concept of *sumak kawsay* (translated as *buen vivir* in Spanish and "living well" in English) has led to the constitutionalization of nature's rights in several South American countries, notably Bolivia and Ecuador (Fatheuer 2011).

Is this diversification of discourses on sustainability conducive to the emergence of a revamped and greener global development paradigm? Would such a paradigm shift increase the effectiveness of the multilateral environmental governance structures that have been painstakingly developed over the past 50 years? This chapter approaches these eminently complex questions by focusing on the case of China, and more particularly on the concept of "ecological civilization" (EC, 生态文明) it has developed over the past decade, as it was transforming from a veto-wielding power, resisting international commitments to address global environmental problems, into a potent leader of environmental governance. While many welcome China's increased global involvement, others have expressed skepticism. The debate, as in other policy fields, concerns whether a rising China will support or break the global governance system. However, if one considers that the current global system of environmental governance is defective, then the question should no longer be about maintaining or breaking the status quo but rather about how China will influence the direction, scope, and outcome of its reform.

This chapter demonstrates that the reception of the Chinese concept of EC by the international community has been mixed. I argue that this lukewarm reception by the rest of the world is due in part to the fact that Chinese leaders have not clearly proposed EC as a competing paradigm for global development. Instead, it has more often been presented either as a Sinicization of sustainable development (UNEP 2015) or as an element of a nationalist discourse in which a supposedly superior "Chinese model" is offered to the rest of the world (see, e.g., Zhang 2008). It is also due to the discrepancy between the more ambitious and radical interpretation of EC and China's environmental governance practices both domestically and internationally. My contention is that the ambivalence of China's practice affects its contribution to the ongoing reforms of the global climate change and biodiversity regimes.

I begin by providing a brief overview of academic debates regarding the failure of multilateral environmental governance, highlighting the importance of global policy paradigms embedded in a global culture of modernization. Then I introduce the Chinese concept of EC, discussing its implications for global environmental governance in conjunction with the new Chinese foreign policy concept of "community of common destiny" (CCD, 人类命运共同体). Next, I analyze several Western intellectual and academic reactions to the concept of EC, which have initiated its inclusion in the global debate on sustainability and yet show little agreement on its meaning and implications. Finally, I evaluate the impact of EC on China's practice of multilateral environmental governance in the fields of climate change and biodiversity.

Global values, policy paradigms, and the failure of global environmental governance institutions

The reasons adduced for the failure of global environmental governance to prevent the acceleration of predicted environmental crises are varied, reflecting different theoretical positions on what it takes to ensure international cooperation in an anarchic world. For some, this failure can be explained by a lack of political leadership from powerful nations, especially the US, and the use of a "veto" power by large polluters and "megadiverse" developing countries[1] against legally binding commitments that would constrain their economic growth (Brenton 2013; Sell 1996). From this perspective, only a conversion of the global hegemon (the US) or its replacement (e.g., by China) can bring about a durable solution. For others, this failure is due to the fragmentation of global environmental governance (Biermann et al. 2009), with over 1,300 multilateral environmental agreements (MEAs)[2] forming what Young summarized as "a messy patchwork made up of a collection of disparate pieces that do not fit together to form a coherent whole" (2008: 17). Repeated calls to build a world environmental organization and international environmental court have been made over the past decade in order to resolve this fragmentation, streamline enforcement, and ensure compliance with global norms. Still other researchers have argued persuasively that there is intrinsic governance value in the diversity and even partial redundancy of MEAs, which enables flexibility and innovation and also facilitates the emergence of new, potentially more ambitious international practices (Keohane & Victor 2010; Orsini et al. 2013). The problem, they contend, is not one of weak global organization but rather of weak institutions adopted to regulate the behavior of states and relevant economic actors within MEAs (Young 2008). Pushing this argument further, many environmental theorists have argued that the failure to adopt adequate institutions is fundamentally rooted in the value system of the current world economic order, which has put the pursuit of industrialized prosperity above respect for planetary ecological limits (e.g., Gare 2017; Pan 2016, 2020, this volume), and the associated economic-liberal, capitalist paradigm underpinning economic globalization (Bernstein 2002; Klein 2014).

As mentioned previously, a key target of criticism has been the concept of sustainable development, which claimed to resolve the tension between environment and development that emerged on the global stage in the 1970s. Originally defined as "development that meets the needs of the present without compromising the ability of future generations to meet their own needs" in the 1987 Brundtland Commission Report, *Our Common Future*, it since has been more precisely understood as "the capability of maintaining, over indefinite periods of time, specified values of human wellbeing, social equity and environmental quality" (Leach et al. 2010: xiv).

Sustainable development embodies the promise that every nation can achieve modern prosperity while preserving global ecological resources. Such a concept would go well beyond the compromise reached between developed countries that wanted to restrict global growth (especially in the developing world) for environmental protection and developing countries, especially China and India, that claimed their right to development. This promise was institutionalized as the overarching principle of the United Nations' environmental action at the Rio Earth Summit in 1992. As shown in Figure 2.1, it was reiterated, with few amendments, during the following two decades until becoming completely identified with the UN development agenda through the adoption of the Sustainable Development Goals (SDGs) in 2015. The latter incorporated the principle that environmental protection is not only a precondition but also a driver of future economic development.

This institutionalization success story contrasts with the failure to halt (or even to slow down) the three major global environmental crises for which multilateral

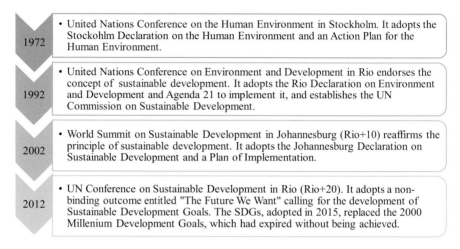

FIGURE 2.1 The institutionalization of the concept of sustainable development

environmental agreements were signed at the Rio Summit in 1992, alongside its adoption in the Rio Declaration: climate change, loss of biodiversity, and desertification. Unlike mere declarations, MEAs cement the development of regimes (i.e., jointly agreed objectives) but also norms, rules, and decision-making procedures around which actors' expectations converge,[3] and on this basis they make commitments to regulate the behavior of economic actors within their jurisdiction.

The objectives of the UNFCCC and CBD – two framework conventions destined to be further elaborated over time – were defined in 1992. For the former, the goal was "to stabilize greenhouse gas concentrations at a level that would prevent dangerous anthropogenic interference with the climate system" (UNFCCC, article 2). The objective of the latter convention was "to promote the conservation and sustainable use of biological diversity, as well as the fair and equitable sharing of genetic resources" (CBD, article 1). However, both have grappled with the implementation of the norm of sustainable development in ways that may have stifled the pursuit of their environmental raison d'être.

The two conventions created and sustained environmental regimes that share some similarities but also display significant differences. Each has led to the adoption of protocols specifying the rules of conduct of member states to achieve the convention's goals. Each also established multilateral scientific bodies (the IPCC and the IPBES, respectively) to accumulate scientific knowledge and inform the international community, even though the IPCC was created in 1988, four years before the signing of the UNFCCC, and the IPBES was created outside the UN in 2012, 20 years after the signing of the CBD. This difference reflects the comparatively low level of international concern for biodiversity issues and the comparative weakness of that regime's institutions. But that weakness also could be attributed to the way in which the goals of the CBD were expanded to include not only the protection of biodiversity but also the use of biodiversity to create technology and wealth as well as compromises about the way in which this wealth should be shared (Chasek et al. 2017). The same mandate is reflected in the scientific mission of the IPBES, which is to "strengthen the science-policy interface for biodiversity and ecosystem services for the conservation and sustainable use of biodiversity, long-term human well-being and sustainable development."[4]

The prominent role of development as a goal of the CBD has had several consequences. First, the US never signed the CBD because it fundamentally disagreed with the inclusion of provisions on genetic resources (even while it has participated as an active observer in CBD negotiations). Second, like the UNFCCC, whose Kyoto Protocol aimed at reducing greenhouse gas emissions responsible for climate change, the CBD also adopted protocols to further its regime. The 2000 Cartagena Protocol and 2010 Nagoya Protocol addressed thorny but arguably peripheral issues pertaining, respectively, to the biosafety of trade in genetically modified organisms and to access to and utilization of genetic resources. But these protocols suffered from defections due to the opposition of big agronomic and pharmaceutical industrial interests (Chasek et al. 2017). Meanwhile, biodiversity protection has been addressed through non-binding programs and targets and other pre-existing conventions like the Convention on International Trade in Endangered Species (CITES, adopted in 1973). These have left many critical areas inadequately addressed, including global commons like the oceans and forests. Third, with more ambitious environmental goals and higher stakes in the outcome of negotiations, the COP meetings of the UNFCCC have been more frequent than those of the CBD (annually rather than every other year) and better structured (with more institutionalized and coordinated negotiation groups). They have secured the direct involvement of higher-level country representatives, with nations sending their heads of states or government to finalize deals and compromises at the UNFCCC, while usually not sending higher than minister-level representatives to the CBD.

That being said, sustainable development concerns have not been absent from the UNFCCC. But instead of being formulated in the goal, they have been addressed through the implementation of the cornerstone principle of "common but differentiated responsibility and respective capabilities" (CBDR-EC), which was akin to finding a balance between ensuring the right of developing countries to develop and reach the level of prosperity enjoyed by industrialized countries on the one hand and containing the growth in global emissions on the other hand. It is now evident that this balancing act failed and that global emissions have increased to unprecedented levels, while reductions were undertaken only by a relatively small group of developed countries that had ratified the Kyoto Protocol. However, the Copenhagen summit in 2009 proved that it was impossible to extend the top-down approach of multilaterally negotiated emissions targets adopted in Kyoto to all developed and developing countries. Negotiations turned into a blame game about who should reduce more, who should have more responsibility, and what was a fair distribution of the so-called remaining carbon budget.

The solution eventually embodied in the 2015 Paris Agreement included a revision of the CBDR principle negotiated between the US and China, with the rhetorical addendum "in light of different national circumstances." It enabled agreement on a universal, legally binding target to limit global temperature increase to 1.5–2°C, and on the fact that this target would be fulfilled by commitments made unilaterally and voluntarily by each member states. Bernstein and Hoffman welcomed "the beginning of a profound conceptual shift in global environmental governance . . . from a collective action problem to a catalytic mechanism to promote and facilitate transformative pathways to decarbonization" (Bernstein & Hoffman 2018: 190). However, this institutional innovation adopted in Paris rested on the promise of a "green industrial revolution" that would generate dividends of green growth, tech, and jobs in front-running nations (Goron & Freeman 2018; He 2011).

Sadly, the voluntary commitments pledged by countries following the adoption of the Paris Agreement have proven insufficient to fulfill the binding 2°C target. Also, with the US withdrawal and increasing global tensions regarding which country will "win" or "lose" the green technology race, the narrative of the green industrial revolution as a spinoff from sustainable development already has revealed significant limitations. Signs of countries dramatically ratcheting up their climate ambitions are hard to find.

As for the CBD, the IPBES reports have made it abundantly clear that the non-binding Aichi Targets adopted in 2010 have not been met (CBD 2018). The widespread recognition of this failure has given rise to demands for the negotiation of a Paris-like agreement that would make biodiversity conservation goals both more stringent and better enforced. Yet, the fact that developmental goals are stipulated alongside conservation goals in the Convention and the fact that most biodiverse countries are developing countries whose economic advancement depends (for some, in large measure) on the exploitation of natural resources have made this endeavor very challenging. As we will see in a later section, China, as the host of the upcoming COP15, faces tremendous pressures to push for more ambitious conservation goals and institutions in Kunming.

In short, the fact that both the UNFCCC and the CBD have been shaped by the idea of sustainable development, and their subsequent failure to achieve their environmental goals due to many countries' pursuit of economic growth, may call for the adoption of an alternative, more ambitious, and perhaps more eco-centric concept to guide UN environmental action. But there are not many candidates. One attractive concept that has emerged in the past decade is that of the Anthropocene, a word that expresses the realization that humans now have the power to alter, and perhaps destroy, fundamental systems enabling life on planet Earth (Kolbert 2015). Although its dystopian take on humanity's environmental impact has mobilized large environmental movements in Western countries, especially among youth, it has not received substantial buy-in from global environmental institutions. Meanwhile, some scholars have suggested that the Chinese concept of EC could provide an alternative development theory capable of revolutionizing the global economic order and bringing about a global ecological transition (Pan 2016; Gare 2017). The rest of this chapter evaluates this possibility by analyzing the Chinese discourse of EC, its reception by Western scholars, and its impact on China's practice of global environmental governance.

The political and cultural meaning of the Chinese concepts of "ecological civilization" and "community of common destiny"

In order to evaluate the potential implications of ecological civilization (EC) for global environmental governance, it is important to understand how it has become a central political value within China and how it has been used by China on the global stage. We also must analyze the political and cultural content of this concept and assess whether it is intended as a domestic or global strategy of development. In this section, I argue that while the value content of EC remains ambiguous, its association with the foreign policy concept of community of common destiny (CCD) in recent years has supported a more active normative engagement of China in global environmental governance.

Until about a decade ago, the environmental agenda of Chinese policymakers revolved mainly around the concept of sustainable development, as defined by the UN. Some Chinese documents now present EC as having taken root in the country's first environmental regulations adopted in the 1970s, even going back to Mao Zedong's thought.[5] But in fact, until the mid-2000s the term "ecological civilization" was used only sporadically by some academics following its first appearance in the translation of a Russian article published in the newspaper *Guangming ribao* in 1985. As illustrated in Figure 2.2, it was the official endorsement by President Hu Jintao in his work report to the 17th Communist Party Congress in 2007 that triggered its emergence in public discourse. Since then, EC has become a central element of the development doctrine of China's party-state; it was introduced in the constitution of the Communist Party of China (CCP) in 2012 and in the constitution of the People's Republic in 2018. Meanwhile, both the CCP and the state apparatuses have built new institutions to implement this doctrine, including the party's "Task Force for the Promotion of Economic Development and Ecological Civilization" in 2013 and the state's revamped Ministry of Ecology and Environment (MEE) in 2018. Party and state organs have also jointly issued a series of central-level documents aimed at greening the party-state. The "Central Opinions on Ecological Civilization Construction" and the action plan issued in 2015, in combination with the "Central Opinions on the Delineation and Adherence to the Ecological Protection Red Lines" issued in 2017, have provided a top-level design for ecological planning. The 2016 "Methods for the Evaluation of the Achievement of Eco-civilization Construction Targets" and the 2019 "Working Rules Pertaining to the Central Environmental Protection Inspections" have instituted a centralized politico-administrative evaluation, control, and sanction of local cadres' environmental performance and responsibility. These new institutions, together with significant legal developments and impressive propaganda deployment, have become landmarks of environmental governance under EC in China, with some

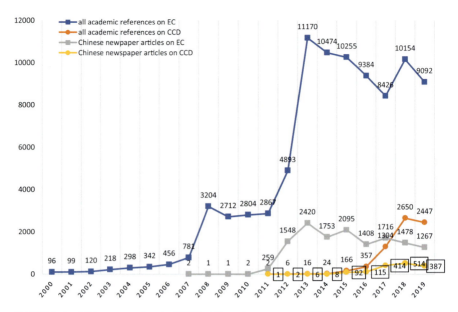

FIGURE 2.2 Chinese academic (2000–19) and newspaper (2007–19) references to the concepts of "ecological civilization" (EC) and "community of common destiny" (CCD)

Source: CNKI database.

Note: The database of academic sources (文献) and newspapers (报纸) were searched with the approximative topics (模糊, 主题) of ecological civilization (生态文明) and community of common destiny (人类命运共同体) on May 14, 2020.

results mostly visible in the reduction of air pollution and the closure of myriad polluting plants across the country between 2016 and 2019.

The institutionalization of EC within the structures of the party-state is important because it anchors EC to China's authoritarian regime and also ties it to the official doctrine of "socialism with Chinese characteristics." As I have argued elsewhere (Goron 2018), even though EC emerged in the 2000s as a way for Hu Jintao to acknowledge the questioning of China's unsustainable development mode in the face of unsustainable economic growth, increasing inequalities, and growing social unrest, its constitutionalization as one of the CCP's core missions has transformed it into a doctrine disseminated by the state propaganda system into every corner of the Chinese society. The use of the term "civilization" (*wenming* 文明) sanctions the inclusion of ecology in the ambit of the CCP's self-defined governing objectives. Since 2012, the so-called five-in-one mission (*wu wei yi ti* 五位一体) encompassing economic, political, cultural, societal, and ecological civilization construction has replaced the former duo of "material civilization" and "spiritual civilization" promoted by Deng Xiaoping in the 1980s in the CCP Constitution. This close association with the CCP determines the political culture that EC carries with it when it is promoted internationally.

However, it is also important to try to decipher the ecological values promoted through this concept, so as to better understand the worldview it proposes, and whether or not it differs from the concept of sustainable development. Since 2013, President Xi Jinping has promoted an EC doctrine that does propose a specific worldview, even though its contours and references have been debated among Chinese intellectuals, by associating it with the discourse on the "Chinese dream of national rejuvenation" (*Zhongguo meng* 中国梦) and the "New Era" (*xin shidai* 新时代). In this sense, EC embodies the belief that environmental problems are solvable and that they will be solved under the leadership of the CCP (Wang 2018: 730). It also represents a promise that the attainment of the right balance between humans and nature will enable prosperity forever; this in essence is the message delivered by Xi Jinping's most quoted EC aphorism: "Lucid waters and lush mountains are invaluable assets" (*lvshui qingshan jiu shi Jinshan yingshan* 绿水青山就是金山银山). Furthermore, in line with the historical materialism that characterizes the doctrine of socialism with Chinese characteristics (Foster 2017), EC has been presented as the next step in the evolution of human civilization, coming after the "primitive civilization" (*yuanshe wenming* 原始文明), the agricultural civilization (*nongye wenming* 农业文明), and the industrial civilization (*gongye wenming* 工业文明) (Ke 2013). In this sense, Marinelli's interpretation is persuasive when he argues that the idea of ecological civilization has become part of "a teleological discourse, characterized by a normative, prescriptive, and also deterministic connotation of progress," with a "recurring projection of the solution into an allegedly perfect future" (2018: 368). The Chinese philosopher Song Tian distinguishes between two interpretations of this vision, which need to be distinguished if we are to understand the ambiguous relationship between EC and sustainable development. According to Tian, the mainstream interpretation of EC is what he calls the "most advanced stage" interpretation, where EC follows the logic of ecological modernization and sustainable development and supports the idea that environmental problems will be solved with more progress in technology and science. A more radical interpretation of EC, which Tian defends against the former, is what he calls a "total transformation" interpretation of EC, which implies a complete overhaul of the culture of industrial civilization, including a rejection of the values of development, economic growth, and the belief in science and technology as a panacea for environmental problems (Tian 2019).

Other elements of the EC doctrine refer specifically to characteristics of China's political and traditional culture, with divergent interpretations indicating a tension between universalism and nationalism. First, because EC is part of "socialism with Chinese characteristics," it has been associated by some with an anti-capitalist critique of global environmental governance institutions, including the theory of ecological modernization and sustainable development. Such concepts are rejected because they are allegedly subordinate to and undermined by the capitalist world economy. Thus, these charges in some ways echo the critique of eco-socialism in the West (Pan 2006; Huan 2007, 2017), but they also have been marshaled to support a nationalist discourse concerning the superiority of China's political regime (e.g., Zhang 2008). Second, the EC discourse also includes references to China's traditional culture, which is then counterposed to the unsustainable canons of modernization (high energy consumption, urbanization, speedy transportation, etc.). Notions from Buddhism, Daoism, and Confucianism, including the principle of "harmony between man and nature" (天人合一; Pan 2016; Zeng 2019) and the discursive valorization of rural societies and minorities' traditional ways of interacting with nature, are all part of this critique of the "industrial culture" (e.g., Wen et al. 2012; for a critical review of EC practice in minority areas, see Zeng 2019). There is no doubt that this cultural, ethical, or religious dimension of the EC discourse has been used in official media to boost nationalism by portraying environmental degradation as something fundamentally "non-Chinese." However, a popular reading of EC among Chinese environmental activists emphasizes the usefulness of these traditional references to encourage change in individuals' and societal values; it supports their advocacy of alternative lifestyles, which are often much more radically green than what the party-state envisages and supports (e.g., of a rural and frugal lifestyle; cf. Cao & Yin 2014).[6] In other words, these environmentalists adhere to the discourse of EC because they interpret it as opening up the possibility of a "total change," whereas 20 years of "sustainable development" in China have led to an ecological disaster.

Just as there have been different interpretations of what EC means for China, there are also different interpretations of its implications for global environmental governance. First, it is important to distinguish between different kinds of influences. One type of global influence can be realized merely by changing China domestically, because of China's size and importance in the world economy. The China Council for International Cooperation on Environment and Development (CCICED), a boundary institution created in 1992 to institutionalize communication between the Chinese leadership and the international community on sustainability, drew the following conclusion: "As China transforms into an ecological civilization domestically, there will be many ramifications for trade and investment both internally and abroad" (CCICED 2018: 6).

An example of this kind of reasoning can be found in the article by Jiang et al. (2013) published in *Climate Policy*, which is intended to show how China's domestic efforts to reduce coal consumption contribute towards achieving the 2°C target. The perspective implies that EC would be primarily a domestic project. It is in line with a traditional Chinese approach to global governance, which considers that solving China's problems is the best way to contribute to global public goods and UN development goals. Consequently, this perspective does not contest the mainstream concepts promoted at the UN. On the contrary, it presents EC merely as a localization of the global norm of sustainable development (SD) and implies that SD and EC are compatible, if not essentially similar.

Another arguably more ambitious way for EC to achieve global influence would be to promote a change in the world economic order from its core, for instance by championing EC as a replacement for the norm of sustainable development. A strong international promotion of EC is supported by the adoption of the foreign policy concept of "community of common destiny" (CCD, *renlei minyun gongtongti* 人类命运共同体), which first appeared in Hu Jintao's report to the 18th CCP Congress in 2012 and has been further developed and promoted by Xi Jinping both domestically and internationally, especially since the CCP's 19th Congress in 2017 (Zhang 2017). The rapid upgrading of this concept, which has become a new cornerstone of China's foreign policy discourse, is evident (as illustrated in Figure 2.2) from the significant increase in newspaper and academic articles recorded in the CNKI database, from just one article in 2011 to 2,650 in 2018. Although the total number of articles on CCD remains smaller than the number of those devoted to EC (over 10,000 articles published in 2018), it is still significant because, contrary to EC, related publications are confined to the field of international relations and foreign policy analysis.

As with EC, interpretations of CCD have varied. For some, it is merely a reiteration of Hu Jintao's peaceful development (*heping fazhan* 和平发展) doctrine, but for others it serves to appease the anxieties created by the more assertive foreign policy launched by Xi Jinping, which broke with Deng's strategy of "hiding the capacity and keeping a low profile" (*taoguang yanghui* 韬光养晦) in favor of "striving for achievements" (*fenfa youwei* 奋发有为; Yan 2014; Zhang 2017). By emphasizing a "common destiny," CCD claims that China's intentions are good and that it wants to work together with other nations to address the problems of the world. To those worried that China would seek to overturn the current global order, it "conveys the message that China wishes to maintain the status quo and has no intention to introduce fundamental changes," but also that it wants to take a more active part in it (Zhang 2017: 198).

In his speech before the UN General Assembly in 2015, Xi Jinping provided a definition of CCD in which green development appeared prominently.[7] It can be inferred that EC and CCD are linked. In fact, they are also connected because they form part of "Xi Jinping's Thought" and legacy, as well as in the way both have been fleshed out with ethical and cultural values drawn from Chinese traditional culture. This combination suggests that China might want to use EC to "strive for achievements" in the field of global environmental governance. Yet, the extent to which it might do so successfully depends on demonstrating the necessity of replacing the current mainstream value of sustainable development by a new development paradigm based on EC, and whether the cultural, socio-economic, and political values projected by EC will appeal to the international community.

The international community's mixed reception of "ecological civilization"

As the international community has become better acquainted with EC, it too has shown some ambivalence about the meaning and values embodied in that concept. We should point out that this acquaintance is fairly recent, since until 2012 EC was not systematically translated as such in English publications; the terms "ecological progress" or "environmental protection" often were used instead, but they failed to convey its specific political value content. Since 2012, efforts have been made by China to hasten the publication of more accurate translations and convey the point that EC was and is more than a synonym for environmental protection. This section provides a preliminary analysis of some representative works written by Western scholars that offer various interpretations of its meaning and its implications beyond China's borders, and thereby it provides a glimpse of the purchase of EC within the international community.

The first significant international publication on EC was issued by the UN Environment Programme (UNEP) in 2015 in collaboration with the Think Tank of the Chinese Ministry of Environmental Protection and the CCICED (UNEP 2015). Titled *Green Is Gold: The Strategy and Actions of China's Ecological Civilization*, this report claims China's "firm supports and active implementation of the concept and actions of sustainable development at the global level" and that "its effort to build an Eco-civilization will make a significant contribution to the 2030 Agenda for Sustainable Development." The foreword, written by UNEP executive director Achim Steiner, similarly presents EC as "one of the national sustainable development models," alongside such concepts as Bhutan's Gross National Happiness, Thailand's Sufficiency Economy, and Bolivia's Living Well. Thus, EC is considered as one of multiple pathways to implementing the UN's SDGs locally. There is no perceptible contradiction or even competition between EC and SD; EC is set within the limited domestic Chinese context, with its strategies, innovations, and projected outcomes considered not only compatible with but also supportive of the UN's Agenda for Sustainable Development.

In fact, many critical scholars also consider that Chinese domestic practices of EC are basically following the mantra of SD that they judge inefficient. For instance, Elizabeth Lord concludes in her doctoral dissertation that China's local practice of EC, "for a large majority, simply means pursuing the economic and political status quo, and integrating some environmental components to the existing model, a process akin to 'sustainable development' where development is still central" (2018: 207).

The second publication I looked at is an article by Adrian Ely and Sam Geall[8] published in the authoritative *China Quarterly*. Based on theories emphasizing the importance of narratives in shaping pathways of action, they argue that EC, in that it embodies "the adoption of a more proactive rhetorical stance on environmental reform and international environmental diplomacy," might be an important signal in the Chinese context that could even "help to underpin a green transformation, one of great consequence if it can be properly harnessed" (Geall & Ely 2017: 1178). This publication thus offers a hopeful view of EC, which – while circumscribing the changes it would bring mainly to "the Chinese context" – suggests that this change could unleash new capacities for global action in the environmental field. Hence, even though they underline the fact that EC is the "first civilizing slogan with global dimension," the impact they expect would be on China's willingness to support multilateral efforts, which could be harnessed by those wishing for more ambitious global environmental institutions, especially European countries and the

UN. They do not argue, however, that EC could be promoted by China as a new global norm and development paradigm.

The third publication is an article by Australian philosopher Arran Gare, published in 2017, which condenses the argument developed in his book, *The Philosophical Foundations of Ecological Civilization: A Manifesto for the Future*. Gare delivers a very strong critique of the concept of sustainable development, which he presents as having crippled efforts to comprehend the ecological crisis, because

> built into the notion of sustainable development is a bifurcation where what really matters is the development of the economy, and the ecosystems of which humans are part are considered in terms of whether they are sustainable under the stress of the developing economy.
>
> (Gare 2017: 132)

According to Gare, SD was adopted with the support of big business to neutralize challenges from an emerging deep green counterculture. The author thus endorses EC as an alternative to a "Western-dominated" ecocidal[9] economic world order. He then goes on to argue that environmentalists should align themselves with ecological civilization because it has been endorsed by China, which "is clearly emerging as a superpower and increasingly will challenge existing power structures in the world" (Gare 2017: 135). Having briefly reviewed China's efforts and mentioned Confucianism and Daoism as cultural underpinnings, he contends that "China will take a leading role in the struggle to create a global civilization, reorienting humanity to overcome the threat to global ecological destruction" (Gare 2017: 138). Gare thus associates a transformative interpretation of EC with a hegemonic transition in favor of China.

The fourth publication, by Sinologist Jean-Yves Heurtebise, argues for a view diametrically opposed to that of Gare, because he argues that EC may be detrimental to global environmental governance. He criticizes EC for harboring the contestable claim that "the essence of the Asian ethos would be 'a holistic harmony' and therefore inherently more eco-friendly than European culture inclined towards dualistic individualisms" (Heurtebise 2017: 8). A leitmotiv of Chinese EC discourse has indeed been that "China should not follow the same environmentally harmful development path of the West" (Pan Yue, cited in Heurtebise 2017: 8), even though China already suffers from the over-exploitation of its environmental resources resulting from three decades of accelerated industrialization and urbanization. As evidence of the way in which culture and nationalism are intertwined, a 2015 editorial in the *People's Daily* claimed that China's "profound cultural heritage of loving and protecting nature" was "beyond reach for other cultures" (cited in Goron 2018: 43). Heurtebise warns that such a discourse is not only inaccurate but also in contradiction with the need for collaborative action among nations to address global environmental problems. From this perspective, EC as promoted by China is potentially alienating the international community and is being used in a way that not only fails to promote major change in the global institutions of environmental governance but also threatens the multilateral efforts made to obtain more ambitious commitments for a higher level of environmental protection from governments, including that of China itself.

The last publication I reviewed, titled *What Is Ecological Civilization?*, was published by researchers at the Institute of Ecological Civilization based in the US. It represents an intellectual movement that regards EC as a global model opposed to that created by modernization and industrialization (Clayton & Schwartz 2019). It stems from philosopher John Cobb, for whom EC is a post-modern project that proposes a hopeful vision for a future global civilization which has secured its own survival on the planet (Clayton & Schwartz 2019). That vision is thus more in line with Tian (2019) and his "total change" interpretation of EC. While the authors pay some tribute to China for endorsing the concept, they insist that this implies much more radical changes including forgoing the objective of modernization. Hence, they proudly state that "in our work in China we have, with some success, made the goal of ecological civilization controversial by suggesting that it subordinates the aim to modernize" (Clayton & Schwartz 2019: 8). Furthermore, John Cobb's EC conception is rooted in the promotion of civil society's actions. In this sense, Clayton and Schwartz effectively support the view advocated by American political comparativist Roy Morrison, for whom ecological civilization was "a call for democracy" and not a call "for better management or stronger authority" (Morrison 1995: 3). That view is at odds with the centralized, bureaucratic, and sometimes authoritarian practices put in place by the Chinese government to reach its ecological civilization goals.

The various publications cited in this section have ushered in a necessary dialogue with China's concept of EC, and they demonstrate both a growing interest in and significant uncertainty regarding its interpretation and implications. These uncertainties are not necessarily a bad thing, as most international norms develop and gain consensus by enabling different actors to project their own meanings and values into them. Sustainable development provides a prime example of such a process. However, as outlined above, this global conversation will be influenced by the way in which China engages the international community and accepts co-construction, implying an internationalization, a loss of control over the discourse, and perhaps the possibility of being held accountable for not living up to the standards of a more radical, more democratic, and more ambitious interpretation of EC.

For now, EC remains by and large unacknowledged by Western societies, and it has no purchase within global environmental and climate movements. EC promotion beyond China's borders has not yet succeeded. Whether or not China is keen on leading a discursive battle at the UN is uncertain. The next section examines whether EC and CCD have influenced China's practice of global multilateralism and, in particular, whether they have propelled China to lead the reforms for more ambitious and effective institutions to halt global climate change and biodiversity loss.

China's practice of ecological civilization in multilateral environmental governance within the fields of climate change and biodiversity

If EC is not yet sufficiently mature to challenge global norms on development and environment, it is important to verify whether the endorsement of that principle has led China to support or resist the existing institutions of multilateral environmental governance. Because China is a big player and potentially wields a veto power over many global environmental issues, its leadership within the framework of multilateral cooperation can make a difference, especially when other major nations, like the US, withdraw.

China has signed and ratified a large number of MEAs, among them the UNFCCC and the CBD. It is one of the largest emitters of greenhouse gases, accounting for 29% of annual global emissions in 2018. Moreover, it is a megadiverse country, harboring nearly 10% of all plant species and 14% of animal species on Earth.[10] However, its participation level in both regimes has been highly uneven. In regard to climate change, China has been a vocal participant ever since the negotiation of the UNFCCC in 1992. But while engaging with the process, the Chinese government has resisted the multilateral imposition of emissions reduction targets. In Chinese eyes, the principle of common but differentiated responsibility implied a recognition of its and other developing countries' right to industrialize, and therefore to pollute, as well as of the moral duty of developed countries to help them "leapfrog" into greener modes of industrialization via financial and technology transfers (Heggelund 2007). The Chinese position has not changed much in the decades since 1992. At the Copenhagen COP in 2009, despite the fact that China had announced a unilateral pledge to reduce the carbon intensity of its economy by 40%–45% by 2020, it vehemently opposed European proposals to include some developing countries in the second phase of the Kyoto Protocol.

The presidency of Xi Jinping, associated with the promotion of EC, has brought significant change. The obligation to address global climate change became aligned with Xi's domestic economic reform agenda and the war on pollution (Hilton & Kerr 2017). Xi claimed that addressing climate change was in China's interest and not a duty imposed by others;[11] accordingly he also encouraged a more active diplomatic effort. China signed several bilateral agreements in the run-up to the Paris COP and, most importantly, reached a pathbreaking agreement with the Obama administration in 2014, which was instrumental in sealing key compromises on the bottom-up and universal structure of the Paris Agreement. In this process, China accepted both the universal obligation for all countries, including developing countries, to reduce their emissions, and to take part in a multilateral review and evaluation of its actions, something to which it had been sternly opposed before.

The change of US administration in 2016 left a vacuum of leadership, and many turned to China to fill it. Geall and Ely (2017) note that Xi's continued commitment to the Paris Agreement, made at the World Economic Forum in Davos, received almost universal praise. Yet, China's capacity and willingness to exercise this leadership have been questioned (e.g., Economy 2017). Xi Jinping has made efforts to maintain the Paris momentum in the years that followed. He hosted a G20 summit in Hangzhou dedicated to the low-carbon transition and joined the Ministerial on Climate Action created by Canada and the EU to replace the Major Economies Forum, which had been led by the US under the Obama administration and was dismantled by its successor. Furthermore, while holding to its developing country status, China made unilateral commitments to provide USD 5 billion of climate cooperation aid to other developing countries. It also has been deeply involved in the negotiations of the Paris Rulebook, especially the enhanced transparency framework, for which it was nominated as a co-facilitator, together with the US.[12] In this context, it played a critical role in resolving a stand-off which opposed the Like-Minded Developing Countries (LMDC, to which China belongs) to developed countries like the US and the EU, regarding whether there should be one set of transparency and reporting rules for all (which the US and the EU wanted) or a different set of rules applying to developed and developing countries (which the LMDCs wanted). Eventually, during the second week of negotiations at the COP25 in Katowice, China's Special Representative for Climate Change Xie Zhenhua announced that China would accept a single rulebook. This change, which enabled the Katowice summit to be a success, was accomplished by the participants agreeing to include a number of flexibilities in the rules themselves, many of which accommodated China's needs. China also insisted that the choice to use these flexibilities would be left out of the review and compliance procedures of the Paris Agreement. Once China and the developed countries agreed on these conditions, the support of the rest of the LMDCs for a single rulebook was immediately obtained.

This episode illustrates China's increasingly skilled climate diplomacy but not necessarily its leadership in bringing about the most ambitious and effective climate regime. Moreover, in recent years China's commitment to act on climate change has shown signs of weakening. Although China already met its 2020 carbon intensity target (40%–45%) in 2017, three years ahead of schedule, its CO_2 emissions rose in 2017 and again in 2018. The objective put forward in its Nationally Determined Contributions (NDC), that they will peak by 2030, is universally considered as conservative and insufficient to keep global temperatures below 2°C.[13] China thus will face tremendous pressure to ratchet up its contributions for 2030, but thus far it has not been particularly proactive in proposing an upgraded NDC.

This coming of age of China's climate diplomacy since 1992 contrasts with its discreet, almost unnoticeable contribution to the CBD process over the same period. Over the past 30 years, China for the most part has not actively engaged with the CBD negotiations, even though it ratified both the Cartagena and the Nagoya Protocols in 2000 and 2016, respectively. This sluggishness is reflected in the paucity of scholarly analyses of China's relationship to the CBD, compared to the already significant literature on its relationship to the UNFCCC. And yet, biodiversity and conservation are hot issues in China not only because of the trade in endangered species, which has been addressed under CITES, but also because of the challenges that China has faced in its efforts to protect biodiversity within its own borders. Notable among those efforts have been the progressive establishment and difficult supervision of a vast network of protected areas since the 1980s and the implementation of the idea of "ecological redlines" in 2017.

EC can be seen as having brought a major change in China's attitude towards the CBD because the country offered to host the COP15 in 2020, which is expected to adopt major reform of the current regime governance structure under the Post-2020 Global Biodiversity Framework. This represents a significant diplomatic challenge, because although a "zero draft"[14] was proposed by a working group co-chaired by Canada and Uganda in January of 2020, little progress has been made in resolving outstanding disagreements between parties on the scope and shape of this framework. As a CCICED report highlighted,

> there is still a great gap between high expectations on the part of scientists and others alarmed at the rapid global ecological damage and biodiversity loss, and existing political will nationally and globally to take sufficient action to guarantee a sustainable future.
>
> *(CCICED 2019: 5)*

The need for strong political leadership is widely recognized. Yet, while China contributed to the Sharm El-Sheikh to Beijing Action Agenda for Nature and People established at the COP14 in 2018,[15] other countries have arguably shown more leadership than China. France, keen on exporting its experience with the Paris Agreement, tabled a Global Pact for Environment at the UN High Level Political Forum in July 2017; Canada hosted a Nature Champions meeting in April 2019 in Montreal, attended by environment ministers and leaders from various non-governmental organizations; and Costa Rica launched a High Ambition Coalition of nations to push for a Deal for Nature on the eve of the UN Secretary-General's Climate Summit in New York in September of 2019.[16]

Civil society's expectations of China as a host have continued to rise, even as the political momentum has failed to build and was crushed by the coronavirus pandemic. According to the CCICED report, "only being a good host for the CBD COP15 is not enough" (CCICED 2019: 8). A workshop report organized by the MEE and the EU underlined that China, as a host, should share its experience, demonstrate its efforts at building an ecological civilization domestically, make a substantial commitment itself, and exercise collective leadership (Rankovic & Shen 2018). However, thus far, the main influence that China has had on the upcoming COP has been visible in the choice of its logo and especially its theme, "Ecological Civilization – Building a Shared Future for All Life on Earth" (see Figure 2.3), which combines the two key discursive elements of ecological civilization and community of common destiny, here extended to non-humans as well. In this regard, hosting the CBD provides a unique opportunity for China to promote these concepts internationally.

By contrast, some observers have questioned China's ability to drive the negotiations for a new and more ambitious governance framework by "leading by example"

50 Coraline Goron

FIGURE 2.3   Logo of the Kunming CBD COP15, with the COP's theme "Ecological Civilization – Building a Shared Future for All Life on Earth"

Source: Logo commissioned by the Ministry of Ecology and Environmental Protection and presented by then Minister Li Gangjie and Acting Executive Director of the CBD Elizabeth Mrema on January 9, 2020. Available at www.cbcgdf.org/English/NewsShow/5008/10951.html.

in showcasing what the term "ecological civilization" means within China itself in the field of biodiversity conservation, by making sufficiently ambitious international commitments, and by pushing a majority of governments to reach ambitious compromises. As underlined by Mike Shanahan in an article published in *China Dialogue* in February 2020, there have been "fears that China will prefer to facilitate dialogue towards *any* agreement rather than drive ambition towards a strong one and risk failing" (Shanahan 2020).

Conclusion

This chapter set out to examine whether China's concept of ecological civilization could contribute to bringing about a more ambitious and effective scheme of global environmental governance. I established the link between global values, policy paradigms, and environmental regimes, highlighting the way in which the policy paradigm of sustainable development, encased in a global culture of modernization, implicitly had prioritized development over the environment and led to the adoption of weak global environmental institutions, notably in the fields of climate change and biodiversity. I then discussed the origins as well as the political and cultural values that China's discourse on ecological civilization has projected both domestically and internationally. I demonstrated the ambiguity of this discourse, which is by turns universalist or nationalist, anti-capitalist or modernist, revolutionary or traditionalist. The mixed reception given to ecological civilization by international scholars reflects these ambiguities, between those hoping to find in EC an alternative development paradigm supported either by a new hegemon (Gare 2017) or the emergence of a new global culture (Clayton & Schwartz 2019) and those who see a mere Sinicization of the concept of sustainable development (Lord 2018), and between those who see China's EC as a catalyst of global change (Geall & Ely 2017) and those who fear a truculent nationalism impeding global cooperation (Heurtebise 2017).

EC is thus one important element of a rising debate about China's shifting role, as it moves from the status of being a global norm taker to that of a norm maker, and the uncertainties surrounding the political, cultural, and socio-economic values it wants to promote internationally. Overall, its potential to concoct and disseminate an alternative paradigm for the world appears constrained, particularly if it is put forward in an antagonistic spirit as part of the evidence of the cultural or political superiority of "socialism with Chinese characteristics" over other ideologies or ways of life. Indeed, as Allan et al. have emphasized, to the extent that the discourse coming from China appears "insular and propagandistic," it is unlikely to form the basis of a vision that could find support among global elites and masses (Allan et al. 2018: 841). Notwithstanding its shortcomings, the concept of sustainable development has the merit of stemming from multilateralism. If EC is to achieve a similar status, it would have to get the international community on board and recognize that an alternative global civilization only can emerge from a multilateral dialogue drawing on multiple cultural resources (Meyer & Telò 2019; Qin 2019).

The analysis of China's recent contributions to the reform of multilateral regimes in the field of climate change and biodiversity demonstrated both that China has made an undeniable contribution to environmental multilateralism and that it has made some attempts, especially in the field of biodiversity, to advance its concept of EC. But when it comes to bringing about more environmentally ambitious and effective institutional forms of multilateral governance, China has not embraced a leadership role. In the field of climate change, it has moved away from a veto position to one that enables it to broker compromises between other veto-wielding powers and the more ambitious parties. In the field of biodiversity, it has thus far displayed limited ability or will to drive the negotiations towards the ambitious outcome to which scientists and civil society generally aspire.

Notes

1 The term "megadiverse" refers to a group of countries that harbor the most biodiversity. According to the UN-sponsored website Biodiversity A to Z (www.biodiversitya-z.org/content/megadiverse-countries), 17 countries have been identified as "megadiverse": the US, Mexico, Colombia, Ecuador, Peru, Venezuela, Brazil, the Democratic Republic

of Congo, South Africa, Madagascar, India, Malaysia, Indonesia, the Philippines, Papua New Guinea, China, and Australia. Together, they account for at least two-thirds of all non-fish vertebrate species and three-quarters of all higher plant species.
2 See the International Environmental Agreement Database hosted by the University of Oregon. Available at https://iea.uoregon.edu/.
3 This definition of regimes is attributed to Krasner and is cited in Orsini et al. (2013).
4 Definition provided by the IPBES on its website: https://ipbes.net/about.
5 This reference was made in the Chinese introduction to the double volumes of *Comments on the Construction of Ecological Civilization in New China for the 70th Anniversary of the People's Republic of China*, distributed at the China and the World International Forum on the Paradigm Shift of Ecological Civilization, held on October 30 and November 1, 2019, in Jinan and co-organized by the Chinese Academy of Social Science and the Jinan municipal government.
6 Cao and Yin give the portrait of Liao Xiaoyi, the founder of the non-governmental organization Global Village, as a model of "Chinese-style" environmentalism. Liao takes a shower once a week to save water, washes clothes by hand and uses the wash water to flush the toilets, eschews cashmere products, and never has bought a car or an air-conditioner – all this in order to reduce her environmental footprint to a minimum.
7 Full speech available at https://gadebate.un.org/sites/default/files/gastatements/70/70_ZH_en.pdf. The objective to "build an ecosystem that puts mother nature and green development first" appears on page 5.
8 Geall is the editor of *China Dialogue*, one of the most read bilingual media sources on China and the environment.
9 Adjective derived from the term "ecocide," which refers to actions leading to the decimation of ecosystems, humanity, and non-human life. Some have proposed that the crime of ecocide be included in the statutes of the International Court of Justice. See https://ecocidelaw.com/the-law/what-is-ecocide/.
10 These numbers are given by the UN Development Program in China portal on biodiversity conservation, available at www.cn.undp.org/content/china/en/home/ourwork/environmentandenergy/in_depth/biodiversity-conservation-.html.
11 Xi Jinping has repeatedly made this statement since he took power. "应对气候变化：不是别人要我们做，而是我们自己要做。"
12 The US negotiating team continued to participate in negotiations until its formal withdrawal in 2020.
13 Climate Action Tracker, China country page. Available at https://climateactiontracker.org/countries/china/.
14 www.cbd.int/article/2020-01-10-19-02-38.
15 This created a platform that was launched in April of 2019 to receive and showcase commitments and contributions to biodiversity from stakeholders. It is hosted on the CBD website: www.cbd.int/action-agenda/.
16 www.campaignfornature.org/high-ambition-coalition.

References

Adler, E. & V. Pouliot. 2011. *International Practices*. Cambridge: New York: Cambridge University Press

Allan, B., S. Vucetic, & T. Hopf. 2018. "The Distribution of Identity and the Future of International Order: China's Hegemonic Prospects." *International Organization* 72(3): 839–69

Bernstein, S. 2002. *The Compromise of Liberal Environmentalism*. New York: Columbia University Press

Bernstein, S. & M. Hoffmann. 2018. "The Politics of Decarbonization and the Catalytic Impact of Subnational Climate Experiments." *Policy Sciences* 51(2): 189–211

Biermann, F., P. Pattberg, H. van Asselt, & F. Zelli. 2009. "The Fragmentation of Global Environmental Governance Architectures: A Framework Analysis." *Global Environmental Politics* 9(4): 14–40

Brenton, A. 2013. "'Great Powers' in Climate Politics." *Climate Policy* 13(5): 541–46

Brundtland, G. H. 1987. *Report of the World Commission on Environment and Development: "Our Common Future."* Available at http://www.un-documents.net/our-common-future.pdf

Cao, B. & W. Yin. 2014. *Ecological Civilization of Contemporary China*. Beijing: China International Press

CBD. 2018. "Updated Assessment of Progress towards Selected Aichi Biodiversity Targets and Option to Accelerate Progress." November. Available at www.cbd.int/doc/c/3824/7957/5bb56cbf504e73b6f00282e9/cop-14-l-02-en.pdf

CCICED. 2018. "Shocks, Innovation and Ecological Civilization. A 'New Green Era' for China and for the World." 2018 Issues Paper. December. Available at www.cciced.net/cciceden/POLICY/rr/Issuespaper/201812/P020181225041727879458.pdf

CCICED. 2019. "Special Policy Study (SPS) on Post-Global Biodiversity Conservation: Building Momentum for a Successful COP 15." June. Available at www.cciced.net/cciceden/POLICY/rr/prr/2019/201908/P020190830112083784945.pdf

Chasek, P., D. Downie, & J. Brown. 2017. *Global Environmental Politics. Dilemmas in World Politics*. Westview, NY: Routledge

Clapp, J. & P. Dauvergner. 2016. "Brief History of International Environmental Cooperation." In S. Nicholson & P. Wapner (eds.), *Global Environmental Politics: From Person to Planet*. Oxon, UK: Routledge, pp. 121–36

Clayton, P. & W. A. Schwartz. 2019. *What is Ecological Civilization? Crisis, Hope, and the Future of the Planet*. Anoka, MN: Process Century Press

Dryzek, J. 1997. *The Politics of the Earth: Environmental Discourses*. Oxford, UK: Oxford University Press

Economy, E. 2017. "Why China is Not a Climate Leader." *Politico Magazine*. June 12. Available at www.politico.com/magazine/story/2017/06/12/why-china-is-no-climate-leader-215249

Fatheuer, T. 2011. *Buen Vivir: A Brief Introduction to Latin America's New Concepts for the Good Life and the Rights of Nature*. Heinrich Böll Stiftung Publication series on Ecology, Volume 17. Available at www.boell.de/sites/default/files/Buen_Vivir_engl.pdf

Foster, J. 2017. "The Earth-System Crisis and Ecological Civilization: A Marxian View." *International Critical Thought* 7(4): 439–58

Gare, A. 2017. "From 'Sustainable Development' to 'Ecological Civilization': Winning the War for Survival." *Cosmos and History: The Journal of Natural and Social Philosophy* 13(3): 130–53

Geall, S. & A. Ely. 2017. "Narratives and Pathways towards an Ecological Civilization in China." *The China Quarterly* 236: 1175–96

Goron, C. 2018. "Ecological Civilization and the Political Limits of a Chinese Concept of Sustainability." *China Perspective* 4: 39–52. Available at http://journals.openedition.org/chinaperspectives/8463

Goron, C. & D. Freeman. 2018. "Industrial Policy in China and Europe's Climate Change Strategies." In M. Telò, X. Wang, & C. Ding (eds.), *The EU-China Partnership: Bridging Institutional, and Ideational Differences between Two Unprecedented Global Actors*. Oxon, UK: Routledge, pp. 204–20

He, L. 2011. "China's Climate-Change Policy from Kyoto to Copenhagen: Domestic Needs and International Aspirations." *Asian Perspective* 34(3): 5–33

Heggelund, G. 2007. "China's Climate Change Policy: Domestic and International Developments." *Asian Perspective* 31(2): 155–91

Heurtebise, J.-Y. 2017. "Sustainability and Ecological Civilization in the Age of Anthropocene: An Epistemological Analysis of the Psychosocial and 'Culturalist' Interpretations of Global Environmental Risks." *Sustainability* 9(8): 1331

Hilton, I. & O. Kerr. 2017. "The Paris Agreement: China's 'New Normal' Role in International Climate Negotiations." *Climate Policy* 17(1): 48–58. Available at http://sro.sussex.ac.uk/71477

Huan, Q. 2007. "Ecological Modernization: A Realistic Green Road for China?" *Environmental Politics* 16(4): 683–87

Huan, Q. 2017. "Criticism of the Logic of the Ecological Imperialism of 'Carbon Politics' and Its Transcendence." *Social Sciences in China* 38(2): 76–94

IPBES. 2019. "Summary for Policymakers of the Global Assessment Report on Biodiversity and Ecosystem Services of the Intergovernmental Science-Policy Platform on Biodiversity and Ecosystem Services." May 6. Available at https://ipbes.net/global-assessment

IPCC. 2018. *Global Warming of 1.5°C: An IPCC Special Report on the Impacts of Global Warming of 1.5°C above Pre-industrial Levels and Related Global Greenhouse Gas Emission Pathways, in the Context of Strengthening the Global Response to the Threat of Climate Change, Sustainable Development, and Efforts to Eradicate Poverty*. V. Masson-Delmotte, P. Zhai, H.-O. Pörtner, D. Roberts, J. Skea, P. Shukla, A. Pirani, W. Moufouma-Okia, C. Péan, R. Pidcock, S. Connors, J. Matthews, Y. Chen, X. Zhou, M.I. Gomis, E. Lonnoy, T. Maycock, M. Tignor, & T. Waterfield (eds.). Available at www.ipcc.ch/site/assets/uploads/sites/2/2019/06/SR15_Full_Report_High_Res.pdf

Jiang, K., X. Zhuang, R. Miao, & C. He. 2013. "China's Role in Attaining the Global 2 C Target." *Climate Policy* 13(suppl 1): 55–69

Ke, J. 2013. "Introduction to the Special Issue on Ecological Civilization and Beautiful China." *Social Sciences in China* 34(4): 139–42

Keohane, R. & D. Victor. 2010. "The Regime Complex for Climate Change." *Perspectives on Politics* 9(10): 7–23

Klein, N. 2014. *This Changes Everything: Capitalism vs. the Climate*. New York: Simon & Schuster

Kolbert, E. 2015. "Enter the Anthropocene." In S. Nicholson & P. Wapner (eds.), *Global Environmental Politics: From Person to Planet*. Oxon, UK: Routledge, pp. 13–16

Laurence, B. & P. Ehrlich. 2016. "Radical Overhaul Needed to Halt Earth's Sixth Great Extinction Event." *The Conversation*. November 8. Available at https://theconversation.com/radical-overhaul-needed-to-halt-earths-sixth-great-extinction-event-68221

Leach, M., I. Scoones, & A. Stirling. 2010. *Dynamic Sustainabilities: Technology, Environment and Social Justice*. London: Earthscan

Lord, E. 2018. *Building an Ecological Civilization across the Rural/Urban Divide and the Politics of Environmental Knowledge Production in Contemporary China*. Toronto, Canada: University of Toronto Press

Marinelli, M. 2018. "How to Build a 'Beautiful China' in the Anthropocene. The Political Discourse and the Intellectual Debate on Ecological Civilization." *Journal of Chinese Political Science*. Online first. Available at https://doi.org/10.1007/s11366-018-9538-7

Meyer, T. & M. Telò. 2019. "Introduction." In T. Meyer, J. de Sales Marques, & M. Telò (eds.), *Regionalism and Multilateralism: Politics, Economic, Culture*. Abingdon, UK & New York: Routledge, pp. 1–14

Mol, A. & G. Spaargaren. 2000. "Ecological Modernization Theory in Debate: A Review." *Environmental Politics* 9(1): 17–49

Morrison, R. 1995. *Ecological Democracy*. Boston: South End Press

Orsini, A., J.-F. Morin, & O. Young. 2013. "Regime Complexes: A Buzz, a Boom, or a Boost for Global Governance?" *Global Governance* 19: 27–39

Pan, J. 2016. *China's Environmental Governing and Ecological Civilization*. Online: Springer
Pan, Y. 2006. "论社会主义生态文明." Lun shehuizhuyi shengtai wenming [On a Socialist Ecological Civilization]. 绿叶 Lvye [Green Leaves]. October. Available at www.zhb.gov.cn/hjyw/200702/t20070206_100622.htm
Qin, Y. 2019. "Transnational Governance and Multiple Multilateralisms." In T. Meyer, J. de Sales Marques, & M. Telò (eds.), *Regionalism and Multilateralism: Politics, Economics, Culture*. Abingdon, UK & New York: Routledge, pp. 48–65
Qin, Y. 2020. "Multilateralism via Inter-practicality: Institutions and Relations." This volume.
Rankovic, A. & Shen Xiaoli. 2018. "First Biodiversity Workshop Summary Report. Sharing Perspectives on CBD Implementation and Options for the Post-2020 Global Biodiversity Framework." EU-China Environment Project. Available at https://www.iddri.org/sites/default/files/PDF/Publications/Hors%20catalogue%20Iddri/201903-biodiversity%20workshop%20beijing%202018.pdf
Sell, S. 1996. "North-South Environmental Bargaining: Ozone, Climate Change, and Biodiversity." *Global Governance* 2(1): 97–118
Shanahan, M. 2020. "Explainer: COP15, the Biggest Biodiversity Conference in a Decade." *China Dialogue*. February 24. Available at www.chinadialogue.net/article/show/single/en/11873-Explainer-COP15-the-biggest-biodiversity-conference-in-a-decade
Tian, S. 2019. "A Reverse Understanding of 'Development': Three Interpretations of Ecological Civilization." *Interculturalites Chine-France* (5): 39–56
UNEP. 2015. *Green is Gold. The Strategy and Actions of China's Ecological Civilization*. Available at https://reliefweb.int/sites/reliefweb.int/files/resources/greenisgold_en_20160519.pdf
Wang, A. 2018. "Symbolic Legitimation in Chinese Reform." *Environmental Law* 48(4): 699–760
Weale, A. 1992. *The New Politics of Pollution*. Manchester, UK: Manchester University Press
Wen, T., K. Lau, C. Cheng, H. He, & J. Qiu. 2012. "Ecological Civilization, Indigenous Culture, and Rural Reconstruction in China." *Monthly Review* 63(9): 29–35
Yan, X. 2014. "From Keeping a Low Profile to Striving for Achievement." *The Chinese Journal of International Politics* 7(2): 153–84
Young, O. 2008. "The Architecture of Global Environmental Governance: Bringing Science to Bear on Policy." *Global Environmental Politics* 8(1): 14–32
Zeng, L. 2019. "Dai Identity in the Chinese Ecological Civilization: Negotiating Culture, Environment, and Development in Xishuangbanna, Southwest China." *Religions* (10): 646. doi:10.3390/rel10120646
Zhang, D. 2017. "The Concept of Community of Common Destiny in China's Diplomacy: Meaning, Motives and Implications." *Asia & The Pacific Policy Studies* 5(2): 196–207
Zhang, W. 张维为. 2008. "生态文明: 中国的机遇." "Shengtai wenming: Zhongguo de jiyu" [Ecological Civilization: China's Opportunity]. *Xuexi shibao*. March. Available at www.china.com.cn/xxsb/txt/2008-03/10/content_12170989.htm

3

CHINESE POWER SECTOR REGULATION

Key lessons for developing nations

Deborah Seligsohn

In 2003 the Chinese government began a long process of increasing its regulation of large stationary polluters – the heavy-industry facilities that burn enormous quantities of fossil fuel, which in China is mainly coal. These are the largest sources of air pollution in China. Power generation is one of the top two polluters in almost every country, except in a few like Brazil that rely heavily on hydropower. Moreover, because of the quantity of pollution produced at a single location, the urgency to protect air quality is great, as is the opportunity to find economies of scale in both abatement technologies and enforcement modalities. As a result, many developing countries would benefit from examining the Chinese experience in air pollution abatement and discover potential applications to their own efforts to control air pollution. The focus here is on traditional air pollutants, the components of smog and haze, rather than the greenhouse gases that contribute to climate change. However, better regulation will also help governments that seek to control greenhouse gases.

In this chapter I will discuss how the Chinese experience can be usefully considered as other large developing countries, such as India, increase their regulation of heavy industry. This chapter is based on a study of the Chinese power sector, and the lessons drawn from the study are particularly useful to that sector, but many of the general concerns, such as methods for monitoring and enforcement, also can be applied to other stationary sources. Power generation is the single largest user of coal in both China and India, as well as in a number of other developing countries. Because coal is the dirtiest of fossil fuels, pollution abatement in the coal-fired power sector is the lowest hanging fruit in terms of least cost abatement of traditional air pollutants.

For many years Chinese cities regularly dominated lists of the world's most polluted urban areas, but in recent years a number of the top ten slots have been replaced by Indian cities (IQAir n.d.). This to a significant degree reflects China's success in controlling air pollution, with its pollution peaking in 2011 and slowly declining, while India has continued to see increases (Krotkov et al. 2016). Over the course of the past decade, the Indian press and civil society have begun to note the Chinese example and in a number of cases have begun to consider the Chinese model as a potentially useful approach to air pollution control.

Indians and Chinese alike are quick to point out their many differences, both political (i.e., that China is an authoritarian system while India is democratic and federal) and cultural (i.e., that India is a multicultural, multilingual state, whereas the vast majority of Chinese are Mandarin-speaking Han). However, the technology China has used was developed in the West, and much of their monitoring and enforcement system has been informed by close cooperation over decades with the US Environmental Protection Agency ("EPA Collaboration with China" n.d.). As this chapter hopes to illustrate, it is fruitful to examine both technical and systems approaches across different regime types and social contexts.

Public outcry over air pollution actually began earlier in India than it did in China, as evidenced by a number of legal cases that date back to the 1980s (Cassels 1989). These lawsuits had considerable influence, but they tended to be city specific; they did not encompass the entire nation or even a complete airshed (the area within which air circulates and pollutants mix). While experts in both countries were engaged on the issue in its early stages, the first major Chinese public discussion emerged when the instant messaging platform Weibo came into wide use. Weibo is essentially the Chinese form of Twitter, though from the beginning it allowed for longer posts than did Twitter (Wang et al. 2015). By 2010 there was considerable public discussion on Weibo. In the winter of 2012–13 the Western press coined the term "airpocalypse" to describe the extreme air pollution events that mark urban areas in both countries (Ferreri et al. 2018). These occur when a temperature inversion or other atmospheric events trap air within a city for a number of days, leading to extremely high air pollution measurements, often above the standard 500 (or hazardous) measurement on the air quality index. Although these types of events were first noted in the West, beginning with Donora, Pennsylvania, in 1948 (Ciocco & Thompson 1961) and the more widely known London Smog of 1952 (Bell et al. 2004), they have become a regular part of life in large, congested Asian cities. Some scientists have suggested they are getting worse not only because of the pollutants discharged but also because climate change is increasing their frequency. By 2015, when New Delhi experienced one of these events during the Paris Climate Change negotiations, the term airpocalypse had been adopted by the Indian press. And in recent years the Chinese experience has received regular media attention in India. Some such references are to actual conditions, while others pertain to monitoring and enforcement. The Centre for Science and Society, in particular, has done considerable work to disseminate high-quality information on the Chinese system.

In 2015 the Government of India adopted tougher pollution abatement standards for the power sector. These standards represent a significant improvement over previous measures. The newest plants have pollution control equipment as modern as that found in the US, Europe, and Japan, although it is less effective at pollution control than at some plants in China today, particularly coal-fired operations. Older power plants continue to operate under regulations comparable to ones that the Chinese promulgated between 2003 and 2010. India's regulations initially were scheduled to take effect by 2017, but the implementation date has been postponed to 2022.

China and India share a number of characteristics, including large and dense populations near major sources of air pollution and overall high levels of emissions. Both factors make it worthwhile to study the Chinese experience when considering India's regulatory future. There are also considerable differences between the two countries' situations, some of which (particularly the variety of sources of air pollution in India) will make pollution abatement in India even more difficult than in China. However, by adopting its new power sector regulations in 2015, the Indian government recognized a truth that Chinese policymakers had come to a decade earlier: while there are many sources of air pollution, the sheer size and the concentration of industrial sources make them particularly worthwhile as a first target of attack.

The Chinese experience has been iterative on multiple dimensions. The Chinese government first adopted tough power sector standards in 2003 with a two-stage phase-in, then raised them in 2011 and added the ultra-low-emissions (ULE) requirements in 2016, by far the strictest in the world. Thus, the standards themselves have toughened over time. But there has also been a considerable learning process in terms of enforcement. Chinese regulators have made changes in goal setting, monitoring, penalties, and rate structures. There are lessons to be learned in regard to all of these areas and choices to be made for other developing countries in terms of the costs of continuing to use coal versus choosing to move more rapidly to cleaner sources. China has found that producing relatively clean coal-fired power in a densely populated and industrialized country requires heavy investments in the power plants themselves, the technology and workforce to enforce the standards, and the means to dispose of the waste from the emissions abatement processes.

In what follows, I review the Chinese experience with an eye towards what might be useful for India and other developing countries. In some sense other countries do not face quite the regulatory hurdles of China, which has approximately ten times as many coal-fired power plants as India does. However, China's progress both in building up the enforcement bureaucracy and in reforming the structure of these energy sectors is worth considering in the context of other countries' energy and enforcement planning.

Standard setting

China faced long-standing air quality issues that had been increasing in severity for decades when it began to implement tougher standards in the early 2000s. As early as the 1990s the leaders of China's environmental establishment argued for a more aggressive approach to air quality regulation (Qu 1992), but it took a leadership change in the early 2000s and structural reform of the power sector for regulators to see an opening for tougher regulations (Seligsohn 2018). Prior to 2003, there was little effective regulation of SO_2 from coal-fired power, none for NO_x, and only limited particulate control. At the time, China was heading towards the peak sulfur levels that the US had seen in the early 1970s.

Coal-fired power plants were the obvious place to initiate a new regulatory regime. China relies heavily on coal for the largest part of its energy supply. Because coal-fired power plants are a stationary source, they are relatively easy to mandate and inspect. They use approximately half of all coal consumed in China (International Energy Agency 2018), making them the single largest source of air pollution. Moreover, the solution to another significant part of China's coal problem, perhaps affecting half of the remaining half, would be (paradoxically) to use more electricity rather than less. If the percentage of coal used in Chinese power-generation seems low (it is much greater than half in both India and the US), it is because of the widespread use of coal directly by both small industries and households. For households, most of the clean-up solution involves fuel switching to liquefied petroleum gas (LPG) and natural gas, but for industry and to some extent for home heating and cooling, the solution is to increase reliance on the power sector both by using more electricity and by using steam from combined heat and power facilities. Large central coal-fired power stations can be fitted with pollution abatement equipment, which would be difficult if not impossible for smaller industrial and household units. Thus, part of the solution to cleaning up China's cities has involved building more power plants. It was thus critical that these plants be clean and efficient.

Prior to 2003, Chinese standards applied only to particulate emissions. Very little attention was paid to the role that both SO_2 and NO_x play as $PM_{2.5}$ precursor chemicals, and despite much discussion of acid rain since the 1990s, there was no actual regulation of these primary sources of acid rain. The 2003 standard (see Table 3.1) reduces the allowable particulate level considerably and brings in both SO_2 and NO_x standards, although the NO_x standard was so lenient that it did not actually require the power plants to use de-NO_x equipment. The SO_2 standard, on the other hand, was sufficiently strict as to require the installation of flue-gas desulfurization (FGD) equipment on almost all plants in China.

With the standards in the 200–600 mg/m³ range (depending on the age and location of the plant), most power plants installed FGDs that removed approximately 90% of SO_2 emissions from the flue gas. What this meant was that most power plants were closed for a two- to three-month period while they added FGDs and additional particulate capture machinery. In some cases, the process required moving other buildings on the power plant grounds in order to make room for the new equipment.

It is worth noting that while pollution standards were being raised, the Chinese government was also systematically closing small coal-fired power plants. Over the period since 2005, the Chinese government has replaced smaller units, starting with quite small ones (under about 10 MW) and then steadily increasing the size of the units required to shut down. By now, most plants under 50 MW have been

TABLE 3.1 Comparison of Indian and Chinese power plant air quality standards

	$PM\ (mg/m^3)$	$SO_2\ (mg/m^3)$	$NO_x\ (mg/m^3)$	Mercury
India December 2015				
Pre-2003 units	100	200–600	600	.03
2003–2015 units	50		300	
2016 onward units	30	100	100	
China Pre-2003 1996 Standard	200–3300	–	–	–
China 2003 Standard	200–600 (2005)	1200–2100	650–1500	–
	50–200 (2010)	400–1200		–
China 2011 Standard	30	100–400	100–200	0.03
China Ultra-Low Emissions 2015	10	35	50	0.03

Sources: Ministry of Environment, Forests and Climate Change Notification, SO3305(E), December 7, 2015, GB13223–1996, 2003 and 2011 Standards, MEP announcement: "全面实施燃煤电厂超低排放和节能改造工作方案" 2015.

closed, as have many that are between 50 and 150 MW as well. For that reason they did not need to address the complex challenges of installing new equipment at the smallest sites. The other major difference is that Chinese standards do not really incorporate the concept of "grandfathering" to protect older facilities from new requirements, as is common in the US and many other countries, including India. While there was some variation in the 2003 regulations, the majority of the variation was regional rather than by date of plant, and in subsequent regulation there has been no grandfathering of any kind.

The 2003 standards proved to be insufficient even after the Chinese resolved the initial noncompliance issues that had meant little progress occurred until after 2006. The standards were incorporated as targets in the 11th Five-Year Plan (2006–10), signaling that compliance was required. Most FGDs were installed between 2007 and 2009, and policymakers were then able to evaluate their effectiveness. The result is that SO_2 emissions peaked in China in 2007 and have declined ever since, even as total coal-fired electricity output has more than doubled.

But even as SO_2 emissions declined, overall pollution levels rose. Both SO_2 and NO_x are major contributors to $PM_{2.5}$, the most serious health concern, as are power-plant particulate emissions themselves. China has a regular standards-review timetable, which in theory requires a regular review every five years, although in practice the timing appears to vary. In any case, the Chinese government through its standard-setting bodies was ready to review the 2003 standard in 2009. The standards bodies (affiliated both with the then Ministry of Environmental Protection [MEP] and the industry itself) recommended the standards be raised to world-class levels. They overcame industry objections and were able to obtain government approval. New standards were adopted in 2011, this time with targets integrated into the 12th Five-Year Plan, which began in the same year.

These new standards required a doubling of FGD capacity at most power plants, all-new NO_x control, and additional particulate abatement equipment. These changes obviously entailed significant expense, as well as downtime for the plants and the need to find space for these facilities. With FGD, for example, plants had the option of adding a second column or doubling the column height of their existing facility. Obviously, adding a second column would be less expensive, but not all plants had sufficient room to add another separate FGD.

These modifications were completed by 2013, but industry, seeing the likelihood of future restrictions on new coal-fired plant building, advocated for a still stricter standard, which became the ULE standard. The ULE standard again required significant plant downtime as additional particulate removal, FGD, and NO_x removal equipment was installed. Some power stations had to once again undergo the redesign of their physical plant and the relocation of buildings. In many cases, at least some existing equipment had to be replaced.

Lessons to be learned

There is a certain appeal to the kind of gradual iterative approach the Chinese practiced with standards gradually being raised over a number of years, but it is worth thinking about what actually happens at the plant level. Each time the standards have been raised, plants have had to redesign their facilities, invest in new equipment, and close for considerable spans of time while the equipment is installed. Raising the standards all at once would have avoided much of this downtime and in many cases reduced the total investment involved. As plants needed to rearrange facilities to fit more equipment within their footprint, they often had to tear down and rebuild items like their original FGD.

The Chinese have also realized over the years that even the modest amount of grandfathering of old facilities found in the 2003 regulation would not enable them to meet their air quality targets.

All of this implies that standards are best set with total carrying capacity in mind. It is less expensive to set a maximal standard and have one installation period for a power plant. It is also worth setting current standards with future electricity production, not current production, in mind. Most developing countries can expect future electricity demand to be greater than current demand and thus to carry even more environmental costs.

Monitoring and enforcement

As seen by the lag between the adoption of new SO_2 standards in 2003 and actual measurable reductions in SO_2 emissions in 2007, effective implementation of standards requires enforcement. China has undergone an important shift in its monitoring from a system that involved periodic on-site spot checks by environmental personnel to one that relies very heavily on continuous emissions monitoring systems (CEMS), with the same personnel continuing to do regular spot checks focused on ensuring technical integrity (Schreifels et al. 2012). At the same time there has been a shift from a system of fines to a much more developed program of integrated pricing and serious penalties, such as plant closures for gross violations.

CEMS is critical to the success of the Chinese system, as it has been to the US system. In fact, officials from the US Environmental Protection Agency (EPA) were involved in helping the Chinese MEP train up in how to operate a supervisory system dependent on electronic monitoring. CEMS alone has not been sufficient, however. In multiple visits to power plants in China, I have been shown how the system is kept under lock and key and subject to surprise inspections by the local Environmental Protection Bureau (EPB). These inspections are regular, occurring in most places on approximately a quarterly basis, but of course the CEMS is also connected directly to local, provincial, regional, and national environmental offices. If these see a discrepancy, they can send out an inspector. I have been told that there were issues with tampering at the beginning, which resulted in the institution of more rigorous observation and inspection.

The Chinese system, again similar to that of the US, relies on a large and robust enforcement workforce, especially at the local level. Even a medium-sized city, such as Yantai in Shandong province, has over 1,000 inspectors. Although it is difficult to find complete numbers, the total environmental enforcement workforce is well into the millions. It appears to be as large as the US EPA's workforce of 15 million. Moreover, it is layered and deep. At the national level the ministry itself is small, but it has several thousand personnel in research institutes that report directly to the ministry, conduct research, and develop policies and standards. Then there are EPBs at every level of government: provincial, county, city, and city district. Moreover, starting around 2005, the ministry began to establish regional offices modeled on the US EPA's regions. The specific purpose of these was to have a mechanism for inspecting and enforcing provincial compliance. The previous challenge for the environmental bureaucracy, as for most bureaucracies within the Chinese system, is that they not only answered to the ministry but also to the local head (governor, mayor, etc.). Creating a layer without any general bureaucratic equivalent increased ministerial control. This level of supervision is critical: both the ability of the ministry to monitor provincial and local behavior and also the wealth of personnel at the very local level that can inspect specific facilities and ensure that their CEMS and abatement equipment are operating effectively.

Monitoring is, of course, critical, but it is unlikely to have had such an impact without an increasingly sophisticated enforcement system. Prior to the 2006 11th Five-Year Plan, the main enforcement mechanism involved issuing fines, which were widely viewed as too low to incentivize compliance. Instead they became a minor cost of doing business. After the imposition of "hard targets" in the 11th Five-Year Plan (in other words, targets that were enforceable, as opposed to "soft" suggested targets), enforcement became more serious and the tools at the government's disposal were more varied. Some of these tools, like shutting down facilities, are extreme. Although shutdown can be used as a threat, it may prove too difficult for government officials to use, because the public and businesses depend on power,

Chinese power sector regulation 63

after all. The real shift for the power sector came in the form of a clever payment system that made the use of pollution abatement equipment self-enforcing.

Prices paid to power plants are set by the national and provincial development reform commissions. Once FGD became required, the payments came in the form of a base rate and an environmental subsidy or surcharge. These costs were borne by the grid company when it purchased the electricity. The payments were set such that the profit for the plant was built into the environmental surcharge rather than into the base rate. The CEMS were connected not just to the environmental bureaucracy but also to the grid company. As a result, the grid company had an incentive to monitor power plants' emissions closely. If emissions rose, they didn't have to pay the environmental surcharge. Similarly, the plants had an incentive to keep the FGD running effectively. Without it, as one electricity expert explains, "there is no profit." Figure 3.1 shows the self-enforcing structure put in place with CEMS.

At the same time, fines were also increased, and local EPBs began to impose them on an hourly basis rather than as one-time charges. The result was that failing to comply with emissions standards has become increasingly costly to the power sector. By 2015, sources told me power that sector executives who failed to run their emissions equipment effectively were losing their jobs – not at the government's behest, but because they were costing their companies money.

This system has become more complex as the standards have tightened. In the 11th Five-Year Plan, the environmental subsidy was just for FGD. Once the 2011 standard and 12th Five-Year Plan goals were set, an additional surcharge was added

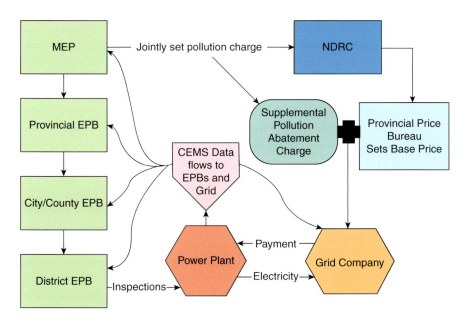

FIGURE 3.1 The self-enforcement payment feedback system

for NO_x control. In the early years, power companies complained that the surcharge payment was not high enough, but over time fees were adjusted and the risks of both fines and shutdowns became greater. As a result, compliance in the power sector has continued to improve.

Lessons to be learned

There are a number of critical lessons to be learned from the Chinese experience with CEMS. First, it only works as part of a comprehensive system of both monitoring and enforcement. CEMS alone will not change behavior, and absent effective inspections and monitoring of the machinery itself, it will simply be tampered with. The Chinese did face tampering issues early in their use of CEMS, but by ensuring sufficient spot inspections along with direct access to the data in real time at every level of government, they appear to have been able to reduce this problem significantly. The key elements of this system are personnel on the ground to conduct inspections and data access throughout the system. Without robust staffing, the Chinese record of pollution reduction would have been unlikely. There have been suggestions that CEMS can act as a substitute for staff, but that has not been the Chinese (nor in fact the US) experience. CEMS is a tool that environmental personnel can use for more effective enforcement.

The second important lesson is the need, as with any other aspect of behavioral change, for effective and timely penalties. The Chinese system of integrating payment with enforcement is particularly effective because it incentivizes the grid company to act as the direct enforcement agency. For any locale with fixed prices for power producers, whether through power purchase agreements or through a regulator, this system of a dual pricing – base price and environmental surcharge – is ideal, making enforcement more effective and less costly. It is not surprising that the Chinese power sector cleaned up a number of years before other heavy-industry sectors, in which progress did not really begin until 2012–15. This pricing model only works where there is a fixed price paid by the buyer, but in these cases it is quite useful.

Regardless of whether the pricing model itself is utilizable, it is essential that noncompliance be costly. A key shift in China was to charge fines on a per-hour basis rather than as a one-off for each incident. That forced plants either to resolve technical difficulties quickly or to power down until abatement equipment could be repaired. The shift thus also incentivizes good proactive maintenance. If firms have a profit motive, costly fines should be effective. Plant closures are obviously the ultimate threat, but their effectiveness depends on whether they can actually be implemented. In earlier years, when electricity was short in China, the threat seemed unlikely to be carried out. At this point, in light of systematic overcapacity, it is less costly for the government to impose closures. The more effective middle route is, in addition to imposing fines, to take environmental performance into account in dispatch rules. If the best performing plants are put on line first, they obviously benefit.

Competition

An often overlooked part of the Chinese system is that state-owned firms compete with each other intensely. As I have shown in previous research (Seligsohn 2018), both standards and enforcement improved as the Chinese electricity sector became more competitive after the single power company was broken into five in 2002. Companies compete with each other for profits, but given the amount of permitting involved in building new power plants, they also compete for government approval. If the government is committed to improving environmental outcomes, competing as the green alternative can be an attractive option for some companies. The result is to raise the standards for the entire sector.

Fuel choice

While this chapter focuses on pollution abatement in the coal power sector, and it is critical to implement effective pollution abatement, no other country in the world has more coal-fired power plants than China does. In expanding power production, it is worth considering whether one way to keep pollution abatement costs down is to choose other sources for generating electricity.

Here, the case of India is instructive. Despite its relatively modest coal-fired power plant capacity in comparison to China, coal is still India's top energy source, accounting for 54% of energy demand (Tiewsoh et al. 2017). Moreover, while India considers itself a relatively coal-rich country, coal dependence has not led to energy independence. India already imports 18% of its coal, and as Ahluwalia, Gupta, and Stern (an illustrious group including a former deputy chairman of the Indian Planning Commission and the UK's Sir Nicholas Stern) outlined in 2016, in a business-as-usual scenario, this dependence would increase to more than 57% by 2047 as coal demand would more than quadruple. By contrast, these authors suggest, if India adopted a more low-carbon strategy (a mix of efficiency and renewables), it could maintain its current coal import level as supply would at most double.

Choosing a more diverse set of fuel options, and especially moving away from fossil fuel dependence in the power sector, would reduce the amount of pollution abatement equipment required. It would also reduce the need to manage the waste products of this abatement. While we want to take the pollution out of the air, it has to go somewhere, and pollution abatement creates a significant solid waste management challenge. Specifically, particulate removal results in ash, and FGD can process sulfur in a variety of ways, but the most common is to produce calcium sulfite ($CaSO_3$), which can be further processed to produce gypsum. Ash management can be a large problem, especially in a country like India, where the available coal contains very high ash content. That residue can be used, but it is often simply a waste that has to be disposed of. Similarly, the gypsum produced by FGD potentially also can be used as a building material, but here too we find challenges. For a time, such gypsum was being imported into the US as a building material, but that trade was subsequently halted after a series of scandals involving contamination

(Michon n.d.). Coal has a number of impurities that can include sulfur, mercury, arsenic, and fluorine. When these and other impurities are captured along with the FGD waste, they result in a product that cannot be used in building construction. While the Chinese still use gypsum from the power sector domestically, interviews in the steel industry revealed that the gypsum produced in that sector is viewed as too contaminated for any subsequent purpose. As a result, heavy reliance on coal-fired power leads to a massive increase in landfill use – a major challenge in densely populated countries. Increasing the emphasis on efficiency and renewables produces a major co-benefit of reducing additional demand for solid waste disposal.

Conclusion

As India and other countries raise their regulatory standards for stationary sources, there is a great deal to be learned from the Chinese example. The major lessons that can be drawn from the Chinese experience include the following.

- Incremental raising of standards increases the total cost. Adopting maximally strict standards to begin with avoids repeated plant closures and redesigns.
- Enforcement personnel are critical, even when plants have CEMS installed. Inspections keep CEMS from being tampered with.
- Setting up a pricing system where the purchaser can act as an enforcement agent promotes compliance.
- Non-compliance demands sure and costly punishment.
- Competition promotes company good behavior.
- Coal is not the only solution. Pollution abatement is costly; an excellent alternative is to increase the use of alternative sources of energy, which also promotes efficiency.

Coal continues to be a major source of energy. It is also a major pollutant. As long as coal is in the mix, countries ought to use best practices to control that pollution. However, they should realize that other alternatives will be cleaner, especially by reducing carbon pollution, which avoids the costs not just of installing and operating expensive pollution abatement equipment but also of disposing of the large quantities of solid waste produced from that captured pollution.

References

Ahluwalia, M., H. Gupta, & N. Stern. 2016. "A More Sustainable Energy Strategy for India." Working Paper No. 328.

Bell, M., D. Davis, & T. Fletcher. 2004. "A Retrospective Assessment of Mortality from the London Smog Episode of 1952: The Role of Influenza and Pollution." *Environmental Health Perspectives* 112(1): 6–8

Cassels, J. 1989. "Judicial Activism and Public Interest Litigation in India: Attempting the Impossible?" *The American Journal of Comparative Law* 37(3): 495–519

Ciocco, A. & D. Thompson. 1961. "A Follow-up of Donora Ten Years After: Methodology and Findings." *Journal of Public Health* 51(2): 155–64

"EPA Collaboration with China." n.d. Available at www.epa.gov/international-cooperation/epa-collaboration-china

Ferreri, J., R. Peng, M. Bell, L. Ya, T. Li, & G. B. Anderson. 2018. "The January 2013 Beijing 'Airpocalypse' and its Acute Effects on Emergency and Outpatient Visits at a Beijing Hospital." *Air Quality, Atmosphere & Health* 11(3): 301–09

International Energy Agency. 2018. "Coal Consumption by Sector in China, 2008–2024." Available at www.iea.org/data-and-statistics/charts/coal-consumption-by-sector-in-china-2008-2024

IQAir. n.d. "World's Most Polluted Cities." Available at www.airvisual.com/world-most-polluted-cities

Krotkov, N., C. McLinden, C. Li, L. Lamsal, E. Celarier, S. Marchenko, W. Swartz, E. Bucsela, J. Joiner, B, Duncan, K, Boersma, J. Veefkind, P. Levelt, V. Fioletov, R. Dickerson, H. He, Z. Lu, & D. Streets. 2016. "Aura OMI Observations of Regional SO_2 and NO_2 Pollution Changes from 2005 to 2015." *Atmospheric Chemistry and Physics* 16(7): 4605–29

Michon, K. n.d. "Chinese Drywall: Health Problems and Property Damage." Available at www.nolo.com/legal-encyclopedia/chinese-drywall-problems-health-effects-32402.html

Qu, G. 1992. "China's Dual-Thrust Energy Strategy: Economic Development and Environmental Protection." *Energy Policy* 20(6): 500–506

Schreifels, J., Y. Fu, & E. Wilson. 2012. "Sulfur Dioxide Control in China: Policy Evolution During The 10th And 11th Five-Year Plans and Lessons for The Future." *Energy Policy* 48: 779–89

Seligsohn, D. 2018. "Corporate Concentration and Air Pollution Governance in China." Unpublished dissertation. University of California San Diego

Tiewsoh, L., M. Sivek, & J. Jirásek. 2017. "Traditional Energy Resources in India (Coal, Crude Oil, Natural Gas): A Review." *Energy Sources, Part B: Economics, Planning, and Policy* 12(2): 110–18. doi:10.1080/15567249.2015.1042172

Wang, S., M. Paul, & M. Dredze. 2015. "Social Media as a Sensor of Air Quality and Public Response in China." *Journal of Medical Internet Research* 17(3): e22

PART II
Trade wars, economic cooperation, and social justice

4

THE CRISIS OF INTERNATIONAL TRADE AND ITS CULTURAL AND POLITICAL IMPLICATIONS

Is the EU's approach contributing to a renewal of multilateralism?

Mario Telò[#]

Introduction: a dramatic change in global trade

For many decades, trade was the main driver of global economic growth, but that is no longer the case. The Trump administration in the US reacted to novel circumstances, including especially the emergence of trading powers such as China and the EU, by disrupting the global multilateral trading system (e.g., by boycotting the World Trade Organization [WTO] and starting trade wars). According to some US scholars, including Ikenberry and Deudney (2018), the country's that approach ran counter to American traditional commitments to multilateralism and free trade. In the US, trade liberalization has enjoyed bipartisan support since 1919. Subsequently, after World War II the US supported the creation of the General Agreement on Tariffs and Trade (GATT, 1947), an international body charged with encouraging freer trade. The GATT managed to reduce trade barriers during many successful rounds of negotiation. Eventually it was transformed into the WTO at the Marrakesh Conference of 1994.

Is the current American hostility to free trade just a temporary aberration? In spite of current talks designed to resolve trade disputes, the agency Allianz Outlook predicts that trade wars will be permanent. Even when negotiators come to partial agreement (as with the temporary truce of December 2019), inevitably such accords are followed by new trade wars, thus sowing distrust and strategic suspicion among the US, China, the EU, and most other trading partners. Despite Joseph Biden's victory in the 2020 presidential election, we should not rule out the possibility – even the likelihood – that a kind of "Trumpism without Trump" may continue to exert an influence on US foreign policy. That would be a factor strengthening hardliners in every country.

President Trump was not the exclusive cause of the current anti-trade mood in the US. He was merely an accelerant and one who weaponized trade issues for domestic political gain. He played on certain negative emotions and perceptions among the public, such as its fear of China. Furthermore, the frustrated US middle class feels that it has been the loser, because trade liberalization certainly has had some negative domestic impacts as have (or so they believe) the current WTO rules. In contrast to the Obama strategy, the Trump administration:

- Raised tariffs against Chinese and EU imports and justifying the consequent trade wars by (implausibly) citing "security concerns."
- Boycotted the WTO panel system, a mechanism for resolving conflicts that lies at the heart of the organization's ability to function, as a "threat to US national sovereignty."
- Withdrew from the Trans-Pacific Partnership (TPP) – a deal signed in 2015 with 12 Asia-Pacific countries – and instead opted for a new kind of bilateral transactional and hierarchical trade arrangement exemplified by the US-Mexico-Canada Agreement (USMCA), an agreement with Mexico and Canada that will replace the North American Free Trade Agreement (NAFTA). (Notice that even the acronym FTA, standing for free-trade agreement, was deleted!)

The aims of this chapter are twofold: to gauge the magnitude and scope of the current upheaval in the system of world trade and identify its historical roots, and to focus on the EU's new trade policy as a possible contribution to an alternative mode of global trade governance.

More than trade is at stake: the political and cultural implications of trade relations

What have European philosophers said about trade since the seventeenth century, and what can they still teach us?

A theoretical dispute relevant to our present concerns arose in the wake of the geographic discoveries of the fifteenth and sixteenth centuries and the first wave of globalization that followed them. In a way analogous to the current debate, there were three alternative visions, each articulated by certain "founding fathers" of trade theory: free-trade liberalism, understood not only as an economic arrangement, but as a moral benefit; mercantilism and state protectionism; and regulated, rules-based trade. To illustrate these positions, we first will consider Montesquieu, who inspired the optimistic arguments of later free-trade and free-market advocates such as Adam Smith and David Ricardo. We then will turn to Colbert's approach in favor of mercantilism and finally to Kant's theory of rules-based trade.

Arguments for unrestricted free trade

Although Montesquieu inspired the famously liberal view of free trade identified with Ricardo and Smith, for whom it was an application of free market capitalist doctrine, he himself defended trade on non-economic grounds. One of the most original social scientists of the last century, Albert Hirschman (1977), presents the normative model of *doux commerce* elaborated by Montesquieu in *De L'Esprit des Lois* (1748/1949) as follows:

- Trade regulates violent political passions and conflicts. Liberalism's genealogy becomes clear in its legal foundations (the theories of rights, of exchange, and of contract).
- Trade renders moral customs sweeter and kinder. By multiplying exchanges and augmenting travelers' knowledge of one another, it makes cultural interplay between peoples possible and facilitates tolerance by overcoming inaccurate prejudices about the "other." Cultural knowledge and socialization thus counteract ethnocentrism and arrogance. Trade eases every kind of human exchange by encouraging intellectual, inter-civilizational communication.
- Trade makes political dialogues and alliances possible. It contains wars and consolidates international peace.
- Trade stimulates the individual (not only the collective) interest in peace, strengthens virtue among merchants and citizens, and enables harmony between individual and societal interests. In short, the individual interest in trade fosters a political interest in peace.
- Individual freedom is associated with trade. The more trade burgeons, the more liberalism develops. By the same token, trade acts to limit the concentration of power and keep authoritarian tendencies in check.

This highly optimistic view of trade (i.e., that liberal globalization benefits everyone) was revived in the decades after the end of the Cold War. In its vulgar form it was popularized by Francis Fukuyama in *The End of History and the Last Man* (1992) and expressed in the trade policies of former British Prime Minister Tony Blair.

Arguments against free trade

In sharp contrast, there has been a school of thought highly critical of free-trade doctrine that underlines its negative effects and favors nationalism and protectionism or even mercantilism. Colbert and the French mercantilists of the seventeenth to twentieth centuries are most closely associated with this position. According to Colbert, exports are good and imports are bad for the economy, hence France should pursue a policy of replacing imports by domestic products. Tariffs should be used to protect the domestic market, especially state-owned companies.

Mercantilism was not confined to France; it had influential advocates in every European country including Germany, where Friedrich List criticized free-trade theory as a tool of British imperialism employed to dominate and subdue other states. The mercantilist tradition has had an impact on theories of economic development in our own time, where it has been cited to justify both protectionism and political/military nationalism.

Moreover, there have been "leftist" arguments against free trade and in favor of protectionism as well, which have origins in the anti-liberal writings of Fichte and Rousseau, both prioritizing the need to protect the domestic social contract by closing the borders to foreign trade. That tradition extended to Marx and Engels, who argued in *The Communist Manifesto* that "in place of the numberless indefeasible chartered freedoms, [the bourgeoisie] has set up that single unconscionable freedom – Free Trade" (1848). Nevertheless, socialist protectionism – represented over nearly two centuries by figures ranging from Ferdinand Lassalle to Jean-Pierre Chevènement, Philip Melanchthon, Jeremy Corbyn, and Samir Amin, among others – has been a minority position unable to balance the mainstream right-wing hegemony on protectionism.

There have been numerous historical experiences with protectionism, autarky, and anti-multilateralist thinking in the twentieth century in countries and eras ranging from Fascist Italy, Nazi Germany, and authoritarian Spain and Portugal to modernizing Brazil and India. But the scheme also was tried in many communist economies built on state planning and following the Soviet model. It failed in all of those instances. Despite those failures, it has been revived in our own day by "populist realists" like Trump and in the many political waves launched against globalization and free trade, especially by several commentators and leaders on the right, most of whom advocate some modernized version of mercantilism in international trade.

Due to the deficiencies and shortcomings of both liberal free-trade doctrine and the mercantilist, protectionist alternatives to it, the idea of legally institutionalized, regulated fair trade gradually has emerged as a third, reasonable option. Before we examine that set of ideas, it is worthwhile to look more closely at the risks of free trade. Asymmetries between costs and benefits, or between the rich beneficiaries and the poor "losers," may intensify. Excessive profits realized through free trade may provoke inequalities within a specific country or in international society or both. Unfair trade and excessive inequality, in turn, disrupt commerce and generate social instability as the gap between rich and poor widens. As critics of Britain's once-dominant free-trade system long have pointed out, trade may provoke consolidation of hierarchies and dependence. Thus, free trade actually may make violence more likely (in contrast to the *doux commerce* hypothesis), as its victims could abandon the legal framework and use force against foreign traders.

Arguments for rules-based trade

For many of those reasons, Immanuel Kant in his essay on "Perpetual Peace" (1795) highlighted the link between trade and the development of transnational ties, because trade multiplies contacts that fall under the twin rules of a "right to visit" and an "obligation to welcome." Still, he argued, trade can encourage peace only if it is rules-based, institutionalized, and legal. In other words, trade must be embedded in a framework that establishes the rules for exchange, punishes infractions and defections, and thus indirectly enhances the level of trust among the trading partners.

One conclusion to be drawn from the arguments presented so far is that we need greater conceptual precision to avoid misunderstandings. First, we must distinguish carefully between economic liberalism, now often called neoliberalism, and political liberalism as a form of rules-based governance. Liberalism is a set of political ideas that does not necessarily coincide with economic liberalism. Those ideas, a legacy of thinkers like Locke, Kant, Hamilton, and J. S. Mill, include transparency and publicity, the rule of law, freedom of religion and the press, democratic voting procedures, and respect for minority rights.

Second, we should acknowledge that the protectionism adopted by Trump is not consistent with liberalism in any of its forms. Liberalism under US hegemony is not equivalent to liberalism per se. From 1944 until well into the 1970s and even 1980s, American trade policy was generally liberal in the broader political sense of promoting comity and trust among trading nations. But in the 1980s, both the US and Great Britain, under Reagan and Thatcher respectively, increasingly pursued a neoliberal trade policy on exclusively free-market grounds.

The point is that we must distinguish the non-hegemonic, rules-based, transparent, regulated, and legitimate liberal scheme of governance imagined by Kant and other liberal thinkers both from Trump's antiliberal protectionism and from the deregulated, neoliberal economic and trade policies pursued, for example, by the IMF under the rubric of the Washington Consensus beginning in 1989.

Worldwide, multilateral trade has slowed, with potentially dire consequences for prosperity, peace, and global governance

The multilateral trading system currently faces daunting challenges. Due to persistent trade tensions, global trade growth has lost momentum. Trade is no longer the main driver of economic development. WTO economists expect growth in merchandise trade volume to fall to 2.6% in 2019 – down from 4.6% in 2017 and 3.0% in 2018. Consensus estimates have world GDP growth slowing from 2.9% in 2018 to 2.6% in both 2019 and 2020. A collapse or paralysis of the system would set global economic governance back by 20 years, thereby undermining the predictability, relative stability, and fairness of multilateral trade relations. This represents a serious, perhaps even an existential, threat to those economic systems that are deeply integrated into global value chains, most notably China, the EU-28, the US, Japan, South Korea, and Canada, as shown in Tables 4.1 and 4.2.

There are several paths the world might take to combat the current negative trend in global trade. Although the different policy alternatives are not mutually exclusive, certain paths seem more realistic under the current international situation, and any given country might find some more appealing than others. One possibility would be to foster alternative growth drivers (e.g., by bolstering domestic market demand). That could work in countries like Germany and China, provided

TABLE 4.1 Shares of the world market for export of goods (2017)

China	16.9% (excluding Hong Kong)
EU-28	15.8% (external trade flows with non-EU countries)
US	11.5%
Japan	5.2%
South Korea	4.3%
Canada	3.1%
Rest of the world	43.2%

Source: Eurostat (online data code: ext_it_introle).

TABLE 4.2 Shares in the world market for import of goods (2016)

US	17.6%
EU-28	14.8% (external trade with non-EU countries)
China	12.4% (excluding Hong Kong)
Japan	4.7%
Canada	3.2%
South Korea	3.2%
Rest of the world	44.1%

Source: Eurostat (online data code: ext_it_introle).

that trade openness was maintained. But whether it would work across the board, and whether it would help to promote peace and global governance, remain to be seen. For that reason, we will focus below on two different options: relaunching/accelerating global trade by unblocking global WTO rounds and reforming the WTO, and fostering regional, interregional, and bilateral arrangements.

Reviving global trade by reforming the WTO

In recent decades the international community has moved from the soft GATT regime that began in 1947 to the binding procedures and decisions of the WTO (1995, "a GATT with teeth"), which has been accepted by 160 countries, including China (2001). Given that there are no winners in retaliatory trade wars, the right path to global economic growth and prosperity (in the best case) could be achieved by reforming and revamping that body. The WTO remains highly relevant for a new, more efficient multilateral system of governance and provides an example of "governance beyond the State" (Weyembergh & Telò 2020). Its main functions are to administer multilateral trade rules, serve as a forum for trade negotiations, and provide a mechanism to settle trade disputes. While all these functions are essential, they are under pressure and in need of reform, yet the latter two will prove to be extremely difficult.

In the context of the quasi-failure of the World Trade Organization/Doha Round negotiations begun in 2000, new issues have come to the surface and the agenda has become more complex. Some of these issues represent serious challenges for any trade regulation reform. They include the following:

1. Updating the rules of the global trading system in response to changes that have occurred since the WTO was established in 1995. Those include intellectual property rights, public procurement, transfer of technologies, and digital trade.
2. Improving the ability of the WTO to monitor states' trade policies and respond to the increased role of state-owned enterprises.
3. Combatting "industrial subsidies" given by some WTO member countries (not only China) that eventually lead to overcapacity and overproduction.
4. Enforcing compliance on notification of state aid. Many countries fail to comply with the WTO's notification requirements. In China, for example, state contribution and subsidies to firms and banks account for 96% of GDP, which is 5% more than in 2013, according to State Council data. The WTO rules in question require countries to notify others that they are engaging in subsidy programs. This is a thorny issue, so much so that some countries have proposed levying penalties for non-compliance.
5. Clarifying which member states count as "developing" countries. Many member states have requested that they be allowed to retain their status as developing countries. But what does – or should – confer that status on a WTO member state? Designation as a developing country matters, because such members may receive "special and differential treatment." Today, ten of the G-20 countries, including China, India, and South Korea, currently claim developing country status at the WTO, even though they are economically advanced in many respects. China, for example, already is an established global economic power as measured by its GDP/PPP (gross domestic product, adjusted for purchasing power parity), although if judged by per capita GDP alone, China indeed remains a developing country. Recently, Brazil decided to forgo developing country status to mark a milestone in its economic improvement. That move could inject momentum into the discussion about setting quantifiable criteria to clarify a country's development status. The EU has endorsed Norway's proposal for a pragmatic approach to the entire controversy. That proposal is more about the kind and extent of the benefits conferred by developing country status than about which countries deserve to be so designated. In particular, it would refuse to grant blanket exemptions from the WTO's duties and rules and would wish for greater precision in specifying exactly what advantages developing countries ought to enjoy. All in all, we can say that the reforms of the WTO desired by the European Union could be a tough sell in the US. Still, several steps towards reform have been taken already.

Obstacles to reforming the WTO

In recent years, a dialogue started between the EU and many relevant WTO members, initially the US and China. The EU has made concrete reform proposals (European Commission 2018), as discussed with Canada and Japan. In 2018,

Canada convened a meeting of trade ministers from 13 WTO member states to discuss reforming the institution. The EU-China top summit met in Brussels on April 9, 2019, to address the same topic. However, thus far the US has rejected the EU's proposals. The Trump administration dramatically changed the US approach to the WTO. Besides launching trade wars, it chose a far riskier course. Citing alleged "security threats," the US attacked the very heart of the WTO, the dispute settlement mechanism (despite the fact that the US has prevailed in 87% of its WTO-adjudicated disputes), by blocking the appointments of members to the WTO's Appellate Body, as will be explained further below.

This heavy-handed treatment of the WTO was justified in the name of putting US interests ahead of those of other countries ("America First"); yet American producers may actually have seen more costs than benefits from such policies, including the loss of overseas markets, higher costs for steel and other imported goods needed for America's own manufactures, and the disruption of supply chains. Some of Washington's more influential politicians (especially in Congress) understand this argument and tried to act as a check and balance on the Trump administration's more extreme moves. Additionally, business leaders sometimes have used that back channel to register their own objections to trade wars and WTO-bashing.

Given that Trump's bid for reelection was defeated, subsequent US policies may revert to previous patterns. Of course, the world needs the US to jointly lead the way on trade policy. The question is how the US as a trade giant could remain a reliable partner beyond its previous hegemonic role. Unless the incoming Biden administration is able to reverse Trump's policies, the EU could face escalating trade wars that result in tit-for-tat retaliation.

In any event, as suggested above, serious differences have emerged in transatlantic relations on the issue of settling international trade disputes. Within the WTO, a very effective supranational dispute settlement mechanism existed for more than two decades. Panels established under that mechanism provided what is essentially a court of first resort. At a higher level sits an appellate body, composed of a permanent staff of judges, lawyers, and officials, that is authorized to issue decisions binding on all members of the organization. Its operation provides an excellent example of "governance beyond the state," in which institutionalized trade rules effectively limit the national sovereignty of even the strongest WTO members. The Trump administration blocked the appointment of new judges to the appellate body, which – by December of 2019 – had fallen below the minimum number of judges (three of the originally envisaged seven) needed to function at all. Thus, de facto the appellate body has ceased to operate, calling into question the core element of the WTO's dispute settlement mechanism. Both technical and substantive debates have begun about reforming the WTO.

Resistances to WTO reform has come not only from the US, with its incremental defections and boycotts. Some developing countries (including India and South Africa) no longer seem to be interested in sitting for serious negotiations, while China, as the country that mostly benefitted from the current globalization, remains a defender of the status quo. The consequence is that WTO is declining as a credible forum and driver for liberalization. Scholars openly address the question of whether the current multipolar global power structure, notably in case of civilizational regionalism, is compatible with multilateral governance (Huntington 1996; Katzenstein 2005; Santander 2016).

Another relevant example of a set of issues involving the WTO concerns the so-called investor-state dispute settlements (ISDS). In such cases private investors submit complaints about government behavior, usually for alleged abuses, discriminatory actions, or arbitrary expropriations. Unlike in the WTO panel system, there is no permanent court with jurisdiction over ISDS cases. In the usual practice of the more than 2,000 already completed trade adjustments, ad hoc panels of independent arbiters (consisting of legal experts, professors, lawyers, and former judges, among others) are created and their responsibilities are defined by the appellants themselves. However, this system is increasingly the target of criticism by public figures. During the previous decade it became a hotbed of controversy on many fronts, especially in trade negotiations among various partners: Comprehensive Economic and Trade Agreement (EU and Canada) (CETA), EU-Japan, NAFTA, TPP, and the Transatlantic Trade and Investment Partnership (TTIP).

The UN Commission on International Trade Law, which was established in 2017, has identified three main problems plaguing ISDS proceedings. First, different panels tend to adopt divergent and inconsistent interpretations of both international law and individual provisions. Second, there are concerns regarding the selection of panel members, their qualifications, and their impartiality (lack of effectiveness and transparency). Finally, complaints have been lodged about excessive costs and the long duration of ISDS procedures and cases. The EU has underlined the link between costs and the first two of these points.

However, according to the EU, such complaints can be addressed fully only through a structural reform of the system. To that end, in April of 2019 the EU proposed to set up a standing mechanism to handle investor-state conflicts. It would have the following features: a panel of mediators, encouraging the amicable settlement of conflicts; a court of first resort, composed of full-time judges selected according to their qualifications and independence; and an appellate body that would be able to correct factual mistakes and errors about law. Critics of the proposal have argued that the procedure is not open to further appeal, either at the domestic or the international level, and that it lacks sufficient protections (e.g., in regard to work, safety, the environment, and food security). Current guidelines for revision include, at a minimum, references to International Labour Organization (ILO) conventions and UN conventions on human rights. The EU proposal is under discussion in the UNCITRAL (UN Arbitration Rules) working group; that discussion underscores the need for greater predictability and coherence in arbitral decisions and ways to resolve the concerns mentioned above. Now that the new EU Commission has taken office with Ursula van der Leyen as President, this proposal could be part of a political strategy designed to strengthen institutional multilateralism, including the WTO's regulatory authority.

In light of the above considerations, is reforming the WTO a real possibility? Our tentative conclusion is that doing so would prove extremely difficult because the organization's 160 member states would have to address and achieve consensus about each of its main functions: administering multilateral trade relations, providing a forum for trade negotiations, and settling trade disputes. Assuming that sweeping reform is at present not a live option, perhaps at least the international community could address the most urgent problem: reform of the dispute resolution system to cope with the recent Appellate Body crisis that arose late last year. But it remains unclear whether this narrower reform endeavor would have a greater likelihood of success. Depending on what transpires under the Biden administration, the EU and China, which mostly have benefited from globalization, would seem to have a special responsibility to collaborate on strengthening the WTO. They must make concessions to WTO rules and procedures and search for ways to revive free trade, ensuring that we don't return to the law of the jungle.

Because, in the current crisis, the main functions of the WTO are all at stake, it might be an error to rely on prospects for reform alone. As Qin (2018) points out, the length and complexity of global trade negotiations have been increasing from the GATT rounds (6 to 67 months) to the famous Uruguay Round (87 months before the great Marrakesh Agreement of 1994) and the WTO Doha Round (started in 2000: 192 months until a final outcome, with the exception of mini-arrangements in Bali and Nairobi). Moreover, the organization remains hobbled by the resistance and non-cooperation of the US, which – if it continues – will jeopardize the whole system of multilateralism. Fortunately, another, more indirect option is available.

Reviving global trade through bilateralism and interregionalism

Given the current paralysis in WTO negotiations, the world's largest trade powers may want to consider bilateralism and/or interregionalism as the next best options for reining in trade wars and averting a Hobbesian war of all against all. The open question is whether and under which conditions these options are compatible with multilateralism.

We need to distinguish the concept of bilateralism (evidenced by the Trump-driven US approach to trade relations, as manifested, for example, in bargaining between the US and South Korea) from that of interregionalism. The second concept shows up in two cases: ties between the EU and the Southern Common Market (MERCOSUR), and "hybrid interregionalism" (relations between the EU and China or between China and Africa). Both concepts, but especially the implementation of interregionalism, can be said to embody a "new multilateralism," provided that they respect its main rules, procedures, and principles. To explore more fully possible alternatives to WTO reform and classic global multilateralism, we also might cite the example of the Comprehensive and Progressive Agreement for Trans-Pacific Partnership (CPTPP) and the Regional Comprehensive Economic Partnership (RCEP), both in the Asia-Pacific region.

Other groups of WTO members have begun to work out their own "plurilateral" solutions to the organization's problems (e.g., one with 76 member states, including China and even the US), mainly by focusing on narrower issues than grand reform. The EU, for instance, has shown its willingness to talk about setting rules for e-commerce. Although plurilateral efforts are no panacea, they can fill important gaps. The EU is particularly committed to interregionalism and regionalism because they correspond to its nature as a regional entity. Its comprehensive approach to trade policy, which reflects a clear legal and strategic background that intended to situate trade within the larger framework of its external relations, is based on several documents: the Lisbon Treaty of 2007, which grants to the European Parliament veto rights in the ratification of trade and investment arrangements deals; the Malmström Report of 2015 ("Trade for All"); and the High Representative for Foreign and Security Policy's 2016 Mogherini Report ("Global Europe").

For the new EU approach to external policies, interregional relations are a crucial test. Here, two preliminary definitions are needed. Regionalism concerns multidimensional and institutionalized relations among interdependent neighboring countries and societies (Telò 2001, 2007, 2014, 2016). Interregionalism, by contrast, refers to multidimensional relations between a regional organization and either a different regional organization or else a large state or a group of states belonging to two or more continents. Interregional relations thus understood have been caught up in the troubled drift of global governance that we have been examining in this chapter (Hettne 2007; Rüland 2006, 2015; Söderbaum et al. 2016; Fawcett et al. 2015).

The list of interregional negotiations started by great powers or regional entities includes the following:

- As far as EU interregional relations from the 1970s to the 1990s are concerned, the literature indicates that such arrangements were not always easy to reach, and their record is various and mixed. Already well-established multipurpose cooperation processes include the following: African, Caribbean, and Pacific Group of States (with Africa and the Caribbean and Pacific regions); the Asia-Europe Meeting [ASEM] with East Asia; EU-Community of Latin American and Caribbean States (with Latin America); and the Euro-Mediterranean Barcelona process (with the northern part of Africa and the southern rim of the Mediterranean). Furthermore, once it became clear the WTO negotiations at the Doha Development Round were deadlocked, the EU launched interregional trade negotiations with every continent as well as with many individual states.
- The US, too, attempted to establish interregional ties, but many such endeavors came to naught (or very little). Some examples of these efforts include the Free Trade Area of the Americas (FTAA), including the entire Western hemisphere; Asia-Pacific Economic Cooperation (APEC); the Trans-Pacific Partnership (TTP), for the Asia-Pacific region with the exception of China; and TTIP. However, FTAA failed, APEC is stagnating, and Donald Trump decided to withdraw from TPP, while TTIP negotiations have been interrupted.

- The Association of Southeast Asian Nations (ASEAN) also has tried to advance interregional schemes of various kinds, including ASEAN+6 (with six other countries of Asia and Oceania); RCEP (with China, Japan, Australia and New Zealand); and ASEAN-MERCOSUR (with the four Latin American countries in the MERCOSUR bloc).
- The Chinese approach to interregionalism is of more recent origin and so cannot be critically assessed yet. First, there is the Belt and Road Initiative (BRI), which is actually a two-pronged (land and sea) scheme to promote interregionalism by linking Europe and East Asia more closely. Second, China has developed extensive and controversial interregional ties with Africa, Europe (via the BRI), and other continents (Feng & Telò 2020).

The Asia-Pacific region is crucial for the future of global trade. The Asia-Pacific Economic Cooperation Free Trade Agreement (APEC-FTA) remains a significant, though failed project. Conceived in 1989 and given a high profile by the Clinton administration (Bergsten 1994), it was supposed to accelerate trade in that region, but it was effectively scuttled by George W. Bush after the 9/11 attacks when his administration decided to prioritize security over trade. China, and more specifically Xi Jinping, revived it as the FTA of the Pacific at the 2014 APEC meeting, although it will probably never fulfill its original promise. However, there may be other emergent frameworks in the post-hegemonic era. For example, no one can ignore the recent success of the trilateral meeting of 2019 involving South Korea, Japan, and China, which supported a quick conclusion of RCEP (at the ASEAN+6 level, from which India defected in 2019). And there may be opportunities for joint leadership by China and Japan in crafting a possible bargain between RCEP and the former TPP, surviving with the acronym CPTPP after the US withdrawal under Trump. Still, the question is open about the leadership in the Asia-Pacific region. The problem of India's nationalism and protectionism lingers: important differences in standards hamper trade. Finally, China has taken the lead in building interregional trade ties and annual summits with Africa.

All in all, the EU, the US, and China have led the push for liberalized trade and fostering interregional cooperation, so we should not rule out the possibility that they could partially replace or supplement the stagnating WTO in this endeavor.

The new EU trade policy as a case study: how well has it been applied thus far?

The European Union is a civilian power, not a military power. It develops its international influence through methods other than military action: cooperation with developing countries, humanitarian aid, partnership agreements, economic and cultural cooperation combined with political dialogue, peacekeeping missions under the title of Common Foreign and Security Policy (CFSP), and the EU's most powerful international tool, trade policy. Along with the US and China, the EU is among the three giants of global trade and is a major trading partner of many countries, as shown in Table 4.3.

TABLE 4.3 EU trade with its main partners (2018)

Imports:

China 20%	EUR 394.7 billion
US 13%	EUR 267.3 billion
Russia 8%	EUR 168.3 billion
Norway 4%	EUR 83.8 billion
Rest of the world 49%	–

Exports:

US 21%	EUR 406.4 billion
China 11%	EUR 209.9 billion
Switzerland 8%	EUR 156.5 billion
Russia 4%	EUR 85.3 billion
Turkey 4%	EUR 77.3 billion
Rest of the world 52%	–

Source: Eurostat (online data code, 2018).[1]

What is new is that since 2006 the EU has pursued a variety of interregional trade initiatives with every continent. We need to determine just how well those efforts have fared thus far. There are several case studies that may shed light on that question.

To begin with, the trade deal between the EU and South Korea, signed in 2011 and ratified in 2015, represents a significant model. It has been a great success in terms of both import and export volumes. Trade is booming between the partners. The agreement has created new opportunities for market access in services and investments and includes provisions in areas such as competition policy, government procurement, intellectual property rights, transparency in regulation, and sustainable development. As a complement to the trade deal, the Framework Agreement of 2010 provides a basis for strengthened cooperation on major political and global issues such as human rights, non-proliferation of weapons of mass destruction, counter-terrorism, climate change, and energy security. This is an overarching attempt at political cooperation with a legal link to the Free Trade Agreement. However, the trade deal risks being suspended unless the ILO convention on labor rights is ratified. The EU in 2019 launched legal action because South Korea had not yet ratified the ILO convention, which was included in the treaty.[2]

In another initiative, the EU worked out CETA, a trade arrangement with Canada, in 2016. That deal is relevant to our analysis for several reasons. First, CETA features a more inclusive agenda that embraces a comprehensive set of issues, from the environment and social welfare to public procurement, "geographic indications," and the precautionary principle. Second, it is an "interconnection treaty" (De Block & Lebullenger 2018; Telò 2018), a regulatory arrangement including a permanent dialogue between both regulatory authorities. Third, it goes beyond the ISDS mechanism discussed above; in fact, the investment court system may evolve towards a multilateral institution. Currently we have more than 2,000 treaties that still employ the old private tribunal system. It is not easy to change the latter in light of recent opposition from the US. However, the EU and Canada agree on this point. Both favor a public, transparent tribunal with appeal rights and standing magistrates. But further legal work is needed on certain questions. First, the Wallonia precedent should be revisited, in which that Belgian province's regional government threatened to block the free-trade agreement between the EU and Canada. Second, and most importantly, legal scholars should take a hard look at the famous "Singapore decision" of May 2017 rendered by the Court of Justice of the European Union (CJEU). The CJEU ruled that there are two aspects of the proposed EU-Singapore free-trade agreement in which "the EU is not endowed with exclusive competence, namely the field of non-direct foreign investment ('portfolio' investments made without any intention to influence the management and control of an undertaking) and the regime governing dispute settlement between investors and States" (opinion 2/15). By contrast, apart from trade issues, transport and (crucially) "sustainable development" are matters of the EU's exclusive competence. The problematic legacy of the Singapore decision is the risk that the EU will have to unpack interregional arrangements and figure out which aspects must be submitted to the member states. This matter will be elucidated further below.

Finally, the negotiation and ratification process was troubled by serious legitimacy deficits. A large share of public opinion in many countries demanded more transparency. The Commission was obliged to make dramatic changes in the way it conducted negotiations, as shown by the endeavors of Commissioner Malmström in 2015–16 for enhanced and deeper dialogue with the EU Parliament and the non-governmental organizations (NGOs) compared with previous Commissioner De Gucht. Regarding the CETA implementation, the statistical data are very positive, for the EU more than for Canada. However, even in the EU some problems persist. For example, the majority of small and medium-sized enterprises (SMEs) are not yet aware of the opportunities offered by CETA, according to the European Parliament's assessment in 2019. Moreover, according to the French Centre d'Etudes Prospectives et d'Informations Internationales review (2015), while the trade gains are evident, insufficient care is paid to the supplementary problems created by CETA by implementing the COP21 objectives. That being said, critics should recognize that CETA may be a model for the post-Brexit relations between the EU and UK.

Besides the advances in treaty-making described above, the EU also has concluded a successful treaty with Japan. Among other things, that treaty, signed in 2017 and entered into force in February 2019, shows that a rules-based global trade order can work well, contrary to Donald Trump's efforts to revert to protectionism. The EU-Japan accord may prove more significant even than those with South Korea and Canada, especially in the wake of the demise of the TTIP negotiations with the US, because it will cover countries that produce 25% of the world's GDP and count some 600 million inhabitants. It provides a paramount model for second-generation regulatory arrangements and will go far towards removing both traditional trade barriers on goods and non-tariff barriers. It will extend to many new areas as well, including services, agriculture, sanitation, sustainable development, public procurement, the digital economy, and intellectual property. Furthermore, this Economic Partnership Agreement was parallel to a second EU arrangement with Japan, the Strategic Partnership Agreement, which represents the first framework agreement between the two entities and strengthens their overall partnership by providing an overarching framework for enhanced political and sectoral cooperation and joint action on issues of common interest, including regional and global challenges.

Nor should we omit a major interregional achievement: the treaty between the EU and MERCOSUR, reached in 2019 and still awaiting ratification by all parties. The outcome of two decades of trade negotiations, it builds on the Interregional Cooperation Agreement between the EU and MERCOSUR, signed in Madrid in 1995. Like the other treaties described above, it includes topics that go beyond trade cooperation, including non-tariff barriers, socio-environmental standards, and the precautionary principle, as well as democratization, human rights, ILO conventions, transparency conflict-resolution mechanisms based on arbitration panels, and capacity-building mechanisms such as technical assistance in training, computer networks, and education.

The EU-MERCOSUR agreement establishes a profound multidimensional, interregional partnership, with far-reaching political and cultural implications. It sends a strong geopolitical signal to the world, in an era of trade wars and amid the WTO's declining role, that two formal customs unions can succeed in setting up a trading and regulatory system in the face of resistance and disapproval from the Trump administration, which spurned multilateralism. However, there are some caveats to the generally positive evaluation of EU regulatory arrangement with MERCOSUR. First, there have been recurring protectionist obstacles due to the potentially fundamental adverse impacts of free trade on sensitive sectors of the economies in both blocs, notably agriculture in the EU and manufacturing in MERCOSUR. These forces continue to lobby against ratification, and they seek to swing national public opinions in their direction. For that reason, internal ratification processes pose a significant challenge on both sides of the Atlantic. Political parties on both continents (e.g., in Argentina, France, and Belgium) have expressed opposition, and protectionist agricultural lobbies have fought it in the EU in spite of carefully calibrated tariff-rate quotas and serious standards-control mechanisms. Because there is strong support in Europe for environmental protection – as evidenced, for example, in the growing strength of Green parties, in Pope Francis's condemnation of deforestation in Amazonia, and in widespread concern over climate change and implementing COP21 – the EU must gain unanimous support in the Council as well as within member states in order to ratify the agreement with MERCOSUR. Furthermore, we should recall that the European Parliament has the final word in such arrangements.

Apart from the aforementioned agreements and negotiations, the EU has other irons in the fire, including possible second-generation free-trade deals with Australia, New Zealand, and the African Union. A direct bilateral agreement with

China, which so far has spanned many years of difficult negotiations, also may be in the works, as indicated by a joint declaration made in April of 2019 by China's President Xi and then EU Commission President Juncker. But let us not be too hasty in welcoming this turn of events. As Thomas Meyer and Qin Yaqing argue in the present volume, it is questionable whether any EU-Chinese agreement truly can succeed unless it addresses the fundamental principles underlying trade and takes the first steps towards building understanding and paving the way for compromise. Finally, we should mention the case of Vietnam. In the wake of the EU-Vietnam trade arrangement of 2016, Vietnam has become the EU's second most important trading partner within ASEAN after Singapore. Negotiating better access for EU exporters to the dynamic ASEAN market is a priority for the EU. As a whole, ASEAN represents the EU's third largest trading partner outside Europe after the US and China. Because it is crucial that the EU initiative should not be perceived as an attempt to divide the ASEAN regional bloc, bloc-to-bloc negotiations should be prioritized. Such negotiations also would indirectly involve China by means of larger associations such as ASEAN+1 (China) and ASEAN+3 (China, Japan, and South Korea).

Beijing's evolving response to the unpredictable post–Cold War world disorder and the increasingly aggressive trade policy of the US, if it proves to be dynamic and assertive, will call into question the existing status quo. The BRI, as China's multidimensional strategic bid for influence in Europe and beyond, affects the entire neighborhood, from Malaysia to Indonesia and from Nepal to other South Asian countries (Ding et al. 2018). Two burning questions for comparative research arise from these considerations. First, is the BRI better understood as a unilateral or a multilateral initiative? And second, is the 17+1 Initiative intent on dividing the EU, given that it includes only 12 of the 27 EU member states plus five countries outside the EU?[3]

China relaunched the RCEP in 2015 as a free-trade arrangement with the ASEAN+6 countries (Australia, China, India, Japan, New Zealand, and South Korea) in response to a perceived threat by the Obama administration's trade and security initiatives. In particular, the Chinese leadership was concerned about the proposal for a transpacific partnership, originally planned as a business-driven agreement between the US and 12 Asia-Pacific countries that was designed to ease trade among friends; it was parallel to security initiatives containing China. The RCEP deepened its cooperation as a reaction not only to the TPP but also to TTIP negotiations between the US and EU, which were perceived as an attempt to set global trade standards that would be imposed on China (Morin et al. 2015). In December of 2019, India defected from the RCEP because it was unwilling to give up the benefits it was receiving from maintaining low standards for international trade and its e-commerce concerns.

Significantly, the RCEP free-trade agreement is strongly supported by ASEAN, which had been deepened by the Kuala Lumpur Declaration of November 22, 2015, that established "political, economic and cultural communities" and also by the approval of the ASEAN 2025 Declaration titled Forging Ahead Together.

RCEP was not boycotted by the front of democratic countries (US allies within the Indo-Pacific Alliance, such as Australia, Japan, and South Korea). The initiative is extremely important for two reasons. First, unlike the TPP but like ASEM, it keeps the ASEAN bloc united and in the driver's seat. Second, it divides the members of the informal Quadrilateral Security Dialogue (a.k.a. the "Quad"), which encompasses the US, Australia, India, and Japan, with potential implications for the "economic-security nexus" in the Asia-Pacific region (Pempel 2005, 2010).

In the wake of Trump's bipolar approach and China's assertiveness, the previous economic-security nexus has become wobbly. The 2019 Chengdu summit among South Korea, China, and Japan was a success, and some arrangements for environmental, trade-related, and technological cooperation look resilient and dynamic in this post-hegemonic era. Research should clarify the hypothesis that a China-Japan joint leadership might bring about a future arrangement between the partially overlapping RCEP and the CPTPP. Could the CPTPP be open to China, or could APEC be revived as a broad APEC-FTA (by 2025), a wider kind of umbrella that would encompass both the CPTPP and RCEP? It is also vital to determine what Japan – a pivotal and powerful member of both the TPP and RCEP – actually wants, in view of its crucial security alliance with the US. A regional free-trade agreement including China, Japan, and South Korea would put into play a new dynamic that would go beyond the old trilateral model of the 1980s, which involved the US, Europe, and Japan.

Thus far, it is difficult to deliver a balanced assessment of the new EU trade policy. On the one hand, the EU was extremely proactive in the Trump era, taking advantage of the vacuum created by US withdrawal from many parts of the world, most notably the Asia-Pacific region and South America. The EU has managed to establish a deeper political dialogue with each partner in the Asia-Pacific, from China to Indonesia, and EU authorities have participated in many regional frameworks, whether as invited guests or as observers.

On the other hand, the limits of the EU approach are also evident: it does not yet directly address the economic-security nexus characterizing these regions, particularly that of the Asia-Pacific. The EU was unable to reassert its influence in Northeast Asian controversies after the failure of the Korean Peninsula Energy Development Organization in the 1990s and in spite of highly relevant trade arrangements. Europe plays no role in East Asian security and territorial disputes concerning matters like sovereignty over the islands of the South China Sea or the interpretation of the "one China" doctrine concerning the status of Taiwan. None of the hard security issues of this crucial part of the planet has been addressed by the EU so far, with the sole exception of ASEM declaratory diplomacy. Numerous countries – from Australia and New Zealand to Japan and South Korea, Thailand and the Philippines – find themselves in the awkward position of having the US as their security ally and China as their top trading partner. The EU, especially Germany at its center, faces difficult dilemmas. While the "normative power" illusion of the 1990s is gone (cf. Fawcett et al. 2015; Levrat et al. 2020), the security dimensions of the EU as a civilian power, market power, and trading power are not yet fully expressed. "Civilian power," in contrast to the rhetoric of normative power, remains a worthy analytical concept: however, in the event of a militarization and securitization of Asia-Pacific controversies, the EU inevitably would be a marginal player, and civilian power would become a euphemism, even a "contradiction in terms" (Bull 1982). Either the EU will become capable of building a hard security and foreign policy core that augments its political weight, based on its trade power and market power, or it will be condemned to international irrelevance and internal division, especially in regard to this critical region of the world.

Several conclusions can be drawn from this brief account of the headwinds now buffeting global trade and efforts by the EU and other actors to overcome them by a new generation of free-trade (or, more precisely, regulatory) agreements.

- Trade negotiations are becoming more complex, time-consuming, and difficult than they once were (Woolkock 2020). However, in many cases they have compiled a record of success in the recent decade.
- New mechanisms of trade conflict resolution caused problems with Japan and the US, but worked in regard to Canada and MERCOSUR, to take two examples.
- Trade negotiators with Vietnam have managed to insert the ILO convention on labor rights (including the principle of free association) into the new agreement, but it is not yet clear whether the deal will be ratified. The case of Korea shows how important the implementation of this chapter of the arrangement is for the EU. Currently, the EU–South Korea trade agreement is in limbo pending Korean ratification and implementation of the ILO convention. This stalemate poses a warning for ongoing EU trade negotiations with China, where what matters is not only market access and reciprocity but also the relevant charter of rights and rule of law.
- Finally, it makes sense to ask whether the EU's new comprehensive approach is serious or merely contingent and instrumental. The negotiating agent, the European Commission, has only limited discretion to upgrade trade deals, given the vital role of the European Parliament according to the Lisbon Treaty (via the ratification process) and the influence of NGOs in fostering democratic legitimacy. Furthermore, since the landmark 2018 Singapore decision by the EU Court of Justice, mixed treaties on investments must be ratified by the European Parliament as well as by member states. All in all, building legitimacy around the deliberations and deal-making of the Commission is imperative. The more inclusive the trade agenda is, the more civil society and elected bodies will want to have their say.

Trade and culture

We saw at the beginning of this chapter that trade is not a narrow economic matter; it also has cultural dimensions that must be taken into account. That insight leads to a series of questions and observations with which we will conclude. What should a comprehensive trade agenda do or say about culture? Does an emphasis on the political and cultural dimension of trade mean that cultural goods should be part of economic-liberal free-trade arrangements?

Negotiations are influenced by national background cultures (Qin 2018) as well as the regulations and laws that govern each country and its national or regional (in the cases of the EU, MERCOSUR, and ASEAN) trading culture.

Industry also has its own culture, as famously exemplified by Fordism, pioneered by the Ford Motor Company in the US during the first half of the twentieth century. Behavioral norms and practices within industries, in the context of national culture, affect the way negotiations play out. It is often the case that cultural norms transcend local and national borders, becoming indicative of the industry generally and not just of the specific countries or locales where they originated. Industrial products are often less influenced by a given country's culture than by industry norms and standards. This fact is especially salient to the digital era, which is dominated by the giants of the new economy. Companies, much like peoples, have their own sets of values, morals, beliefs, and opinions as well as their own dress codes, standards of communication, norms and expectations, and tones and registers. It is also worth noting that within any given company, the financial department is likely to have a different culture and vocabulary than those of its communications and marketing departments.

Two independent variables – GDP and cultural proximity (colonial ties, common borders, and a common language) – matter a great deal, but they differ between sectors. Whereas colonial links influence exchanges in the heritage goods, newspaper and periodical, and visual arts sectors, their influence is, rather surprisingly, less important for audiovisual media. For the economic sector involving "books, newspapers and periodicals and other printed matter," the sharing of a border and/or a language encourages trade. Unlike recorded media, the visual arts and audiovisual media are not influenced by sharing an official language.

Furthermore, regionalism matters: geographic neighborhood has a positive impact on the flows in the visual arts and audiovisual media sectors but does not influence the recorded media sector. The common language is the main factor in the penetration of cultural goods with written content. This factor multiplies the flows. Also, colonial ties certainly shape the preferences of consumers in the importing countries for heritage goods. Is the risk of protectionism increased when cultural goods are being traded?

In addressing the question of trade in cultural goods, a range of policy options is available. At one end of the continuum is a laissez-faire, anything-goes attitude that would not treat such goods differently from any other variety. Cultural artifacts, from that standpoint, would neither deserve nor receive any special legal protections. At the other end of the continuum lie efforts to exclude cultural artifacts from trade negotiations (such as those for the TTIP). The latter approach has been favored by the French in particular and the EU more generally, motivated in large measure by fears of global domination by US media and cultural production. It says that when we negotiate international trade agreements, we should respect internal multiculturalism, preserve local cultures, and prevent excessive uniformity and homogenization as the ultimate outcomes of trade liberalization. But how best to achieve that goal? People have been discussing that very issue for some 20 years, and two approaches seem to have emerged. First, in 1994 the WTO adopted a policy of allowing "cultural exceptions" to broad rules liberalizing trade. Then in 2005, UNESCO agreed on a convention with legal force that would balance the circulation of goods and services, especially between developing and developed countries or between regions and interregional partnerships, against the interest of the less-developed countries in maintaining their cultural traditions and not being overwhelmed by mass-produced goods. These new approaches manifest what we might call a "differentiated universalism": they promulgate broadly liberal trade rules that seek to discourage protectionism but grant exceptions when there are strong cultural reasons to do so, above all the hope of avoiding clashes of civilizations.

Conclusions

From the foregoing analysis, two central conclusions emerge. The first concerns the field of policy recommendations. Assuming that further progress by WTO-level multilateralism, as wished for by classic economic liberalism, is no longer a viable option (Bhagwati 1992), what is at stake is whether what are defined as "next best options" work against or in favor of a new multilateralism. We know that both unilateralism and asymmetrical transactional bilateralism may negatively affect global trade, interregional relations, and multilateralism. The alternative to Trumpian trade wars is not a nostalgic muddling through by old economic liberal FTAs. Upgraded interregional arrangements may provide a way out, provided that the current new multilayered trade multilateralism can become more efficient by including higher standards on matters such as working conditions and environmental protection; more legitimate in a less contingent way; and more driven by the wish of eventually relaunching global multilateralism. In the current century, trade is no longer about mere specific reciprocity but about living standards as well as cultural and political ties between peoples and civilizations. Specific reciprocity is a fundamental and traditional feature of trade arrangements. However, the standards imbedded in trade agreements need to be upgraded and negotiated more holistically to encompass social, environmental, cultural, and legal concerns (rule of law, labor rights), among others. Amid the current global instability, in the event that the US continues to renounce any kind of leadership role, the EU – in alliance with many countries of Asia, Africa, and the Americas – has a special responsibility to undertake enhanced efforts aimed at forging regional and interregional arrangements and strategically framing their geopolitical implications. If these are well designed and thoughtfully applied, they could help revive or even create a post-hegemonic, pluralistic, participatory multilateralism (cf. Qin 2018). Such efforts eventually could spark a revival of the WTO but this time supported by multilayered arrangements, suited to a new generation of regulatory agreements.

Second, this chapter also contributes to international relations theory. It points towards an answer to the vital question of how, in the context of post-realist, neo-institutionalist cooperation theories, students of international relations ought to approach trade. We simply cannot understand what is happening in global trade and its interplay with interregional dialogue without taking into account variables other than the mere cost-benefit calculations of involved actors. Rational choice is not a sufficient explanation. Instead, we must adopt a more inclusive hermeneutic approach. While the weight of rational choice factors (notably states' interests in reducing transaction costs) obviously still matters for purposes of comparative and normative research on trade policy, it is increasingly contained and complemented by other variables. In particular, the relevance of the following non-rational-choice drivers of trade have come to the fore in comparative and normative research in this field.

- *Critical historical junctures.* The emergence of a multipolar world, in conjunction with the global financial crisis of 2008–17, has weakened traditional multilateralism and challenged the role of the WTO and (correspondingly) strengthened interregional arrangements as the second-best option in regard to international trade.
- *Political-security factors* (cf. Risse & Börzel 2016). These factors may gain importance either on the basis of a revived Cold War climate, such as Western ambitions to contain China, or China's effort to foster a bipolar confrontation with the US (Yan 2019), or in the context of a new multilateral trend.
- *Subjective factors*, including ideas, projects, discourses, cognitive and cultural background and dynamics, and mutual perceptions (Katzenstein 2005; Acharya 2014). Such factors cannot be ignored without paying a high price in terms of both scientific research and mutual understanding between partners.
- *The influence of civil society.* Civil society plays a definite role in shaping trade policy. However, to analyze that role correctly we must take into account institutional factors (such as party systems, national constitutions, and in the case of the EU, its constitutive treaties and decisions of the Court of Justice) as well as the results of comparative regional studies.
- *The issue of legitimacy.* In normative terms, strengthening interregional trade and deepening trade and cultural ties require not only output legitimacy (efficiency) but also input legitimacy (Telò 2017), which depends less on ephemeral or "contingent" successes in matters like boosting GDP (Scharpf 1999). The fundamental question for our future research agenda then becomes how to build an accountable and participatory multilevel democracy.

Notes

\# This chapter was revised slightly in November of 2020 to reflect the results of the US presidential election.
1 We remember that Turkey signed a Customs Union with the EU in 1995; that Norway is a member of the European Economic Area (EEA; i.e., of the single market); and that Switzerland has signed a similar Institutional Framework Agreement between the European Union and the Swiss Confederation. The 1997 partnership agreement with Russia was due to be renegotiated but was halted in 2012.

2 In line with Chapter 13 and Annex 13 of the Korea-EU FTA, and reaffirming their commitment to cooperate on the implementation of ILO conventions, South Korea and the EU agreed at the fourth meeting of the Committee on Trade and Sustainable Development in Seoul on September 9, 2015, to launch a cooperation project under the EU Partnership Instrument on the implementation of ILO Convention no. 111. The point of this meeting was to ascertain more precisely how the convention was being implemented in both South Korea and the EU Member States. ILO Convention no. 111, which deals with discrimination in employment and occupations, was signed in 1958. The first three Articles read as follows:

> "a. Any distinction, exclusion or preference made on the basis of race, color, sex, religion, political opinion, national extraction or social origin, which has the effect of nullifying or impairing equality of opportunity or treatment in employment or occupation;
> – any other distinction, exclusion or preference which has the effect of nullifying or impairing equality of opportunity or treatment in employment or occupation as may be determined by the Member concerned, after consultation with representative employers' and workers' organizations, where such exist, and with other appropriate bodies."
>
> "b. Any distinction, exclusion, or preference in respect of a particular job based on the inherent requirements thereof shall not be deemed to be discrimination."
> "c. For the purpose of this Convention the terms employment and occupation include access to vocational training, access to employment and to particular occupations, and terms and conditions of employment."

As noted above, the objective of the meeting between South Korean and EU representatives is to contribute to improving the implementation rate of the Convention in both Korea and the EU member states. The research for this project will result in a detailed comparative analysis of the implementation of Convention no. 111. However, EU Commissioner Cecilia Malmström said on July 5, 2019: "The EU-Korea trade agreement has produced large economic gains for both sides. Trade needs however to go hand in hand with workers' rights. We agreed on that when we put the agreement in place in 2011. Despite some steps in the right direction, nine years later Korea has still not delivered on its commitments. Therefore, at this stage, we see no alternative than to ask for a panel, while of course remaining open to further dialogue to find a mutually agreed solution. This move shows the importance that the EU attaches to sustainable development in our trade agreements."
3 Those countries are Bulgaria, Croatia, the Czech Republic, Estonia, Greece, Hungary, Latvia, Lithuania, Poland, Romania, Slovakia, and Slovenia, plus Albania, Bosnia and Herzegovina, Macedonia, Montenegro, and Serbia.

References

Acharya, A. 2014. *The End of American World Order*. London: Polity Press
Bergsten, F. 1994. "APEC and the World Economy." In R. Garnaut & P. Drysdale (eds.), *Asia Pacific Regionalism*. Sydney: Harper, pp. 218–25
Bhagwati, J. 1992. "Regionalism versus Multilateralism." *The World Economy* 15(5): 535–55
Bull, H. 1982. "Civilian Power Europe: A Contradiction in Terms?" *Journal of Common Market Studies* 21(2): 149–70
CEPII. 2015. "Evaluation macroéconomique des impacts de l'accord commercial et économique entre l'Union européenne et le Canada." Paris. Available at www.cepii.fr
De Block, C. & J. Lebullenger. 2018. *Génération TAFTA/CETA: Les nouveau partenariats de la mondialisation*. Montréal: Université de Montréal

Ding, C., X. Zhang, & M. Telò (eds.). 2018. *Deepening the EU-China Partnership: Bridging Ideational and Institutional Differences*. Abingdon, UK: Routledge
European Commission. 2018, July 5. "WTO-EU's proposals for WTO modernization. Note for the Attention of the Trade Policy Committee." Brussels: European Commission
Fawcett, L., M. Telò, & F. Ponjaert (eds.). 2015. *Interregionalism and the EU*. Abingdon, UK: Routledge
Feng, Y. & M. Telò (eds.). 2020. *China and EU in the Era of Regionalism and Interregionalism*. Brussels: Peter Lang
Fukuyama, F. 1992. *The End of History and the Last Man*. New York: Free Press
Hettne, B. 2007. "Interregionalism and World Order: The Diverging EU and US Models." In M. Telò (ed.), *EU and New Regionalism*. Burlington, VT: Ashgate, pp. 75–105
Hirschman, A. 1977. *The Passions and the Interests*. Princeton, NJ: Princeton University Press
Huntington, S. 1996. *The Clash of Civilizations and the Remaking of World Order*. New York: Simon & Schuster
Ikenberry, J. & D. Deudney. 2018. "Liberal World: The Resilient Order." *Foreign Affairs* 94(4): 1–15
Kant, I. 1795/2016. *Treaty for a Perpetual Peace. A Philosophical Essay*. London: Allen & Unwin
Katzenstein, P. 2005. *A World of Regions*. Ithaca, NY: Cornell University Press
Levrat, N., R. Marchetti, & F. Ponjaert (eds.). 2020. *Framing Power EU*. Abington, UK: Routledge
Malmström, C. 2015. "Trade for All." Brussels: Report of the EU Commission, pp. 10–20
Marx, K. & F. Engels. 1848/2018. *The Communist Manifesto*. London: CreateSpace Independent Publishing Platform
Mogherini, F. 2016. *EU Global Strategy*. Brussels: EEAS
Montesquieu, C. 1748/1949. *The Spirit of the Laws*. New York: Hafner
Morin, J., T. Novotna, F. Ponjaert, & M. Telò (eds.). 2015. *The Politics of Transatlantic Trade Negotiations*. Burlington, VT: Routledge
Pempel, T.J. 2005. *Remapping East Asia: The Construction of a Region*. Ithaca, NY: Cornell University Press
Pempel, T.J. 2010. "Soft Balancing, Hedging, and Institutional Darwinism: The Economic-security Nexus and East Asian Regionalism." *Journal of East Asian Studies* 10: 209–38
Qin, Y. 2018. *A Relational Theory of World Politics*. Cambridge, UK: Cambridge University Press
Risse, T. & T. Börzel (eds.). 2016. *The Oxford Handbook of Comparative Regionalism*. Oxford, UK: Oxford University Press
Rüland, J. 2006. "Interregionalism: An Unfinished Agenda." In H. Hänggi, R. Roloff, & J. Rüland (eds.), *Interregionalism and International Relations*. London: Routledge, pp. 295–313
Rüland, J. 2015. "The Unintended Consequences of Interregional Democracy Promotion: Normative and Conceptual Misunderstanding in EU-ASEAN Relations." In L. Fawcett, M. Telò, & F. Ponjaert (eds.), *Interregionalism and the European Union*. Abington, UK: Routledge, pp. 267–83
Santander, S. 2016. *Concurrences Régionales dans un Monde Multipolaire Emergent*. Brussels: Peter Lang AG
Scharpf, F. 1999. *Governing in Europe: Effective and Democratic?* Oxford, UK: Oxford University Press
Söderbaum, F., F. Baert, & T. Scaramagli (eds.). 2016. *Intersecting Interregionalism*. Dordrecht, The Netherlands: Springer
Telò, M. (ed.). 2001/2007/2014. *European Union and New Regionalism*. Burlington, VT: Ashgate

Telò, M. 2016. *Regionalism in Hard Times: Competitive and Post-liberal Trends in Europe, Asia, Africa, and the Americas*. Abingdon, UK: Routledge

Telò, M. 2017. "The Emerging Conflict between Democratic Legitimacy and the EU's Common Commercial Policy Risks for the EU as a Civilian Power and for the Multilateral Order." *Annals of the Fondazione Einaudi*, Turin, Italy. January 12

Telò, M. 2018. "L'EU Face à la Multiplication des Interconnections Commerçiales Interrégionales et à Leurs Implications Politiques." In C. De Block (ed.), *Generation TAFTA: Les nouveaux partenariats de la mondialisations*. Rennes, France: Presses Universitaires de Rennes, pp. 37–55

Weyembergh, A. & M. Telò (eds.). (2020). *Supranational Governance at Stake*. Abington, UK: Routledge

Woolkock, S. 2020. "Commercial Policy: The European Union and the World Trade and Investment Order." In A. Weyembergh & M. Telò (eds.), *Supranational Governance at Stake*. Abington, UK: Routledge

Yan, X. 2019. *Leadership and the Rise of Great Powers*. Princeton, NJ: Princeton University Press

5
EU-CHINA ECONOMIC AND TRADE RELATIONS IN THE HARD TIMES OF THE WORLD ECONOMY

Ding Chun and Zhang Xiaotong

We are probably entering a long dark tunnel of world history. The world economy is swinging back into a recessionary phase of the business cycle, witnessing a slowdown of trade and investment, and enduring a proliferation of trade restrictions. Globalization, based as it is upon free capital flows, is now the victim of unprecedented setbacks. Competition among the great powers is on the rise and geopolitics has come roaring back. In some countries, as exemplified by Trump's America, economic nationalism is becoming fashionable again as it was during the interwar period and the 1970s. COVID-19, a rapidly surging epidemic, has spread fear on a global scale; that, in turn, is dragging the world economy into a recession. Policymakers in the EU and China cannot turn their back on those contexts. That being said, the two economic powers of continental size, the EU and China, still are adhering to multilateralism, resisting trade protectionism, and cooperating in the fight against the coronavirus. Their policy options, represented by China's Belt and Road Initiative and the EU's multilateralism plus interregionalism, are of utmost importance in the struggle to defeat the protectionist and isolationist pivot of the spirit of our time.

The dual rise and revival of Europe and China are among the most significant historical events to have taken place since World War II, and each has contributed decisively to the formation of an increasingly multipolar world. Economic and trade ties stand out as the core of EU-China relations, and both of those have complicated spillover effects upon political and cultural circumstances as well. The basic logic of EU-China relations displays a three-step process, starting from trade, spilling over into the political sphere, and finally fostering a plethora of cultural links. EU-China relations have experienced a high degree of institutionalization by this time, an advance that provides multiple, multilayered platforms for crisis management and problem resolution.

The US has been a conspicuous factor in EU-China relations ever since the earliest days of diplomatic interaction between the People's Republic and the European Economic Community (EEC). The US is now pivoting towards economic nationalism and exiting from global economic leadership. Therefore, the EU-China relationship is facing a new tri-party complexity ("triplexity"), with the US as the major unpredictable factor. That being said, the EU now increasingly plays the role of a linkage power in this new triplexity, forging issue links and taking positions either for or against the US to advance the Union's pragmatic and normative goals (Zhang & Xie 2016). Equally noteworthy is the EU's trade-security linkage as part of its geo-economic policy agenda. Now that the US has left a vacuum in the Pacific, the EU is pushing ahead with multiple initiatives there (cf. the EU's free-trade agreements, or FTAs, with Japan, Vietnam, Korea, Singapore, and ASEAN, and the comprehensive investment treaty negotiations with China).

Hard times of the world economy

The world economy is drifting back into a sluggish phase. The spread of the coronavirus on a global scale is adding fuel to the fire. World trade started to decelerate from the first quarter of 2018 (see Figures 5.1 and 5.2). The deceleration of trade in 2018 was driven primarily by Europe and Asia due to their large share in world imports (37% and 35%, respectively). After recording strong increases in 2017, Asia saw its trade growth moderate in 2018. Meanwhile, Europe's exports stagnated throughout the year while its imports gradually declined.

Global foreign direct investment (FDI) flows continued their slide in 2018, falling by 13% to $1.3 trillion (see Figure 5.3). The slide is due to the cyclical nature of the world economy and increasing economic policy uncertainty (see Figure 5.4). An index of economic policy uncertainty based on the frequency of phrases related to uncertainty in press accounts has risen consistently over time, peaking at 34.1 in December of 2018, a period that coincided with the US federal government shutdown and US trade negotiations with China. In the meanwhile, foreign investment restrictions and regulations are on the rise (see Figure 5.5).

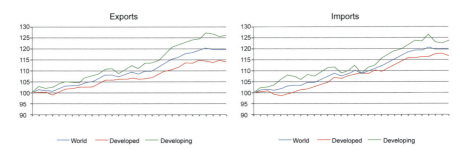

FIGURE 5.1 Slowdown in global trade growth

Source: WTO and UNCTAD.

EU-China economic and trade relations 97

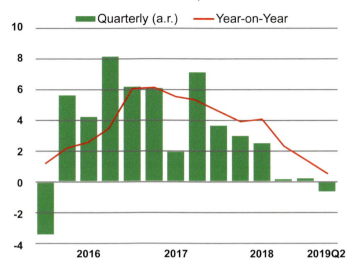

FIGURE 5.2 World trade growth
Source: OECD Interim Economic Outlook, September 2019.

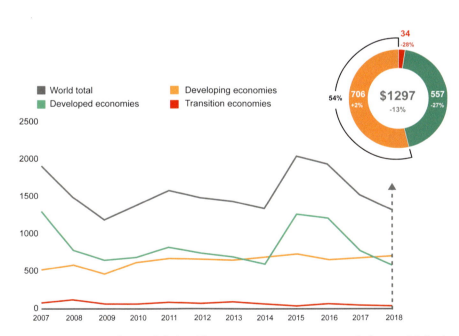

FIGURE 5.3 FDI inflows, global and by economic group, 2007–18 (billions of dollars)
Source: World Investment Report 2019 (UNCTAD).

FIGURE 5.4 Global economic policy uncertainty

Source: World Bank report.

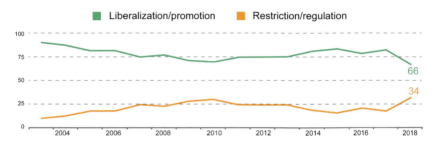

FIGURE 5.5 Foreign investment restrictions and regulations are on the rise

Source: UNCTAD, Investment Policy Hub.

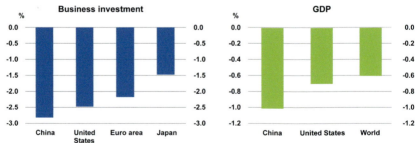

FIGURE 5.6 Impact of 2019 US-China trade restrictions

Source: OECD Interim Economic Outlook, September 2019.

Among all the economic policy uncertainties, the US-China trade war stands out most, because it may significantly impact the world economy and business environment (see Figure 5.6). And of course, China's and Europe's economic slowdowns do not help either. China is implementing the so-called supply-side reform, phasing out backward production capacity and spurring innovation. These reforms are necessary to upgrade China's economy. However, the schedule of the reform effort coincides with the hard times now being experienced by the world economy, and that has caused trade frictions. The EU's economy is still trying to recover from the global financial and sovereign debt crises, with the policy fix largely relying on European economic governance reform. However, the EU's internal sclerosis, the Brexit, the immigration crisis, and the geopolitical crisis pose major challenges.

An overview of EU-China economic and trade relations

China is the EU's second largest trading partner, while the EU is the largest trading partner of China (see Figure 5.7). It is noteworthy that such a close trade interdependence has been achieved within a relatively short time span. When the EEC established diplomatic relations with China in 1975, bilateral trade accounted for only 1% of the EEC's total external trade, whereas in 2018 it accounted for 15%. As far as investment goes, the EU's outward FDI to China maintains a steady level while the EU's internal FDI from China has been growing more quickly in recent years (see Figures 5.8 and 5.9). Equally noteworthy are the dramatic changes of trade structure between China and the EU. China is moving from the semi-periphery to the core of the world economy by selling Europe more and more manufactured high-tech products rather than raw materials and labor-intensive products, as in the past. Intra-industry trade is increasingly replacing inter-industry trade in EU-China trade relations (Ding & Ji 2019).

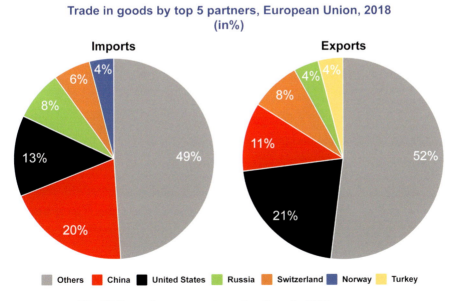

FIGURE 5.7 The EU's top five partners in trade of goods, 2018

Source: EUROSTAT.

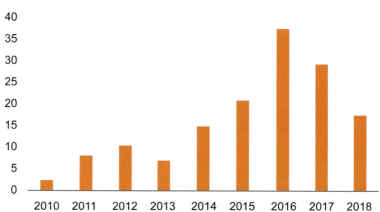

FIGURE 5.8 Chinese FDI in the EU
Source: EUROSTAT.

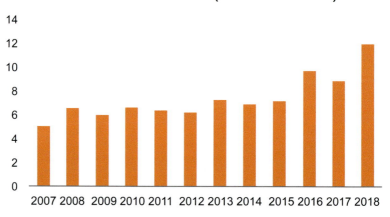

FIGURE 5.9 EU outward foreign direct investment (OFDI) to China
Source: EUROSTAT.

There are many positive elements in the EU-China relationship. The two powers have no fundamental strategic geopolitical conflicts and share a common stance on promoting multilateralism and halting or mitigating climate change. Economic relations have been the anchor of the Sino-EU relationship as consolidated through existing mature mechanisms, including the EU-China Economic and Trade Joint Commission, the EU-China Summit, and a newly established High-Level Economic and Trade Dialogue (HED). Equally important, the economic and trade foundations have given birth to a series of political, cultural, and people-to-people dialogues. As former Chinese Premier Wen Jiabao (The State Council of People's Republic of China 2010) said, "People-to-people exchanges are the bridge linking peoples' hearts and increasing mutual understanding and trust, and therefore lasting longer than economic and trade exchanges."

However, both sides have unresolved concerns, in particular on economic and trade issues. China has become the major target of the EU's anti-dumping and anti-subsidy inquiries with half of the ongoing EU investigations involving China. The conflicts over Chinese steel exports to the EU are a core issue in Sino-EU trade frictions. Based on the surrogate country approach, the EU accuses Chinese steel producers of dumping, and it repeatedly imposes high tariffs as a penalty. Back in 2005, there was a dispute over textile imports into the EU with domestic European manufacturers losing out to cheaper Chinese imported goods. The EU and China have finally reached an agreement ending the conflict over textiles, which poisoned their relations for several weeks. There is actually a long list of Chinese items subject to EU trade defense instruments, but generally speaking, the EU and China have been able to manage these trade disputes.

The US has always been a player, visible or invisible, in EU-China economic and trade relations. While EU-China textile negotiations were going on, parallel US-China textile negotiations also were taking place. The US factor was inevitably taken into consideration by the Commission negotiators. Then Commissioner Mandelson tactically linked the two negotiations to gain an advantageous bargaining position. First, the commissioner leveraged US power to pressure China. Second, he distinguished his approach from that of the US so as to win China's favor in negotiating a quick arrangement, six months earlier than the US-China deal. Now the Trump factor is worsening EU-China trade relations, and EU policymakers are making démarches in the context of the US-China trade war.

The EU's démarches in the context of the US-China trade war

Starting in March of 2018, the EU-China economic and trade relationship became, to a significant extent, subject to the dynamics of the US-China trade war. The latter began on March 22, 2018, when the Trump administration announced on the basis of its "301 investigation" that punitive tariffs would be slapped on some USD 50 billion worth of imports from China due to intellectual property infringement. China immediately counterattacked, marking the outbreak of the US-China trade war.

The EU has to find its way in a triangular relationship vis-à-vis the US and China. The EU's interest is threefold: tame China, bring the US back, and save the WTO. As the former EU trade commissioner Cecilia Malmström remarked, "A core concern of the past decades is our response to China. It has moved from being a developing country, to a strategic competitor of the EU and the US" (European Commission 2019b). A new EU communication defines China as "a cooperation partner, an economic competitor in the pursuit of technological leadership, and a systemic rival promoting alternative models of governance" (European Commission 2019a). As the European policymakers see matters, "the EU and the US often agree on the diagnosis of what the global challenges are and the threat that they pose. But they do not always agree on the cure" (European Commission 2019b). President Trump's economic nationalism and multiple "exits" from multilateral institutions have eroded transatlantic trust. The WTO is becoming a new battlefield in transatlantic relations.

Between March of 2018 and the conclusion of the first phase of US-China trade negotiations on January 15, 2020, the EU's démarches in the context of the US-China trade war could be divided into three phases: (1) March 2018 through July 2018; (2) July 2018 through December 2019; and (3) January 2020 until now.

Phase 1: saving the transatlantic alliance (March 2018 to July 2018)

The Trump administration's decision to impose duties on the EU's steel and aluminum came as a surprise to the EU. Starting on June 1, 2018, the US imposed duties of 25% on steel and 10% on aluminum imports from the EU under Section 232 of the 1962 Trade Expansion Act, citing national security grounds. For the EU, it was a ridiculous and provocative move against multilateral efforts to fight China's steel overcapacity, one that surely would damage the transatlantic alliance. As the EU trade commissioner Malmström said (European Commission 2018b):

> The EU shares similar interests with the US, but deeply disagrees with the US on working methods. . . . [W]e are concerned about the form that response has taken: (1) Blocking appointments necessary for the dispute settlement function of the World Trade Organization. (2) Imposing global trade-restrictive measures on steel and aluminium, and trying to justify them on national security grounds. (3) Taking unilateral trade measures against China and (4) Using increasingly aggressive rhetoric at allies.

It was a crisis moment for the transatlantic alliance. In the eyes of the Commission (2018b), the Trump administration's measures were undermining decades of US foreign policy and Western partnership. The EU's economic diplomacy is, to a large extent, designed to bring the US back and save the transatlantic alliance. The most decisive measure is Juncker's proposal (The White House 2018) for a "3 zero deal" with the US, namely, zero tariffs, zero non-tariff barriers, and zero subsidies on non-auto industrial goods. The EU also agreed to import soybeans and liquefied natural gas from the US. With the "3 zero deal," the EU and the US arrived at a ceasefire in July of 2018.

In the meanwhile, the EU maintained pressure on China in regard to further market openings, intellectual property protection, public procurement, and state-owned enterprises (SOE), and cooperated with China in establishing a working group on WTO reform at the EU-China HED on June 25, 2018, which signaled support for multilateralism (Jing 2018).

Phase 2: saving the WTO and dealing with the China question (July 2018 to December 2019)

Although the Juncker-Trump deal helped bring about a ceasefire across the Atlantic Ocean, the rifts are still there. A case in point is the WTO reform. As EU trade commissioner Malmström explained (European Commission 2018a):

> now the United States have made the appointment of arbitrators dependent on changing the system. And soon we will not have enough staff to operate. Within a year we will run out of arbitrators, then the system will collapse – and the rules cannot be enforced, so they will have no meaning.

That being said, the EU and the US have shared interests in dealing with China. As Malmström remarked, "It is clear that no matter what happens in terms of our relationship bilaterally, we must continue to work together on China and the WTO" (European Commission 2019b).

This phase witnessed an escalation of the US-China trade war. In September of 2018, the US imposed 10% duties on USD 200 billion worth of Chinese exports, and China immediately retaliated by imposing 5%–10% duties on USD 60 billion worth of imports from the US.

In the background of an escalating trade war between the US and China, the EU found itself in a more advantageous negotiating position vis-à-vis China, because China needed the EU's support and the European market. The EU-China Bilateral Investment Treaty (BIT) has been moved forward by both sides.

Phase 3: geopolitical commission, geopolitical trade policy? (January 2020 onward)

The US and China signed a Phase One trade agreement on January 15, 2020. This ceasefire came 18 months later than the EU-US ceasefire represented by the Juncker-Trump "3 zero deal" signed in July 2018. The Phase One trade agreement requires structural reforms and other changes to China's economic and trade regime in the areas of intellectual property, technology transfer, agriculture, financial services, and currency and foreign exchange. It also includes a commitment by China to make substantial additional purchases of US goods and services in the coming years (Office of the US Trade Representative 2020).

The Phase One deal was struck as the new EU institutions kicked into gear. In her mission letters to her colleagues, EU Commission President Von der Leyen (2019) labeled her organization as a "geopolitical Commission." As the EU's top diplomat Josep Borrell put it, "We need to speak more the language of power, not to conquer but to contribute to a more peaceful, prosperous and just world"

(Barigazzi 2019). Borrell cited Dutch Prime Minister Mark Rutte as saying that "if we only preach the merits of principles, and shy away from exercising power in the geopolitical arena, our continent may always be right, but it will seldom be relevant." While the EU's geopolitical priorities are Eastern Europe, the neighborhood, and Africa, they also extend to the wider world.

On the economic and trade fronts, WTO reform, the US and China, and Africa are given priorities. With the US, the Commission needs to work towards a positive, balanced, and mutually beneficial trading partnership, whereas with China the Commission will step up negotiations on a Comprehensive Agreement on Investment, with the aim of concluding a deal by the end of 2020 (Von der Leyen 2019).

By labeling her Commission as a "geopolitical Commission," is Von der Leyen defining geopolitics in terms of commercial interest and distinguishing friend from foe by the standards of geopolitics? As the new EU trade commissioner Phil Hogan has remarked, China's growth, geopolitical ambition, and distinctive model of state capitalism have generated an ongoing debate in the European Union. He raises the question of how the EU might best balance the challenges and opportunities that China presents (European Commission 2020). The year 2020, he adds, will be particularly important as the EU engages directly with China through a series of high-level events. The EU-China Summit was to take place in China in the spring, and additionally there will be a leaders' meeting in Germany in September. He concludes that investment negotiations will be a key tool in the effort to rebalance the relationship with China (European Commission 2020).

A new triplexity in the making?

As EU trade commissioner Hogan (European Commission 2020) said:

> we are faced with a very complex web of challenges in relation to trade and geopolitics. And there are few challenges more complex than China. . . . While I was in Washington, the US and China signed a Phase One trade agreement. This emphasises the complexity of global trade relationships.

Within this complexity, there emerged what we call the "triplexity" of EU-US-China trilateral interrelationships.

This triplexity emerged during the hard times of the world economy and may lead to new critical junctures in world history. Globalization is being challenged. Populism is on the rise. The US-China trade war, along with the sudden outbreak of the COVID-19 pandemic in China and other parts in the world, might lead to the decoupling of the world's major economies, including the US, Europe, and China.

This triplexity confronts policymakers with a negotiating context in which "triangulating" modes of thought are a must. Every move by one party out of the three has implications for the other two. This negotiating context may even possess a global dimension. A decision about any one of the bilateral or trilateral relationships among the three has a significant impact on global economic governance in this era of globalization.

The triplexity has three policy manifestations: President Xi Jinping's "Community of Common Destiny for All Mankind," inspired by Karl Marx and represented by the Belt and Road Initiative, the Asian Infrastructure and Investment Bank, and Chinese efforts in working with the international community to fight COVID-19; the EU's liberal multilateralism, inspired by liberal Enlightenment thinkers such as Immanuel Kant and represented by the WTO and the EU's interregional trade agreements; and US President Trump's economic nationalism, inspired by mercantilism and represented by the "America First" slogan and escalating trade wars.

The future of EU-China economic and trade relations will be conducted within this triplexity context during the hard times of the world economy and politics. Linkage politics would be a major feature of triplex negotiations. Although the US is a third party, it is still linked up by the EU in the latter's negotiations with China. We must bear in mind that the EU and the US have many common interests, such as the protection of intellectual property rights and market access. However, EU and US policies differ on a crucial point: the EU's post-hegemonic multilateralism versus the Trump administration's nationalist unilateralism. This crucial difference means that the EU will be an autonomous actor in the triangular relationship.

The EU-China economic and trade relations, facing both opportunities and challenges, need to be addressed in an innovative and feasible way. The litmus test would be the success (or failure) of the EU-China investment treaty negotiation, which has major implications for European investors. For the Chinese side, European-Chinese connectivity, including trade, investment, finance, and people-to-people exchanges, would be crucial. The newly established China Import Expo may serve as a good platform for such exchanges. The battle against COVID-19 may spur further EU-China cooperation. But for the two authors of this chapter, the biggest challenge confronting EU-China economic and trade relations is the increasing mistrust between the two sides, which probably has resulted from the changing zeitgeist and long-unresolved issues. Therefore, it is highly advisable that both parties should foster an amicable environment for interactions. To achieve this, the joint endeavors by the Chinese and European epistemic communities will have a modest role to play.

References

Barigazzi, J. 2019. "Borrell Urges the EU to be Foreign Policy 'Player, Not the Playground.'" *Politico*. Available at www.politico.eu/article/on-foreign-policy-josep-borrell-urges-eu-to-be-a-player-not-the-playground-balkans/

Ding, C. & H. Jis. 2019. "中欧关系70年：成就、挑战与展望" [The Seventy-Years of China-EU Relations: Achievements, Challenges and Outlook]. *世界经济与政治论坛* [World Economic and Political Forum] 6: 136.

European Commission. 2018a. "Saving the WTO." Available at https://trade.ec.europa.eu/doclib/docs/2018/november/tradoc_157494.pdf

European Commission. 2018b. "Transatlantic Trade in Turbulent Times – Speech by Cecilia Malmström, European Commissioner for Trade." Available at https://ec.europa.eu/commission/presscorner/detail/en/SPEECH_18_4604

European Commission. 2019a. *Joint Communication to The European Parliament, The European Council and The Council: EU-China-A Strategic Outlook*. Strasbourg: European Commission, p. 1

European Commission. 2019b. "The Next Transatlantic Project." Available at http://trade.ec.europa.eu/doclib/press/index.cfm?id=1992

European Commission. 2020. "Speech by Commissioner Phil Hogan at the Publication of Business Europe's Strategy Paper on EU-China Economic Relations." Available at https://ec.europa.eu/commission/commissioners/2019-2024/hogan/announcements/speech-commissioner-phil-hogan-publication-business-europes-strategy-paper-eu-china-economic_en

Jing, F. 2018. "EU, China to Set Up Working Group on Trade Reform." *The China Daily*. Available at www.chinadaily.com.cn/a/201807/12/WS5b473f97a310796df4df61c1.html

Office of the US Trade Representative. 2020. "Economic and Trade Agreement Between the United States of America and The People's Republic of China, January 15, 2020, Fact Sheet." Available at https://ustr.gov/sites/default/files/files/agreements/phase%20one%20agreement/US_China_Agreement_Fact_Sheet.pdf

The State Council of People's Republic of China. 2010. "温家宝总理在中欧文化高峰论坛上的致辞" [Address to China-EU Cultural Summit by Premier Wen Jiabao]. Available at www.gov.cn/ldhd/2010-10/07/content_1716439.htm

The White House. 2018. "Remarks by President Trump and President Juncker of the European Commission in Joint Press Statements." Available at www.whitehouse.gov/briefings-statements/remarks-president-trump-president-juncker-european-commission-joint-press-statements/

Von der Leyen, U. 2019. "Mission Letter to Phil Hogan." *European Commission*. Available at https://ec.europa.eu/commission/sites/beta-political/files/mission-letter-phil-hogan-2019_en.pdf

Zhang, X. & N. Xie. 2016. "联系权力：欧盟的权力性质及其权力战略" [Linkage Power: The EU's Power Nature and Its Power Strategies]. *欧洲研究* [Chinese Journal of European Studies] 3

6

TOWARDS A COMPREHENSIVE APPROACH TO TRADE AND SOCIAL JUSTICE

Renato G. Flôres Jr.[#]

Sixty-three substances, among them some rare-earth minerals, are vital for the daily operation of an advanced economy. Consider the US, for instance: of those 63 substances, it needs to import fully one-third of them. Of the remaining 42, imports of 17 provide between 50% and 98% of the country's annual needs. Furthermore, imports supply as much as 49% of the remaining 25. If, by any chance, the US finds itself without even half a dozen of those vital substances, it might feel compelled to bribe, invade, or even destroy anyone or anything in order to ensure its steady supply, at minimal levels. In the United Nations' euphemism, the country will "use all necessary means" (i.e., go to war).

The above stands out as just one among myriad examples showing that trade relations are far more diverse and potentially far less peaceful and straightforwardly beneficial than many people think. Optimists, or candid souls, like to proclaim the opposite in unqualified terms, often relying on – while gravely misunderstanding – Kant's much-cited (though much less often read) 1795 monograph, *Zum ewigen Frieden: Ein philosophischer Entwurf*. Actually, as I have argued elsewhere (Flôres 2013), even the great Kant's text has at most a tangential relationship with the trade nexus, because it refers to a specific context and has in mind a broader purpose.

However, this chapter is not intended as a discussion of attributions rightly or wrongly used, nor will it portray trade as a miraculous elixir to cure many of the present global governance problems. Notwithstanding, drawing on history and real-life situations, the next section briefly discusses a few realities and misunderstandings about trade, which show that this activity can sometimes qualify as an instrument of war.

Adopting a more modern perspective, I next try to frame trade as a series of economic, non-financial exchanges among countries. This provides a clearer view of the likely convergences in a seemingly chaotic environment of cultural divergences and increasing multipolarity of conflicts, international choke points, and identities.

Despite a few positive signs to the contrary, as outlined below in fidelity to the spirit of this volume, I offer suggestions about how to secure, as far as possible, a multilateral approach to trade and economic relations and enhance its potentially cooperative and humanitarian aspects. As is reiterated in the conclusion, multilateralism – despite its inherent shortcomings – remains the bedrock upon which we must build in order to guarantee a continuous path towards a fairer, more comprehensive, and efficient approach to trade.

Not a novel issue: a few examples

Colonial rule in India offers a fertile ground for discussing the highly debatable benefits of increased (and forced) trade. As has been widely recognized, trade between India and Great Britain was mostly controlled by a firm known as the East India Company. To put it in plain language, the company monopolized the India trade, (mis)using that country for its own selfish purposes for over a century. Shashi Tharoor, a former UN under-secretary-general who served under the late Kofi Annan, offers numerous examples of British misdeeds, which had only one goal, regardless of consequences and negative side-effects: trade profits (Tharoor 2018).

The British-India railway system – traditionally claimed to have improved communications and general welfare – was designed with the sole purpose of facilitating and speeding up the transport of textiles and other export goods from the producing centers to the ports, with total disregard for population spread and development needs.

Another example relates to trade sanctions and blockades used by the powerful to put pressure on their enemies or, even worse, any nation arbitrarily considered so. From the British continental blockade during the Napoleonic Wars[1] to the numerous sanctions inflicted these days by world leaders acting arbitrarily upon innocent, often impoverished populations in countries considered "dangerous" or "guilty of misbehavior," millions of civilians have paid dearly for the alleged benefits of "peaceful trade."

A related point reminds us that historical periods of flourishing trade, such as the zenith of the Roman Empire, the golden era of the Ottoman Empire, or the Pax Britannica, were made possible by an often overlooked but crucial detail. Without the very efficient Roman legions (the highest-performing army of its time), the sultan's fearsome Janissaries' elite units, or the powerful and unrivalled British Navy ("Britannia rules the waves," as tradition would have it), these periods of flourishing trade would have been unconceivable. In all these cases, pax was secured not by trade but rather by force: force-secured trade.

A final illustration concerns the vast area of trade in raw materials and basic agricultural goods, in which several examples of unfair practices and sheer exploitation can be provided. They range from the original Cotonou Agreements, a disguised form of modern colonialism via trade flows, to blunt, indirectly forced assurances of supply. The latter continue to doom African communities and nations to the condition of being either monoculture producers or victims of neo-extractivist policies, dependent on the exports of a single agricultural commodity or raw material.

The list could be lengthened considerably, but three conclusions seem undeniable:

- The first is the intrinsic relationship between trade and power. Trade quite easily can deteriorate into a vicious cycle of domination, abuse, and oppression. As noted earlier, institutions and the multilateral approach are one (partial) solution to these outcomes, and we shall return to them later.
- Second, we desperately need to discard, once and for all, a false, idyllic view on trade, which only blurs the facts and makes more difficult the design of constructive and effective policies.
- Third, as dangerous as the idyllic view is an über-enthusiastic and encompassing approach that uses trade deals as a way to solve or deal more effectively with global commons issues like environmental degradation or inhumane labor conditions. Such an approach crams the trade agenda with questions that, more often than not, would be handled better in another forum.

The examples given in this section, and the framing in the next one, call attention to the dangers of extrapolating from the very essence of trade. At bottom it is nothing but a non-financial flow of goods and services among nations, not a panacea for half of the world's injustices and illnesses.

Perhaps, as a coda, it is fitting to cite a passage from the *Confessions* by Saint Augustine of Hippo: a good name to be cited in a forum praising cultural diversity, as he was a dark-skinned (very likely) Berber[2] from the outskirts of the Roman Empire. Augustine remarks that, having perceived the splendor and immensity of divine grace, he felt immediately compelled to strive for it. Nevertheless, taking into account that his present life was hardly bad at all and that the blessings of grace would require a great self-transformation, he – with blunt frankness – asked God to give him the grace, just not yet!

Free trade is somehow like Saint Augustine's perception of grace: we all recognize its unquestionable value and nearly divine (perhaps too divine) virtues, but we do not want to experience it right now.

Trade as a non-financial interaction among nations

Trade can be looked at within the broader scope of non-financial interactions among countries. This perspective provides both an enlarged and a more reasonable view of its relevance and impacts. Trade in goods cannot be dissociated from foreign direct investment (FDI) and several instances of services trade or from migration (or movement of persons) and the important cultural aspect of such exchanges. A better and more encompassing survey of the underlying economic structures and functions at stake helps in identifying the real motives behind and benefits derived from trade.

On the domestic front, economies may make a variety of different state and market arrangements, operating with more or less imperfect markets and more or less state intervention, and usually being plagued by monopolies and oligopolies, whether visible or not. In more than a few countries, states are significant partners in key enterprises.

Interactions between these structures offer no guarantee of peaceful relations; rather, one frequently encounters harsh competition and Schumpeterian destruction. In an apparent paradox, trade can be a tool for imposing uniformity or spurring rapid, sometimes undesired globalization rather than a means to foster diversity.

When one considers Walmart, Benetton, or Zara; Samsung, Apple, and Huawei; or Amazon and Ali Baba, it becomes apparent that large companies, rather than nations, are fighting for greater international sales and market share, even if the parent country offers some support. This fact undercuts many of the classical findings and theories about how markets should work and forces any given nation to confront not only economic but also complex juridical and geostrategic issues and policy choices.

Thanks to the fragmentation of production and the forging of international value chains, around 80% of trade in goods takes place among fewer than 1,000 large world manufacturers. A much broader and more modern economic logic than the familiar setting imagined by David Ricardo is needed to illuminate these phenomena. In Ricardo's scenario, the English exported wool to the Portuguese in order to buy port wine from them. Thereby, (localized) comparative advantages could be invoked as a shrewd solution to the problem of supplying the citizens of each country with the goods they wanted in the cheapest, most efficient manner.[3]

Globalized world competition no longer centers on supplying competitive versions of a specific good. Although the latter still exists, the main focus today is on rules, norms, and standards embodied in technological decisions and innovations. The Transatlantic Trade and Investment Partnership (TTIP) and Trans-Pacific Partnership (TPP) were not trade agreements in the classical sense but instead the means to establish common rules, norms, and standards for an enlarged "Western World core" designed to leave China out in the cold. On this newly rigged trade battlefield, China either would have to survive by operating under different standards or eventually would be constrained to adhere to those of that core.

Though the European Union cocoon of encompassing regulations has proved more resilient than expected, and the current US administration has done an about-face with the abortion of the TTIP and the significant weakening of the TPP, conflict clearly continues under the aegis of administered trade.

What is often, and wrongly, called the US-China trade war is actually a struggle over technological supremacy, with its most prominent bone of contention being 5G technology, in which – to the great surprise of the US – China so far has developed a better product. That is a fact discreetly acknowledged even by Western firms like the German multinationals that are now partnering with China in the Belt and Road Initiative and the US firms themselves that produce devices and equipment for the Chinese 5G standard.

By recognizing that the scope of trade motivations is broader than previously understood, beyond adding a list of problems germane to the internal conflicts of the advanced economies, one can better distinguish the multiple strategic objectives implicit in the protection structure of a given economy.

The reference to migration at the beginning of this section was made not only for the sake of completeness but also because trade and migration are now treated in a similar fashion by governments. If a certain flow of migrants is undesired, ways are created to stop it irrespective of broader social, humanitarian, or legal considerations or even a "collective welfare" reasoning. Likewise, if a certain flow of goods is considered menacing in some way, it is contained by higher tariffs or "special agreements," regardless of economic considerations or, again, collective welfare reasoning.

And yet every nation needs trade; in fact, we all need trade in this however imperfect, unfair, or over-globalized world. There is no way out.

How can we reconcile the aggressive, disruptive aspects of present-day trade with a more harmonious, minimally fairer, and more welfare-enhancing international version of the same?

Are there positive signs on the horizon?

Among their other functions, institutions and rules have the task of reining in unbridled behavior in economic activities as well as too aggressive animal spirits among agents, be they firms or nations. In the case to be reviewed here, two such institutions are predominant: the United Nations (UN) and the World Trade Organization (WTO).

The good news is that both institutions still exist, have competent staffs and, whenever possible, play by multilateral rules. The more discouraging news is that both of them are in a state of flux, albeit in different ways.

The WTO is in the worse shape of the two because its Appellate Body has been closed since early December of 2019 for lack of a quorum, and many of its functions and attributes have come in for questioning and criticism. At the core of the crisis lies the US-China rivalry, with the former complaining about China's actions since that country joined the WTO on December 11, 2001. The American side broadly charges that China betrayed the hopes of those who facilitated its accession, while China firmly denies this and explicitly preaches in favor of the organization and the multilateral approach to trade, from Geneva to the Davos World Economic Forum. The paralysis in the Appellate Body is solely due to the fact that the US has used its veto power to block the nominations of several new judges.

Within this context, it is almost inevitable that the actions taken by several of its members start to bump up against the limits of what is allowed by WTO rules, if not to violate them outright. Again, the recent US-China trade pact, signed in mid-January of 2020, is a blatant example of an administered trade deal, something that would be unacceptable according to certain articles of the WTO's rules.

The UN is somewhat better off in spite of its many contradictions, relative lack of credibility, and lack of representativeness within the permanent membership of the Security Council, which drives that body's legitimacy deficit. However, the Secretariat has been struggling against these negative trends and is involved in discussing and conducting an encompassing reform of the institution.

The new realities in the world trade arena have had the positive, albeit indirect, effect of awakening some key actors. In this vein, on June 28, 2019, after 20 years of negotiations and to the surprise of many experts, the free trade agreement between the EU and MERCOSUL/MERCOSUR (a.k.a. the Southern Common Market) was signed in Brussels. The agreement still must be ratified by the 27 EU and four MERCOSUL/MERCOSUR members as well as by the European Parliament, a process expected to take around two more years.

The present state of affairs in the EU, and the Europeans' temptation to use the agreement to "punish" MERCOSUL/MERCOSUR countries for their supposed environmental or human rights misdeeds, together with the persistence of the EU's protectionist agricultural and meat lobbies, mean that the agreement is not yet a done deal. Ratification, it is also worth noting, could also be jeopardized by a single MERCOSUL/MERCOSUR member.

The EU also has been trying to pursue an active trade policy towards Asia, having worked out a trade treaty with Japan and prepared another one with South Korea. Nor has the EU forgotten Canada, the other North American partner.

In sum, the global picture cannot be considered totally gloomy, given that some actions and measures have been moving along positive lines. However, there is not yet enough evidence to say that global trade relations have begun a positive trend, either. More remains to be done, and the next section tries to identify some of the tasks that need to be addressed

Five suggestions

Based on the arguments presented so far, I offer below the following suggestions, hopefully realistic and feasible ones, that may enable us to improve on the present situation.

I regard the first two to be the most pressing, given the urgent need to revive and strengthen the WTO and eliminate the bottlenecks that block it from acting. The third proposal goes against the common understanding among nearly all public officials involved in trade negotiations. Nevertheless, awareness that matters have gotten out of hand is starting to grow among the constituencies directly involved in trade – sectoral and regional business associations, consumers, and specific civil society groups and representatives[4] – a trend that I believe will progressively gain momentum. The fourth suggestion may be deemed utopian and I concede that it is, in the short run. But, aside from the conceptual links it has to the previous suggestion, the two together mark a position considered fundamental for restoring trade to its proper niche and enhancing its positive, even its non-violent side.

Finally, the fifth suggestion reminds us that, in spite of being frequently cited, the idea of cultural diversity – reasonably codified in the key 2005 UNESCO (United Nations Educational, Scientific, and Cultural Organization) Convention on the Protection and Promotion of the Diversity of Cultural Expressions – rarely has been raised in the discussion of global governance issues. As pointed out in the conference that gave rise to this book, diversity plays an important role at this moment when multiple modernities and voices struggle to be heard[5] in a world where diversity is misinterpreted. It must also have a significant place in the trade arena, as will be argued below.

First, sustain and reinforce the WTO at all costs. The WTO needs immediate attention and must resume its full functioning. The pending questions must be faced head-on. It should be noted that the positions and criticisms of the US, while thoroughly partisan, are not necessarily always wrong, especially in the matter of the overextension of the duties and attributes of the dispute settlement mechanism. These must be duly considered. The one-member, one-vote system opens the door to many tricks and injustices, but it was a hard-fought victory and probably remains the best option we have, given the alternatives. Therefore, it must be vigorously and actively supported.

Second, stop thinking of the WTO as the only organization capable of reforming trade. The WTO has become unable to tackle the broad variety of problems existing nowadays and must be complemented by other institutions and actions. On one hand, new mechanisms should be created to deal with transnational companies' trade flows, given their inherently asymmetric character and their weight in global trade in goods.[6] On the other hand, joint, coordinated work with other multilateral agencies should be encouraged and given a dramatic boost. This is not exactly new, as successful earlier experiments like the association between sanitary and phytosanitary rules with the Food and Agriculture Organization's Codex Alimentarius testifies.

Telecommunications and internet issues – comprising standards, the allocation of frequencies, services, and basic regulations, in their trade-related aspects – overlap considerably with the International Telecommunications Unit (ITU). A joint task force on coupling and identifying basic general WTO-ITU rules seems a must.

Third, revamp the present outlook of trade deals. As discussed above, trade agreements are not a panacea and should not be used as a weapon to tackle or inhibit behavior considered adverse in other areas. Present-day negotiations are frequently undemocratic, lack transparency, and ultimately favor specific groups and cartels.

One way to attack this problem involves streamlining the objectives of the agreements by focusing on trade – which producers, sellers, buyers, and consumers all clearly desire – and discarding the ever-increasing string of extra (and external) conditions and annexes that have been attached to the treaties for at least the past three decades, giving way to what have been named mega-regional trade agreements.

A related imperative is to recover the true meaning of and legitimate concern for the word "development." Keeping that word and its significance in mind, trade negotiators, when they go about making deals that involve both advanced and less developed economies, will be obliged to take proper account of the opportunities that might otherwise be foreclosed for the economically subordinate partner under the new reality. This does not imply by any means that agreements will become less profitable for the advanced economies, but only that they will neither stifle nor condemn the other side to a relationship of total or semi-dependence.

Moreover, trade must cease being taken as a proxy for the solution of all failures of governance and the regulation of common goods. Climate change and carbon footprints, unfair labor practices, potential violations of basic human rights, broad competitiveness gaps, and geo-strategic rivalries all must be addressed in their proper fora; the current, apparently "smooth and easy" way to enforce supposedly good practices through trade eventually will turn out to be a boomerang, stalling the agreements themselves while doing little to solve the other problems,[7] meanwhile stoking anger, contentiousness, and costly or useless debates.

Fourth, ban, or at least greatly restrict, the use of trade as a tool of war, for many of the same reasons detailed above. A collective effort should be pursued to curb the use of trade for other purposes than trade itself. In particular, and in an instance not covered before, the imposition of trade sanctions on specific states, though known to be inefficient, unfair, and usually inhuman, continues to proliferate despite its nefarious consequences. A convention on abolishing the use of trade sanctions in international relations would be a step in the right direction. It is amazing that, despite the effervescent rhetoric on human rights, concrete actions to enforce them are extremely rare or moribund, to say the least. In principle, the United Nations would be the right venue to host the convention. Eventually, it should (ideally) be universally adopted and brought under the WTO umbrella.

Fifth, make room for diversity in the trade debate. The narrative on diversity is full of beautiful sentiments and invoked in nearly every situation, but very few concrete actions respecting the essence of the concept are to be found. Seriously incorporating diversity into the trade debate does not mean using trade to promote or enforce diversity – something that, besides being artificial, would undercut the third suggestion made above. But it does mean always keeping in mind first that in theory, trade may increase diversity by offering a larger scope of goods and varieties to the consumer.[8] In the real world, however, trade quite often reduces or eliminates diversity by snuffing out practices, habits, and local usages and bankrupting small-scale producers that added to the cultural assets of a given nation or region. The EU, and most notably France, cleverly and properly has used the concept to protect some basic features of its audiovisual sector, while less cleverly (and with a heavy protectionist accent) shielding its agriculture (again notably that of France). Ironically, the EU sometimes is reluctant to accept the same argument when it is made by African and South American countries.

The interplay between the 2005 UNESCO Convention and the WTO rules has been very little studied and should be given much more attention in our *tempi sconvolgenti*.

Conclusion

In a world where peaceful cooperation among diverse states, regions, and cultures is at stake and global governance is undergoing huge transformations – leading some to raise the alarm that nuclear proliferation may resume at a faster pace (cf. Flôres 2020) – it is important to identify simple and workable ways to preserve two basic values of the existing order: a few global institutions with planetary participation, even if they do require serious reforms, and the multilateral principle for a core of key decisions and areas.

Both elements are vital for the subject addressed in this chapter: international trade. Of the five suggestions presented in the previous section, at least three require immediate, serious action to counter the menacing trend towards chaos and hubris in trade relations. Already, the latter are drifting down a dangerous path towards increasing reliance on and belief in managed trade. That, in turn, could intensify the distorting elements, particularly in the social and cultural areas, not to speak of economics, that trade may introduce.

At the heart of these problems we identified a naïve view of trade, disconnected from reality, that has been generating analyses and related solutions that only aggravate the problems. But this is not the only objection to simplistic views of trade. Quite a few observers also have a tendency to misinterpret trade as a universal remedy for many unresolved global governance issues.

The main message of this chapter is that trade should be treated, represented, and negotiated as trade and nothing else. In short, it should be seen as an important non-financial economic transaction among nations, one that is neither the way nor the proper instrument to tackle other transactions or global deficiencies. Although in the end all activities obviously are interrelated, lumping many of them together into a single negotiation is a formula for wasting precious time and other resources. It also complicates any clear identification of the goals and impacts of trade.

This streamlined, more objective approach does not exclude fundamental concerns about local populations, cultural diversity, and development. These are all matters that, somewhat mysteriously, have been disregarded of late by the advocates of mega-trade agreements. Those negotiators at times seem to operate in a world of identical, faceless agents.

A more comprehensive, fair, realistic, and efficient approach to trade should tread this new path – boldly and without delay.

Notes

\# The entire text is my sole responsibility and does not speak for any person or institution beyond myself.
1 See Borges de Macedo (1962) for a perceptive analysis of the continental blockade.

2 Augustine's iconography in Western art usually whitens considerably the color of his skin, in an interesting example of the difficulty of accepting diversity.
3 This is true despite the fact that the very concept of "comparative advantage" is quite elusive and not correctly understood by many, who easily confuse it with "absolute advantage." Paul Samuelson, to his credit, liked to say that Ricardian comparative advantage remained one of the most subtle and difficult-to-grasp economic concepts.
4 As an example of how this awareness or uneasiness has begun to emerge in public fora, we could cite the panel discussion "Just Like US: Exclusive Trade in the Trump Age" that took place in the 2020 Raisina Dialogue in New Delhi, India. It was evident that many participants, especially one member of the German Parliament, felt uncomfortable with excessively ambitious agreements. This member also was active in the parliament's group for international economics and trade, so he was quite familiar with the subject matter. (The video of the panel is available at the ORF site on the Raisina Dialogues.)
5 See the books related to the previous three years of the Institute of European Studies of Macau (IEEM) Conference, of which Meyer et al. (2019) is the most recent iteration.
6 Unfortunately, there is no space to further elaborate this point here.
7 In some of the papers contained in Baru and Dogra (2015), one can sense – even at that date, when the TPP and TTIP were still taken for granted – the feeling that something might be wrong with these mega-agreements.
8 And then, in terms of economic theory, increasing the consumer's utility (provided the proper utility function is employed).

References

Baru, S. & S. Dogra (eds.). 2015. *Power Shifts and New Blocs in the Global Trading System*. Oxford: Routledge, for The International Institute of Strategic Studies

Borges de Macedo, J. 1962. *O Bloqueio Continental: Economia e Guerra Peninsular*. Lisbon: Ed. Gráfica Portuguesa

Flôres, R. G., Jr. 2013. "Conclusion: Dismissing the Kantian View of Trade and Peace." In L. Coppolaro & F. McKenzie (eds.), *A Global History of Trade and Conflict since 1500*. London: Palgrave Macmillan

Flôres, R. G., Jr. 2020. "Back to Nukes? Global Governance's Transitional Moment." In L. Grigoryev & A. Pabst (eds.), *Global Governance in Transformation: Challenges for International Cooperation*. London: Springer Nature

Meyer, T., J. de Sales Marques, & M. Telò (eds.). 2019. *Cultures, Nationalism and Populism: New Challenges to Multilateralism*. London & New York: Routledge

Tharoor, S. 2018. *Inglorious Empire: What the British did to India*. London: Penguin Books

PART III

Which global governance and multilateral peacekeeping?

7

MULTILATERALISM IN CRISIS

A European perspective[1]

Michael Zürn

The year 2016 was a fiasco for multilateralism. Every part of the globe, but especially – and paradoxically – the West, witnessed a revival of nationalism. Almost everywhere in Western Europe, authoritarian-populist parties such as the Freedom Party of Austria (FPÖ) and the Alternative for Germany (AfD) created niches for themselves in the party systems of their respective countries (see, e.g., Inglehart & Norris 2017). In addition, British voters decided by a narrow majority to quit the European Union. Finally, in the US – to general astonishment and more than a little murmuring – Donald Trump was elected president. All of these political forces consistently have opposed open borders for people and goods, rejected any transfer of competence to political institutions beyond the nation-state, and emphasized unconditional national sovereignty. They are not afraid to enter into coalitions with authoritarian potentates like Vladimir Putin of Russia, Recep Tayyip Erdoğan of Turkey, and Viktor Orbán of Hungary, who have attacked the political independence of the courts and the media and regularly disregarded basic individual rights in their own countries. Even the occupation of the Crimea, contrary to international law, did not stop Putin from playing a central role in this network. At the same time, some of the world's rising powers have shown a deep dissatisfaction with global governance and multilateralism in its present form. Thus, it is evident that multilateralism faces a crisis today.

Let us begin with a simplified definition: multilateralism means that governments should seek joint solutions, but ones in which all the countries involved put forward their own points of view (cf. Ruggie 1992; Keohane 1990). Currently, the prospects for multilateral gatherings of this kind appear to be rather dim. Multilateral meetings, when they are held at all, are tension filled and rarely produce tangible results. Still, the heads of governments continue to assemble in multilateral forums such as G20 summits.

Nevertheless, the crisis concerns more than multilateralism in the narrow sense. It affects not only multilateral meetings but also norms, rules, and existing practices in the global realm (Qin 2014). It is more far-reaching, amounting to an overarching crisis of global governance and especially of the international political system that emerged in the 1990s. Why did the crisis happen? This chapter offers an endogenous explanation that lays the blame on the procedural weaknesses of the global governance system. As I will argue, this crisis is really about the deficit of legitimacy. Moreover, the failure to produce successful legitimation narratives is built into the system. The institutionalization of inequality and a technocratic bias in the justification of authority are responsible for this failure. A look at the most important challengers of the global governance system shows that they all more or less explicitly focus their criticisms on these legitimacy deficits.

The crisis of the global governance system

We can speak of a global political system when three conditions are fulfilled (Zürn 2018). First, the actors that potentially participate in it must acknowledge that at least some rudimentary global common goals (such as peace) and at least some collective goods (such as a sustainable ecosystem) exist outside the national sphere. Furthermore, it should take a concerted, joint effort on the part of those actors to achieve such goals. Actors that deny the need for joint, collective action merely represent national, parochial interests. Second, for a robust global political system to exist, there must be international institutions and organizations like the World Trade Organization (WTO) and the United Nations that, in cases of doubt, are able to enforce the common good even against the short-term interests of individual members. To achieve those aims, they must rely mostly on non-coercive (soft) power. Thus, to wield influence they must first of all recognize such institutions as authoritative decision-makers in some spheres. Third, in a true global political system, these international authorities should be willing to defend their actions before those who are affected by the measures they take. That self-defense can rely on their supposedly sound decision-making and/or on good arguments. International policies need to be justified in the eyes of a broad audience comprising both national publics and governments as well as the imagined world society.

A global political system possessing these three characteristics – orientation to the common good; the presence, at least in principle, of international authorities; and claims of justification submitted to global fora – was established after World War II but only developed fully after the fall of the Berlin Wall. A global political system of this shape is inevitable if international problems are to be dealt with in a politically effective way. The global political system depends on the acknowledgment of a shared common fate that transcends parochial concerns. The recognition of the global system as authoritative in some matters implies that so-called national interests and particularistic goals can be neither the sole nor the preeminent normative reference points. While the scheme of global governance is required for many reasons, the concrete forms it has assumed – as is the case with all political systems – are not necessarily either just or peaceful. It is also marked by power asymmetries (Western dominance), unequal opportunities for participation (veto powers and weighted voting), and material inequalities (huge differences in capacities between states). Furthermore, deficiencies such as these regularly provoke contestation, which often expresses itself in the form of protests and resistance (Wiener 2014; Daase et al. 2016). Rising powers challenge Western dominance, anti-globalization movements target neoliberalism, right-wing populist parties aim at corrupt cosmopolitan elites, and Islamic states condemn Western decadence.

The global political system emerged in two phases, both shaped decisively by the US. As World War II drew to a close, Presidents Roosevelt and Truman, especially, took the lead in creating a new world order by founding the Bretton Woods institutions and the United Nations. The order symbolized by those institutions was expanded and deepened during the brief unilateralist phase (Krauthammer 1990) following the end of the Cold War. During that era, liberal elements such as the emphasis on human rights and the creation of an open world economy acquired enhanced significance.

Against this background, the radical rhetoric and actions of the previous US president evidently sought to undermine the normative bases of the global political system. Consider, for example, the Trump administration's National Security Strategy (NSS), which was particularly worrying and paradoxical. Trump's foreword to this document made leaders like Putin, Erdoğan, Orbán, and Xi Jinping almost appear by comparison to be apologists for global governance. It is precisely the three normative bases mentioned above that Trump challenged. He began by rejecting out of hand the very idea of a global common good. In his view, it was competition – especially among "rival powers" such as Russia, China, and the US – that characterized the world order. The NSS made it clear that, in the Trump administration's view, those countries endanger American global influence. To quote directly from the foreword, "[The US] Administration's National Security Strategy lays out a strategic vision for protecting the American people and preserving our way of life, promoting our prosperity, preserving peace through strength, and advancing American influence in the world" (2017: 11). Shared interests, collective assets, and the global common good are not mentioned at all. Peace is equated bluntly with American dominance. By the same token, political institutions designed to realize common interests are made to seem superfluous. In the document, the US withdrawal from the Trans-Pacific Partnership and the Paris Agreement on Climate Change are cited as successes for Trump's policies. And finally, neither the president's foreword nor the NSS document as a whole ever conveyed the impression that it was addressed to people, groups, or governments outside the US. There was not even an attempt at a justification of the policy vis-à-vis all those who are affected by it. Rather, criteria were adduced that, in their nationalist one-sidedness, undermined the normative foundations of the global political system: protection of the American homeland, promotion of US prosperity and economic security, defense of US borders through military strength, and a further increase in the US impact on the world. In other words, the world community and cosmopolitanism had no place in Trump's vision of the international order.

Such resistance to global governance generates a predicament. Just when a strong global political system is more necessary than ever, it seems to be unusually weak. In order to avert the global climate crisis through active measures, prevent another crash in the financial markets, contain the new giants of the digital economy, avoid a renewed arms race, and limit trade wars and superpower rivalries between the US and China, a strong global governance system is needed. But now, at precisely the wrong time, the institutions of global governance are under radical attack, while the normative principles on which they rest are being rejected.

It is possible to distinguish a variety of challenges and challengers that the global political system is now facing. These include:

- Authoritarian leaders such as Vladimir Putin, Recep Tayyip Erdoğan, Jair Bolsonaro, and Viktor Orbán, who place a special emphasis on national sovereignty and criticize the actual practice of international institutions.
- Authoritarian-populist groups or parties in consolidated democracies led by the likes of Marine Le Pen, Donald Trump, and Geert Wilders that treat international institutions as instruments of a cosmopolitan class that infringe on national interests.
- So-called rising powers such as China, Brazil (which, under Bolsonaro, looks to have slipped into the first group), and India (partially also falling into the first group) that acknowledge the necessity of international institutions in principle but want to free them from Western dominance.
- Fundamentalist religious movements, especially in the Middle East, that regard international institutions as tools wielded by godless Westerners to control others.
- Transnational non-governmental organizations, such as Association pour la Taxation des Transactions financières et pour l'Action Citoyenne (Association for the Taxation of Financial Transactions and Citizens' Action) or Occupy, which have an anti-capitalist stance and, for the most part, target other (albeit often stronger) international institutions.

Criticisms, therefore, range across a wide spectrum. They are directed against both the normative foundations of the global political system and concrete international institutions and their practices. Judith Kelley and Beth Simmons, in a forthcoming article, sum up the current state of affairs succinctly: "Global governance has never seemed more necessary, and yet so under attack."

How did the crisis come about?

It wasn't until the 1990s that the global political system attained its mature form. Once the Cold War had ended, the Security Council was able to expand its activities and intervene not only in disputes between states but also in domestic disputes within states. Quite a few of these interventions were aimed at preventing humanitarian catastrophes. As a result, the idea gained ground that the international community was responsible not merely for the safety of individuals but also for the integrity and preservation of entire states. Thus, for example, the International Criminal Court was established so that those accused of war crimes could be called to account. Global trade practices were further liberalized and supplemented by a strong WTO. The International Monetary Fund (IMF) and the World Bank became the central actors in international financial policy. Furthermore, a multitude of other agreements and political authorities came into being in the environmental sphere as well as in the areas of communications and transport. All in all, the authority of international institutions increased as dramatically after 1990 as it had after World War II (see Telò 2014: 145–57 for an account regarding the EU). Figure 7.1 shows the growth of international authority as measured by decision-making proceedings in 36 international organizations. By this criterion, an international governmental organization has authority if it can make binding decisions to which not all member states need agree (either majority decisions or the delegation of competences to independent authorities).

It is precisely this global political system with comparatively strong international institutions that has come under fire in the last ten years. How could this system, brought into existence only in the 1990s, find itself in such a serious crisis so soon? The simplest explanation is that the global political system has produced bad results. But if we look at some highly aggregated developments since 1990,

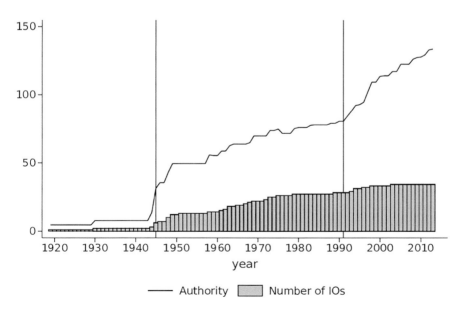

FIGURE 7.1 Rise of international authority

Source: Zürn (2018: 111).

124 Michael Zürn

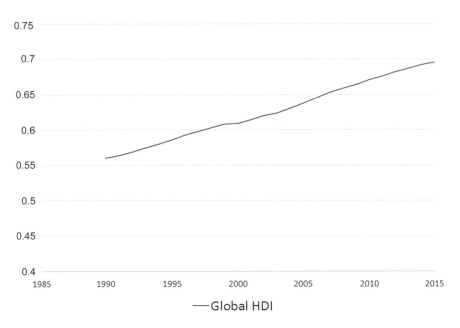

FIGURE 7.2 Global Human Development Index

Source: "Human Development Report," United Nations Development Programme (Zürn 2019: 10).

then the picture that emerges is a remarkably positive one. First, since the 1990s, the Human Development Index (HDI), an indicator of national prosperity, has increased as sharply as it ever did before, as shown in Figure 7.2.

Second, inequality – as measured by the global Gini index – has clearly decreased, above all because many people in China and other Asian countries as well as in parts of Latin America and Africa have escaped from absolute poverty and now belong to the "global middle class" (cf. Milanovic 2016). This upward trend in global development is illustrated in Figure 7.3.

Finally, Figure 7.4 shows that the number of conflicts involving the use of military force has also declined to a historically low level.

Why, then, has what appears to be a highly successful international order fallen into such disfavor? There are two commonly given explanations for this phenomenon. The first points to the sweeping changes that have shaken the international power structure. With the ascent of rising powers, the distribution of power in the international system has been altered drastically. In relative terms, the economic strength of the Western industrial nations has diminished considerably compared to that of the fast-growing economies in Asia and in parts of Latin America and Africa.

China clearly is the only rising power that can be regarded as on a par with the US; actually, it is by now one of the two superpowers. In addition, some regional powers in the Global South, such as India, Brazil, and South Africa, need to be

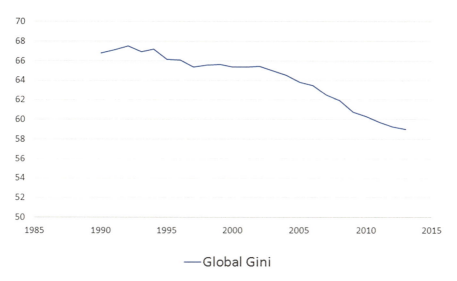

FIGURE 7.3 Global Gini Index
Source: United Nations Development Programme (Zürn 2019: 10).

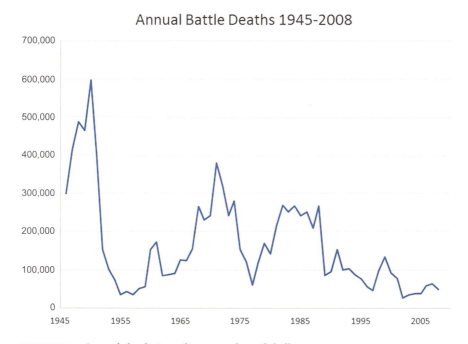

FIGURE 7.4 Annual deaths in military combat, globally
Source: United Nations Development Programme (Zürn 2019: 10).

taken seriously as players in the international system. The changed distribution of power leads to a situation in which the new and rising powers regard the global political system as a Western artifact that disadvantages the Global South. Accordingly, there is significant demand for an adjustment of the international institutions to reflect the new realities of power (Zangl et al. 2016; Stephen & Zürn 2019).

The second explanation is based on the fact that the liberal alignment and open borders that are characteristic of the global political system, especially within Western industrial countries, have created economic and cultural losers. It is these losers of the globalization process, above all in the consolidated democracies, that demand the strengthening of border controls and wish to uphold national sovereignty against the impositions of the global political system (cf. Rogowski 1989; Kriesi et al. 2012; De Wilde et al. 2019).

Each of these explanations, however, highlights only part of the problem. The thesis that the new international distribution of power is responsible for the crisis of multilateralism disregards the fact that, in many respects, the greatest and most fundamental challenges to the global political system are to be found within the Western world. To cite one instance, the thesis that lays blame on the political consequences of growing inequality within societies does not take sufficient account of the fact that many of the winners of globalization in the Global South also have taken a critical stance towards the global political system. Similarly, in the Global North, Austria, France, and the Netherlands – countries where authoritarian populists first made political inroads – are precisely those societies in which inequality has increased the least, if at all.

Thus, these two explanations can account for only some the challenges facing the global political system. Those explanations hold that the crisis of the global governance system is caused by changes that are exogenous to it. But they overlook the crucial mechanisms that have elicited so much dissatisfaction about and resistance to the global governance system. This observation leads us to a third explanation, one that is endogenous to the global governance system and, to some extent, incorporates the aforementioned dominant but partial explanations.

The crisis as a problem of legitimation

The global political system, which attained its full extent and capacity in the 1990s, exercises international authority. Authority is a form of political power. To offer only a few examples, the global political system can use violence when it intervenes to protect human rights, as the Security Council of the United Nations has done; it can prescribe austerity policies, as in cases that have pitted the IMF and private rating agencies against countries in Latin America as well as in Southern Europe; it can overrule national policies designed to protect national industries through the dispute settlement mechanism of the WTO; it can demand that costly measures be taken to protect the global environment (e.g., the Paris Agreement); and much more. The interplay of these sectoral authorities is what entitles us to call it a system of global rule.

Global governance post-1990 involves the assertion of authority and political control, the exercise of which, however, must be legitimized. On its face, the verb "must" in this context should be understood to have a normative significance. Since Hobbes, modern political thought not only has insisted on the necessity of political authority; it also has made clear that collective limitations upon individual freedom of action can be legitimized only under specific conditions and when orderly decision-making procedures are observed. Thus, for modern thought (if not before), the normative obligation to provide grounds for the exercise of political authority translates directly into an empirical imperative. This is a point that Max Weber made roughly 100 years ago: "Normally," he writes, the emergence of authority is "bound up with a constant attempt to arouse and maintain belief in its 'legitimacy'" (2013: 451). From this empirical perspective, belief in legitimacy is what is at stake even in the operation of the system of global governance. Given multiple modernities, beliefs in legitimacy may vary depending on the level of economic development and the kind of culture that we are talking about (Meyer & de Sales Marques 2018).

But what are the conditions under which legitimacy can be attained within a political system? Above all, its attainment requires a convincing narrative on the basis of which the necessity and desirability of global governance can be justified. Such a narrative must include grounds for its functional necessity while also communicating political visions and imagined goals. In addition, it has to refer to decision-making procedures that create legitimacy. Finally, and most fundamentally, a system of rule needs to apply its regulations in ways that will be considered impartial. To be clear, collective rules never are completely impartial; they always favor some groups more than others. But they need to be applied impartially: like cases should be adjudicated in like ways. To put it differently, unless rule is rules based, it won't be able to foster belief in its legitimacy.

For a long time, the Western democracies were unusually successful in generating belief in their legitimacy in this manner, especially after the end of World War II. The functional necessity of statehood was undisputed in the face of external threats, including the task of constructing a welfare state with a comprehensive range of objectives. At the same time, the Western democracies long were sustained by faith in progress and the recognition accorded to decisions democratically reached, then applied following the rule of law. Can the global governance system learn something from this experience? Yes, but only indirectly, for it cannot simply take over the rhetoric of democracy and the rule of law lock, stock, and barrel. Credible narratives of legitimation cannot be formulated in a vacuum, nor can they be created exclusively for purposes of manipulation. They have to be complemented by the appropriate political practices.

There are two peculiarities in the practices of the global political system that hamper the development of such a legitimacy-creating narrative or even render it impossible. One is the lack of sites where the coordination of various international institutions could take place in a transparent way. Democratic political systems within a national framework resolve conflicts of aims between, say, economic and environmental interests through the intervention of either the head of government, the constitutional court, the parliament, or (as a last resort) public opinion. Within the global political system, there are no such institutions that can be considered as effective as those are in the national context.

Conflicts between the international trade and environmental regimes, for instance, have occurred with increasing frequency since 1990, but they are not settled by any meta-authority. As a result, world society has no public venue in which to discuss disputes over conflicting aims. Rather, issues are dealt with and debated, if at all, within the confines of institutionally defined sectors. There is no overarching debate that can fuel political competition between different visions of the global order and between the worldviews upheld by diverse societies. Consequently, technocratic efforts at legitimation predominate at the international level. The validation of international authority takes place primarily on the basis of expertise and effectiveness, not via democratic deliberation, political participation, elections, or a sense of community. This technocratic legitimation frequently fails to justify the extent to which international institutions sometimes encroach on matters of national sovereignty. The predominant technocratic legitimation narrative cannot be stretched much further. In short, military interventions by the international community of states or the enforcement of austerity policies cannot be justified exclusively on technocratic grounds.

Moreover, the global political system lacks an effective separation of powers. Rules are applied inconsistently, which violates the principle that like cases should be adjudicated in like ways. For the most part, international institutions are dominated by a small number of executives from powerful states. They are the ones who dominate the entire process of rulemaking and rule application, hence there is an asymmetry of power that violates the principle of legal equality. The problem can be illustrated best by reference to the UN Security Council. The five permanent members of the Council with veto power have a vital role in making legislative decisions (e.g., what counts as endangering world peace?), in the executive application of such decisions (e.g., does a particular action endanger world peace?), and in the implementation of any interventions that may result (the militarily strongest states are required to carry them out). And all this is done in the absence of any clearly spelled-out jurisdiction. Because of this "institutionalized inequality," similar cases are not treated in a like manner by the Security Council, and this is a systematic flaw. Thus, the Security Council's operations flout the most basic of all sources of legitimation: that a public authority should apply the rules impartially.

As a consequence of these two legitimation problems, the global governance system has developed an authority-legitimation gap. While the political authority of the global political system grew dramatically, efforts to establish its legitimacy were far from having the desired effect. That is, the expansion of the scope of political authority at the international level began to outstrip belief in its legitimacy.

In fact, all the critics of the global political system mentioned above base their resistance to it on the system's legitimation problems.

- Authoritarian leaders such as Putin, Erdoğan, Narendra Modi, and Orbán criticize international institutions' double standards, and for that reason they demand a return to unalloyed national sovereignty.
- Authoritarian populist groups in consolidated democracies turn against the out-of-touch liberal cosmopolitans who allegedly have the final say in the system – which is, essentially, a criticism of technocratic supremacy vis-à-vis the ostensible will of the national majority.
- Rising powers wish to set up different international institutions that will give them rights to participate and make their voices heard more in proportion to their increasing power and wealth.
- Islamic fundamentalist religious movements see international institutions as the spearhead of a Western imperialist policy that serves the continuing subjugation of Islam.
- Transnational non-governmental organizations insist upon the democratization of international institutions so that they can reverse the neoliberal orientation of the latter and their instrumentalization by large-scale US and European corporations.

Of course, these justifications do not always square with the motives that underlie them. Political justifications frequently promote interests of a very different kind. Criticism can serve as a front for the ambitions of authoritarian regimes that seek supremacy, veil the expansionist power politics of rising powers, and (last but not least) mask attempts to protect one's own economy and population from the adverse effects of global competition. These strategic aims, and the related skepticism about international institutions, may be expressed in the form of criticism of international authorities' lack of legitimacy. This reasoning further highlights the legitimation crisis of the global political system.

What is to be done?

Does this analysis suggest that it is necessary to trim and shape the influence of the global political system in such a way that its legitimacy might be saved by other potential sources of legitimation? And is it really necessary to limit the influence of international institutions, as many critics of global governance are demanding?

My answer to these questions is a decisive "no." The functional necessity and normative desirability of international institutions make any such strategies fundamentally unacceptable. It is much more a matter of developing measures that would reinforce the legitimacy of those institutions. To preserve the global political system, we must mount an intellectual defense for it. Only then will it be possible to counter the main danger we face today and to repel the attacks on international institutions. It will be a long, drawn-out struggle that will be carried on at the national and international levels simultaneously. Three measures are especially necessary for the purpose.

First, the proponents of the global political system must move from defense to offense, openly and proactively advocating for a cosmopolitan worldview as a policy that reflects their deepest values and commitments. The inclination to come to reasonable agreements at an international level and to promote them at home as if there were no viable alternative may be the simplest strategy in the short term, but it is costly in the long term because it hampers debate and blocks open-ended public disputation about world politics. Defenders of the global governance system must stand up and be counted as they advocate for the legitimacy and preservation of international institutions. To sell the latter domestically as if they were a necessary evil is an approach that undermines their legitimacy in the long run.

Second, debates on the right way to achieve the common good within European and international institutions need to be more transparent, and there should be room for oppositional views. In order to ensure that discontent with the policies of international and European institutions does not always get translated into criticism of those institutions themselves, potential political opposition within them has to be enabled and accepted. The global governance system must allow for debates about international regulatory needs. These debates must be open to all governments as well as to all members of national societies and the world society. In the absence of global debates about world governance, there can be no successful legitimation of international institutions.

Third, the EU must seek coalition partners for the global political system in the Global South. A long-term effort to establish coalitions of this kind is a much more promising prospect than simply gambling on dubious deals with authoritarian leaders. Adopting such a policy would be a way of helping to make international institutions more legitimate and thus more effective. Both are urgently necessary.

Note

1 This chapter represents an extension, revision, and translation of M. Zürn (2019), "Der Multilateralismus in der Krise: Legitimationsprobleme im globalen politischen System," in *Deutschland & Europa: Zeitschrift für Gemeinschaftskunde, Geschichte und Wirtschaft Friedens- und Sicherheitspolitik in der Europäischen Union*, no. 78. Stuttgart, Germany: Regional Center for Political Education Baden-Württemberg, pp. 8–13. Reprinted by permission. Available at www.deutschlandundeuropa.de/78_19/frieden_sicherheit_eu.pdf.

References

Daase, C., N. Deitelhoff, B. Kamis, J. Pfister, & P. Wallmeier (eds.). 2016. *Herrschaft in den Internationalen Beziehungen*. Berlin: Springer

De Wilde, P., R. Koopmans, W. Merkel, O. Strijbs, & M. Zürn (eds.). 2019. *The Struggle over Borders: Cosmopolitanism and Communitarism*. Cambridge, UK: Cambridge University Press

Inglehart, R. & P. Norris. 2017. "Trump, Brexit, and the Rise of Populism: Economic Have-nots and Cultural Backlash." *Perspectives on Politics* 15(2): 443–54

Kelley, J. & B. Simmons (forthcoming). "Governance by Other Means: Rankings as Regulatory Systems." *International Theory*

Keohane, R. 1990. "Multilateralism: An Agenda for Research." *International Journal* 45(4): 731–64

Krauthammer, C. 1990. "The Unipolar Moment." *Foreign Affairs* 70(1): 23–33

Kriesi, H., E. Grande, M. Dolezal, M. Heibling, D. Höglinger, S. Hutter, & B. Wüest. 2012. *Political Conflict in Western Europe*. Cambridge, UK: Cambridge University Press

Meyer, T. & J. de Sales Marques (eds.). 2018. *Multiple Modernities and Good Governance*. London & New York: Routledge

Milanovic, B. 2016. *Global Inequality: A New Approach for the Age of Globalization*. Cambridge, MA: Harvard University Press.

Qin, Y. 2014. "Continuity through Change: Background Knowledge and China's International Strategy." *The Chinese Journal of International Politics* 7(3): 285–314

Rogowski, R. 1989. *Commerce and Coalitions: How Trade Affects Domestic Political Alignments*. Princeton, NJ: Princeton University Press

Ruggie, J. 1992. "Multilateralism: The Anatomy of an Institution." *International Organization* 46(3): 561–98

Stephen, M. & M. Zürn (eds.). 2019. *Contested World Orders: Rising Powers, Non-governmental Organizations, and the Politics of Authority beyond the Nation State*. Oxford, UK: Oxford University Press

Telò, M. 2014. *European Union and New Regionalism: Competing Regionalism and Global Governance in a Post-hegemonic Era*. London & New York: Routledge

Trump, D. 2017. "National Security Strategy of the United States of America." Available at http://nssarchive.us/national-security-strategy-2017

Weber, M. 2013 [1921]. "Kapitel III: Typen der Herrschaft." In K. Borchardt, E. Hanke, & W. Schluchter (eds.), *Max Weber Gesamtausgabe, Band I/23. Wirtschaft und Gesellschaft. Soziologie*. Tübingen, Germany: Mohr Siebeck, pp. 449–591

Wiener, A. 2014. *A Theory of Contestation*. Berlin: Springer

Zangl, B., F. Heußner, A. Kruck, & X. Lanzendörfer. 2016. "Imperfect Adaptation: How the WTO and the IMF Adjust to Shifting Power Distributions among their Members." *The Review of International Organizations* 11(2): 171–96

Zürn, M. 2018. *A Theory of Global Governance. Authority, Legitimacy, and Contestation*. Oxford, UK: Oxford University Press

Zürn, M. 2019. "Der Multilateralismus in der Krise: Legitimationsprobleme im globalen politischen System." In *Deutschland & Europa: Zeitschrift für Gemeinschaftskunde, Geschichte und Wirtschaft Friedens- und Sicherheitspolitik in der Europäischen Union*, 78. Stuttgart, Germany: Regional Center for Political Education Baden-Württemberg, pp. 8–13. Available at www.deutschlandundeuropa.de/78_19/frieden_sicherheit_eu.pdf.

8
HUMAN SECURITY, CLIMATE CHANGE, AND MIGRATION

A European perspective

Nuno Severiano Teixeira, Joana Castro Pereira, and Susana Ferreira

As the process of globalization deepens, security challenges intensify, calling into question the state's capacity to address them on its own. Events related to climate change and large-scale migration stand among the overwhelming challenges that our societies face today. While shifts in the international arena, in this era of mounting turmoil and convulsion, endanger the core values supporting global governance, the growing interconnectedness and complex nature of these security threats need to be addressed through a collaborative and multilateral approach. This is very clear in the case of the European Union (EU), whose member states have struggled to find a common voice to address shared challenges, such as climate change or migration.

In its latest global risks report, the World Economic Forum (WEF 2020) listed extreme weather, climate action failure, natural disasters, biodiversity loss, and human-made environmental disasters as the top five global risks likely to loom largest within the next decade. Of these, it identifies climate action failure, biodiversity loss, extreme weather events, and water crises as among the top five in terms of impact. We are experiencing a planetary emergency that threatens the future of life on Earth and requires unprecedented global coordination. Despite both growing public awareness of the ecological crisis that the planet is facing and ever more urgent calls for climate action across the globe, particularly among the youth, and the trajectory of greenhouse gas (GHG) emissions and policies since the Paris Climate Agreement was signed in 2015, coupled with the recent increase of conflict in the international system, make the prospects of an ambitious global response very dim for the foreseeable future. As major emitters such as the US, Brazil, and Australia display skepticism regarding the anthropogenic character of climate change and hostility towards international action aimed at mitigating the problem, attention turns to the European Union as the most environmentally committed actor and in its capacity to keep the momentum of the Paris Agreement alive (Evans & Gabbatiss 2019).

Climate change and migration have become intimately related in the last decades, and new (albeit controversial) concepts such as "environmental migration" and "environmental refugees"[1] have emerged. Despite the difficulties in ascertaining the impact of environmental factors on people's decision to relocate (Martin 2010: 397), one thing is certain: Climate change will exacerbate the existing migratory pressure, especially in some specific regions, requiring global efforts to meet these challenges.

While the phenomenon of international migration remains an exception, representing just 3.5% of the world population, its scale has increased. Already there are an estimated 272 million migrants worldwide, surpassing the UN's own projections for 2050 (IOM 2019). However, major migration and displacement events have taken place in recent years, whether motivated by violent conflicts or by severe political, economic, and social instability, and triggering several humanitarian crises, most notably from Syria and Yemen in the Middle East to Venezuela in South America.

These unprecedented migratory dynamics have turned the Mediterranean Sea into the world's deadliest migration corridor. As the migratory pressure in this region intensified in the second decade of the twenty-first century, the EU has found itself at odds with its common migration and asylum policies.

Relying on theoretical reflections about the concepts of security and human security, both of which highlight the human side of today's risks, this chapter provides an overview of the climate change and migration crises in Europe. We will present, assess, and compare the EU's responses to both. To what degree is the EU able to address these issues at a multilateral level? And are the Union's climate and migration policies consistent with the demands of human security?

What are we talking about when we talk about security?

What do people mean when they refer to "security"? We do not know for sure, because the absence of a consensus is the sole point of agreement that has been reached on the matter. Security is an essentially contested concept. Despite the lack of agreement, scholars have been nearly unanimous in thinking that it needed greater clarity and have tried to provide better definitions of it. One such attempt, dating back to the 1950s, is credited to Wolfers (1952). Recently revisited by David (2013), it envisages security in both objective and subjective terms: objectively, as the absence of objective threats to the fundamental and vested values of a community, and subjectively, as the fear (or lack thereof) that those values might be under threat. In the 1990s, Buzan et al. (1998) modified Wolfers's concept, defining security simply as the search for freedom, or the liberation from all threats.

On the whole, a theoretical genealogy of the concept reveals two fundamentally different philosophical approaches to security. According to the first of these, security pertains to *having*. It is viewed as a commodity that is attained through ownership and the accrual of material goods: wealth, arms, power (economic, political, and above all military). From this perspective, the greater the power, the greater the security.

By contrast, according to the second approach, security pertains to *being*. It is viewed from a relational perspective and understood as a relationship between actors whose final goal is emancipation: the liberation from all threats, issuing in a state of well-being, universal justice, and full respect for human rights. Precisely that trust-based relationship is what truly can deliver security. In other words, security does not emerge from the exercise of power based on the notion that to ensure security for some, others necessarily must be deprived of their share. Instead, it stems rather from cooperation that makes provisions for the security of all.

These two strains, either explicitly or (more commonly) in a veiled way, pervade not only the whole theoretical debate raised by security studies, impacting the issues that flow from it and lie at the core of the discipline, but also the security policies of the actors, conditioning how they set their priorities – specifically, whether they mainly should emphasize military prowess or developmental assistance in the fields of environment and human rights.

When we talk about security, the chief question is: security for whom? Who is to be protected from threats? In a nutshell, who or what is the referent of security?

In traditional security studies of a realist persuasion (so-called strategic studies), there was no doubt whatsoever: The referent was the state, such that security meant the state's security. This concept of security, moreover, was invested in and legitimized by the concept of national interest. That novel concept, in the American context, was enshrined in the US National Security Act of 1947 as "national security." From then on, security in the field of international relations came to be understood as the study or exercise of national security (or, in Europe, national defense).

Towards the end of, but mainly after, the Cold War, the concept of security underwent a process of enlargement and further development, and the referent was shifted from the security of the state to the security of the people. But whether "people" meant the individual, or society, or humankind as such remained very much under contention. Disagreements on this issue spawned a growing literature (cf. Anderson-Rogers & Crawford 2018; Fukuda-Parr & Messineo 2012; Shinoda 2004).

In traditional, essentially state-centric security (or strategic) studies, threats unequivocally originate in other states and potentially involve the use of force, particularly of a military nature. For that approach to security, then, what matter are inter-state armed conflicts and the use of military power. But once the referent shifts from state security to popular security, the nature of what constitutes a threat is considerably broadened. Threats need not be exclusively military in character but may also incorporate economic, societal, environmental, political, or identitarian aspects. If we regard security (in Wolfers's or Buzan's sense) as liberation or at least relief from threats against fundamental or acquired rights, then for many people across the world, climate change, poverty, epidemics, and scarcity of natural resources like water or food all can pose problems as grave as, or even graver than, armed conflicts. In such cases, the threat in question does not loom from another state, it does not have a military nature, and it does not even pertain to the use of force. What is more, military means are useless to fight it. In short, if from a traditional viewpoint security equals state security and relies on the use of force, in this more contemporary perspective security is the security of people, which cannot be achieved primarily by relying on those methods.

What are we talking about when we talk about human security?

With the end of the Cold War, the concept of human security began to take root. Historically, that concept has been associated with the 1994 Human Development Report on Human Security, drafted by Mahbub ul Haq under the auspices of the UN (MacFarlane & Khong 2006). The report argued that, over the previous decades, the traditional concept of security had been interpreted narrowly, emphasizing freedom from external aggression and protection of national interests, on the one hand, or safeguards against the nuclear threat, on the other. In this sense, the traditional concept was focused more on the state than on individuals. The report sought to build a bridge to the United Nations Charter, written in 1945, wherein the question of security rested on the dynamic between "freedom from want and freedom from fear," ensuring that individuals did not fall victim to violence or poverty.

As the report argued, human security should be understood as a concern for human life and dignity broadly conceived; it would go beyond exclusive preoccupation with the threat posed by weapons. It was also a universal concept, relevant to all people, whether from wealthy nations or poor states. It was focused on people in general, as the concern was about how they live in the societies to which they belong, how they express their political and social choices, whether they can access the market economy and enjoy social opportunities, and whether they live in peace or in conflict. In this sense, the report identified seven core components that together express the full scope of the concept of human security: economic security, food security, health security, environmental security, personal security, community security, and political security. Now that the bipolar conflict was over, the time had come to bring forth human development as the main concern for the international community (Kaldor 2011: 2).

However, the comprehensiveness of the definition of human security embodied in the report generated deep criticism. As Sabine Alkire points out, the main assessment was that, because of the unclear interconnection between human development and security, the report in the eyes of many had an "idealistic" component and "naïve" recommendations (Alkire 2003: 20–21). These criticisms helped to substantiate the concept of suman security in two dimensions: one broad and the other narrow.

The concept's broad dimension, in line with the 1994 Human Development Report, holds that human security is "concerned with human vulnerability overall, and therefore encompasses all forms of threats from all sources." In other words, it includes, in addition to organized political violence, other threats such as natural disasters, disease, climate change, hunger, and economic problems (Fukuda-Parr & Messineo 2012: 5). By contrast, the narrow formulation advocates a less holistic view. Assuming that the broad version is too comprehensive to be useful, critics contend that the quest for human security must be limited primarily to protecting individuals against political violence and coping with specific threats; a focus on long-term strategies for achieving sustainability and promoting human development allegedly would take security studies too far afield. As a result, the problems to be addressed turn out to be relatively traditional, such as armed conflicts, human rights abuse, insecurity, and the fight against organized crime. Contrary to the broad view, proponents of the narrow approach seek to prevent the concept of human security from becoming a shopping mall of threats too numerous and diffuse to be addressed fruitfully

Established in 2000, the Commission on Human Security put forth an independent report in 2003 seeking to bridge these disparate definitions of human security. Building upon the definition presented in 1994, it refrained from listing all potential threats to human security, instead advancing a set of elementary rights and freedoms that every human being should enjoy as a "vital core." Its main contribution was to stress the importance of involving multiple actors beyond the state, such as non-governmental organizations (NGOs), regional organizations, and civil society, in managing human security. In this sense, it has clearly shown that "the empowerment of people" was to be seen as "an important condition of human security," emphasizing that "security and human security are mutually reinforcing and dependent on each other" (Fukuda-Parr & Messineo 2012: 6).

In sum, the question of human security falls within a broad concept of security that over time has shifted its referent from the state to people, and from the individual and the society to the whole of humankind. The process of securitization (Emmers 2010) makes it possible to address not only the issues of poverty and political and identitarian violence but also those of food security, pandemics, climate change, and migration.

Security and climate change

Climate change is accelerating and its impacts are increasing. The period from 2015 to 2019 comprised the warmest five years on record. Levels of GHG in the atmosphere have reached a new peak, with carbon dioxide growth rates approximately 20% greater than in the previous five-year assessment period. Sea level rise, the melting of ice, and extreme weather also have accelerated (WMO 2019).

According to the 1.5° Centigrade report by the Intergovernmental Panel on Climate Change (IPCC; 2018: 4), "human activities are estimated to have caused approximately 1.0°C of global warming above pre-industrial levels." Under current policies, global temperatures may exceed 1.5°C by the mid-2030s, 2°C by the mid-2050s, and 3.2°C by 2100 (CAT 2019a). A global warming increase of 2°C may trigger tipping points in the biosphere that would move the planet towards an irreversible "hothouse effect" (Steffen et al. 2018).

The nationally determined contributions (NDCs) that parties made under the Paris Climate Agreement are mostly insufficient to safeguard the planet's climate. Assuming that the pledged actions were carried out, global warming still would increase by nearly 3°C by the end of the century, placing the Earth at a potentially catastrophic level of climate change (CAT 2019a; see also Pereira & Viola 2018). It would result in severe risks to global and food security, with a combination of high temperatures and humidity jeopardizing normal human activities, as well as bringing about significant species extinctions that in turn would have adverse, cascading effects on the functioning of entire ecosystems and the vital services they perform for humanity (IPCC 2014). Limiting the Earth's temperature rise to 1.5°C – the aspirational goal of the Paris Climate Agreement – is crucial for saving the majority of global species (Warren et al. 2018) as well as for safeguarding low-lying island states from sea level rise and the poorest countries from climate extremes (UNDP & Climate Analytics 2016). However, international climate cooperation faces several challenges that hinder progress towards achieving the temperature goals set forth in the agreement (cf. Lewis et al. 2019; Jiang et al. 2019). As a result, the risk of a climate event capable of destabilizing the international system during this century cannot be ruled out.

Climate change is the primary indicator of the Anthropocene, the Earth's new geological epoch, in which humanity has become the main agent of planetary environmental change (Crutzen & Stoermer 2000). Complex, unstable, and dangerous, the Anthropocene generates several forms of insecurity that threaten ecosystems, societies, economies, and ultimately the survival of humanity. The planet's new geological reality evidences the unbreakable link between nature and society as well as the entanglement of human and non-human beings and ecologies (i.e., the fact that life on the planet results from complex relationships and interdependencies among species). Human security is inseparable from reorienting our activities and considering the needs and rights of other beings that also depend on healthy ecosystems and allow people to flourish. In sum, the Anthropocene challenges dominant conceptions of security, which assume that threats are limited to outside agents and the existence of an external and stable environment and recognize states or human populations as the only subjects to be secured (see, e.g., Burke et al. 2016; Dryzek & Pickering 2018). In other words, the environment is no longer stable. The key takeaways here are that decision-makers cannot continue to ignore the possibility of a high impact environmental event (Mabey et al. 2011) and that environmental and climate threats to security stem from prevailing production and consumption patterns and lifestyles (Dalby 2017). Accordingly, security practices must move beyond the conventional notion of states protecting their territories and populations from external political/military risks and focus instead on building a new development paradigm centered not only on human populations but also the ecosystems and non-human communities that enable life as we know it on Earth (Cudworth & Hobden 2018). Security and survival require profound reflection on the economic, political, societal, and moral structures and assumptions that gave rise to the dangerous new geological reality facing human civilization in the twenty-first century.

In the context of the Anthropocene, calls for an ecological conception of climate security are emerging. Climate security discourses and practices focusing on securing ecosystem resilience and ecological processes as well as on the impacts of human-induced climate change may have the potential to protect the most vulnerable across space, time, and species. Such an approach could safeguard the rights and needs of impoverished and vulnerable populations, future generations, and non-human living beings through measures to mitigate the scale and gravity of change and to increase ecosystems' capacity to preserve resilience after stress, thus helping to ensure their continued functioning (cf. McDonald 2018). Simply put, human security is inseparable from ecological security.

Unfortunately, as we will show, the EU's environmental and climate strategy of the past few years has not been consistent with ecological resilience and, as a consequence, with human security.

Climate change impacts on Europe

For the past four decades, temperatures have been rising in Europe. The European average temperature in 2018 was one the three highest ever recorded (Copernicus 2019). Anthropogenic climate change has increased significantly the likelihood of extreme weather and climate events in Europe, and it is already having adverse and wide-ranging ecological, human, and economic impacts. These include species migrations and extinctions affecting forestry, agriculture, fishery, and human health; increased flood risks and erosion along coastlines resulting from sea level rise; more frequent and severe heatwaves that potentially could harm human health while enhancing the risk of electricity blackouts and forest fires; infrastructure damage in the realm of transportation; and economic losses in tourism and leisure activities resulting from less favorable climatic conditions (EEA 2017).

Climate change is likely to affect the availability of water in the continent, putting additional pressure on southern regions already experiencing water stress, while other parts of Europe are projected to confront more frequent floods, and low-lying regions are threatened by sea level rise and storm surges (EEA 2018a). Projections indicate that Southeastern and Southern Europe will have the highest numbers of critically threatened sectors and domains. The coastal regions and floodplains of Western Europe are also hotspots. In the Alps and on the Iberian Peninsula, ecosystems will suffer serious impacts. Economic costs are expected to run high. In a 2°C warmer world, the annual total damages from climate change in the EU could reach EUR 120 billion, an amount equivalent to 1.2% of current GDP. In a globalized and highly interconnected world, the situation potentially will be further aggravated by Europe's vulnerability to climate change impacts outside the continent through numerous pathways, including the trade of agricultural and non-agricultural commodities, infrastructure and transport, human migration, finance, and security risks. Spillover effects to the increasingly complex value and supply chains of European products, many of which are linked to distant geographies, can be expected to increase in the coming decades (EEA 2017).

EU citizens' perceptions of, and attitudes on, climate change

According to the latest Eurobarometer report on climate change (European Commission 2019a), over 90% of EU citizens see climate change as a serious problem. Sixty percent believe it is one of the most critical problems confronting the world (an increase of 17 points compared to 2017), and almost one-quarter consider it to be "the single most serious problem" facing humanity (a percentage increase of 11 points from 2017). In 2019, climate change has overtaken international terrorism (54%) as the world's second most pressing problem for EU citizens, after poverty, hunger, and lack of drinking water (71%). There is widespread public support for national and EU actions to mitigate climate change and transition to a climate-neutral economy by 2050. Over 90% of Europeans agree that GHG emissions should be reduced to a minimum to make the EU economy climate-neutral by the middle of the century and that their national governments should set ambitious targets to increase the share of renewables in their respective energy matrixes. Approximately 80% think that more public financial resources should be invested in the transition to clean energies, even if it means cutting subsidies to fossil fuels, a percentage representing an increase of 5 points compared to 2017, and that taking action on climate change will encourage innovation and increase the competitiveness of EU companies. In addition, over 70% of Europeans agree that limiting EU's fossil fuel imports can increase energy security and bring economic benefits, and nearly 80% believe that EU expertise in clean technologies should be used to assist other regions in their mitigation efforts, a move that would also benefit the bloc economically. Finally, 70% agree that adaptation measures to the adverse impacts of irreversible climate change can positively affect citizens.

Most EU citizens consider national governments, business and industry, and the EU's institutions as the main actors responsible for addressing the climate crisis. However, the percentages of Europeans admitting that responsibility also lies within themselves personally and taking individual action to help fight climate change have increased since 2017, from 22% to 36% and from 49% to 60%, respectively. Still, according to the European Commission (2019a), the most common actions are waste reduction and recycling (75%) and cutting down on consumption of disposables (62%).

The EU's response to the climate crisis

The EU is the world's third largest GHG emitter after China and the US, accounting for nearly 9% of the global total (Olivier & Peters 2018). The energy sector generates approximately 80% of the EU's GHG emissions (EEA 2018b).

Between 1990 and 2017, the bloc reduced its overall emissions by 19% (Olivier & Peters 2018). Since international climate negotiations began in the late 1980s, and despite growing obstacles, the EU has played a leading role in global climate governance, advocating binding international agreements, setting its own binding emissions reduction targets, and providing significant funding for assisting developing countries in their climate change mitigation and adaptation efforts (see, e.g., Afionis 2019; Delbeke & Vis 2015; Pereira & Viola 2018).

During the 24th Conference of the Parties of the United Nations Framework Convention on Climate Change, held in Katowice in December of 2018, the EU assumed the role of instrumental leader and worked with China and members of the High Ambition Coalition to ensure consensus on the "Paris rulebook," a deal on implementing the Paris Climate Agreement (Pereira & Viola 2018). In advance of these negotiations, and leading by example, the EU presented its strategic long-term vision for a climate-neutral Europe by 2050 and reaffirmed the bloc's commitment to climate finance activities. In addition, the EU shared its vision on possible pathways to mitigating climate change and ensuring transparency, review, and compliance with the provisions of the Paris Climate Agreement. Moreover, the EU Council expressed its deep concern about the conclusions found in the IPCC's recently published 1.5°C report, thereby demonstrating intellectual leadership (Parker & Karlsson 2018). However, despite European efforts, in light of scientific findings and demands the rules agreed to at Katowice are weak (Evans & Timperley 2018; Höhne & Tewari 2018; Neuweg et al. 2018). As argued by Parker and Karlsson (2018: n.p.), "effective leadership demands credibility and the ability to convince prospective followers that one is acting on behalf of the common good. To date, the EU has not convinced enough governments around the world to match its . . . goals" – which nevertheless are insufficiently ambitious.

The EU's climate and energy targets for 2020 envisage cuts of at least 20% in GHG emissions compared with 1990 levels; a 20% increase in the share of energy consumption from renewables; and a 20% increase in energy efficiency. Key EU targets for 2030 include a reduction of at least 40% in GHG emissions below 1990 levels; an increase of at least 32% in the share of energy consumption from renewables; and an improvement in energy efficiency of at least 32.5%. To achieve these goals, the EU finances and regulates climate and energy action. No less than 20% of its budget for the 2014–20 period (EUR 206 billion) should be spent on climate action. In 2018, the European Commission proposed a new budget of EUR 1,134.6 billion for the 2021–27 period; 25% of that expenditure (nearly EUR 284 billion) is to be allocated to climate change mitigation and adaptation activities. In addition, through its emissions trading scheme (ETS) the EU is reducing GHG emissions from the power sector and major industry in a cost-effective way. Other policy and regulatory actions include:

- The establishment of binding annual emissions reduction targets in the sectors not covered in the ETS – construction, agriculture, transport (excluding aviation,

which is part of the ETS), the non-ETS industry, and the waste sector – for each EU member state.
- The binding of national renewable energy targets.
- Measures to promote building renovation to reduce energy use and improve the energy efficiency of new buildings.
- Mandatory emission reduction targets for new vehicles.
- A legal framework for the environmentally safe use of carbon capture and storage technologies.
- A regulation to ensure that emissions from land use are totally cancelled out by an equivalent removal of carbon dioxide from the atmosphere (through, for example, afforestation and improved forest management).

Moreover, the EU is building an Energy Union based on the following long-term objectives: sustainability, security of supply, and competitiveness. Each member state will develop national climate and energy plans for the 2021–30 period and report on implementation progress every two years, while the European Commission will monitor the EU's progress as a whole. Both the EU and its member states also will develop long-term strategies for the period of at least three decades from 2020 onwards. Finally, the EU also has adopted a strategy to adapt to the irreversible effects of climate change founded on three main objectives: promoting action by member states, building a "climate-proof" EU, and advancing better-informed decision-making. Member states are encouraged to forge adaptation plans, and the European Commission provides funding to assist them in their efforts. Adaptation in the most vulnerable sectors (e.g., agriculture and fisheries) and more resilient infrastructures are promoted, and gaps in adaptation knowledge are addressed (European Parliament 2019).

The EU is on track to meet its climate targets. The EU's climate commitments are, however, insufficient. If all countries followed the European level of ambition, the Earth would potentially warm between 2°C and 3°C by 2100 (CAT 2019b). In 2018, the European Parliament and various EU member states called for a new emissions target of 55% below 1990 levels by 2030, which would still be insufficient to achieve the temperature goals of the Paris Climate Agreement and ensure ecological resilience. In some sectors, the EU lags behind the action needed for stabilizing the climate and preventing adverse climate-induced ecological impacts. For example, a conducive framework for facilitating the task of car manufacturers in achieving new emissions standards and quotas for low or zero emissions vehicles is still missing; more investment in public transport and rail infrastructure is needed; a European ban on installing coal, oil, and gas heating in new buildings is essential and should be made a top priority; and in 2018, nearly two-thirds of emissions in the power sector in the EU still came from coal-fired power stations, which absolutely must be phased out sooner than what is currently projected. These goals could be partially funded by shifting resources currently used for natural gas infrastructure, which will not only increase EU dependency on energy imports and compromise energy security, but also put at risk the fulfilment of the Paris Climate Agreement goals (CAT 2019c).

It should also be noted that the EU is set to fail its 2020 biodiversity protection commitments due to poor implementation of existing nature, water, and marine legislation; lack of coherence between biodiversity policy and other relevant sectors and policies (agriculture, fisheries, forestry, and energy); and insufficient financial resources and maintenance of perverse subsidies, which reveal political unwillingness to take biodiversity loss seriously and resistance by those with vested interests in the status quo. Without assertive nature conservation and restoration action, the resilience of the EU's ecosystems in the face of the climate emergency will be further compromised (EHF 2019; WWF 2019).

Over the past few years, the EU's environmental, climate, and energy policies have faced several obstacles: resistance by the coal-dependent Eastern states; the rise of populism; the French political crisis precipitated by popular rejection of the carbon tax and the low approval rates of President Macron; Germany's struggle to phase out coal; and the turbulent Brexit (the UK exit process from the EU) negotiations (Pereira & Viola 2018). Nevertheless, 2019 brought two promising signs: the Greens became the EU's fourth parliamentary political force in the May elections, and in December of 2019, the European Commission launched a "Green Deal" to make Europe climate neutral by 2050. In spite of all challenges, the EU remains the most committed actor among the major climate powers. Its leadership will be key in raising the ambition level of the project of climate change mitigation in the foreseeable future.

Migration, politics, and security

During this new millennium, characterized as it is by unprecedented levels of human mobility, migration issues have risen to the top of the political agenda, as "high politics" and security concerns. This development has been accompanied by a maturing of the migration field. The latter has begun to move beyond the mainstream discipline, as is evident in the proliferation of research on the impact of the EU's decision-making processes (Lahav & Guiraudon 2007: 3).

European migration studies emerged as a new field of research within migration studies in the 1980s with the political construction of migration within the European project. Nevertheless, until that moment, research on migration in Europe had followed the main tradition on migration studies, focusing on *internal* migration and *international* migration, e.g., Polish migrants living in Europe and America (Pisarevskaya et al. 2019: 3).

The production of knowledge about European migration over the past three decades is quite extensive and involves a diversification of theoretical approaches to this phenomenon, which at the same time has acquired growing political prominence. In this sense, a whole body of literature has focused on the development of European migration policy, especially the framework and mechanisms within which such policy is made (Straubhaar & Zimmerman 1993; Zimmermann 1995; Guiraudon 2000). Simultaneously, the development of cooperation among EU member states on migration has led to the appearance of studies on the regimes governing migration at a regional level, such as in Eastern, Central, and Southern Europe (Arango et al. 2009; Okolski 2012).

From the very beginning, numerous studies have focused on the security logic of EU migration and asylum policies, and the consequent adoption of restrictive measures and mechanisms. The establishment of the Schengen system created the new image of "Fortress Europe" (Ireland 1991; Kofman & Sales 1992), and policy developments within the areas of freedom, security, and justice have emphasized the connection between migration and internal security in the EU. Furthermore, the September 11, 2001, attacks occasioned a turning point in European migration studies and their growing association with security issues, which has translated into a burgeoning literature on the securitization of migration (Huysmans 2000; Kicinger 2004; Lazaridis & Wadia 2015). That literature aims to understand the ways in which migration poses a threat to security and how discourses and practices have conceptualized migration as a security issue. In this regard, a clear trend worth mentioning, pertaining to the restrictive character of the EU's immigration and asylum policies, highlights the criminalization of migration. This strand of the literature focuses on both domestic developments in terms of member states' legislation and the EU's practices of detention and deportation, and it ranges from the protection of human rights to the sociology of crime and security in migration studies (Parkin 2013).

Some recent studies have moved to include the external dimension of the migration policy, assessing the relationship between immigration and foreign policy (Wolff 2015), while others have focused on the migration-development nexus of the EU policies (Lavenex & Kunz 2008). We can also trace a body of literature dedicated to migration governance that explores the impact of European governance and the dilemmas presented by new forms of migration (Geddes 2003; Ferreira 2019).

Pressing migratory dynamics

Over the last decades there has been mounting unease in the EU regarding irregular migratory flows across the Mediterranean by virtue of its association with transnational threats, particularly human smuggling and trafficking. As a consequence of the September 11 attacks in the US, these concerns have become more pressing, linking irregular migration with (Islamic) terrorism and other forms of cross-border organized crime (Lutterbeck 2006: 59). At the same time, the perception of these flows as a humanitarian challenge has grown stronger due to rising death tolls among those attempting passage across the Mediterranean.

The increasing instability along Mediterranean coasts in the second decade of the twenty-first century has highlighted the migratory pressure in this region and caused two major refugee crises, in Libya and Syria. The enduring political and social tensions have translated into long-term conflicts, changing the migration patterns in the basin (Ferreira & Rodrigues 2020).

The scale of migration in the region has been unprecedented, reaching a maximum of 1.8 million arrivals to the EU through the Mediterranean in 2015.

Thousands more have followed them in subsequent years (Frontex 2019). Thus, the Mediterranean Sea has become a clandestine gateway to reach Europe, despite a significant decrease in the number of detections since 2016, with 139,000 detections of illegal border crossings at the EU's sea borders in 2019 (Frontex 2020: 9).

Mediterranean migration routes have undergone significant alterations throughout the last decade, becoming ever more dangerous and intensely exploited by human smugglers. As a consequence, the death toll registered is unparalleled, turning this sea into the most lethal migratory corridor of our time, with a total of over 19,200 deaths recorded between 2014 and the end of 2019 (IOM 2020). Although the trend since its peak in 2016 (when 5,000 deaths were recorded in the Mediterranean) is towards a significant decrease in number of mortalities, the figures are still daunting, and they reveal the ineffectiveness of the measures taken by the EU to cope with the humanitarian tragedy.

As the number of migrants arriving on European territory increased throughout 2015 and 2016, tensions within the EU escalated, given the reluctance of various political leaders to take collective action and share responsibility equitably as a way of managing the migratory pressure. While countries such as Germany adopted an open-door policy (at least initially), other member states, such as Hungary and Croatia, started raising walls and fences to deter and deflect those population movements (Ferreira 2016). Those newly fortified borders, complete with fences and barriers, call into question the values of the so-called area of freedom, security, and justice supposedly created through the application of the EU's Charter of Fundamental Rights.

The EU's migration regime

The pace of and the pressures exerted by migration flows along Europe's borders have challenged the EU's approach to migration management and cast doubt on the efficacy of mechanisms in place regarding its migration regime (migration, asylum, and borders). Despite the lack of European solidarity – demonstrated by the behavior of many member states – and constant setbacks, progress has been made in the adoption of a somewhat effective answer to the management of these flows through the adoption of the European Agenda on Migration and revision of the EU's asylum policy.

The EU's struggle to manage the mounting migratory pressure has stoked growing discontent and anti-immigrant feelings within the populations of EU member countries. It also has fueled the consolidation of new far-right parties, which represents a danger to the EU's future approach to migration. According to the latest Eurobarometer report on "Public Opinion in the European Union," published in December of 2019 (European Commission 2019b), immigration evidently has become the Europeans' major concern, as 34% of those polled consider it as the most pressing issue facing the Union. This concern reaches its highest proportions in Malta (66%), Cyprus (60%), and Slovenia (53%), while in Austria it is tied for first place (27%) with climate change (European Commission 2019b: 17–18).

Turning to the chief sources of worry at the national level, immigration ranks fifth, at 17%, a figure considerably lower compared to the one in the autumn of 2015, when it peaked at 36% (European Commission 2019b: 21). It is the most mentioned issue in the frontline countries of Malta (65%), Greece (47%), Cyprus (29%), and Italy (25%, here on a par with the economic situation), as well as in certain major host countries, including Belgium and Germany at 26% each and Austria at 20% (European Commission 2019b: 24).

Regarding key policies, the survey highlights the strong support of two-thirds of European citizens for a common European Asylum System (66%). There is a shared agreement on this issue among 26 member states, ranging from 89% support in Cyprus and 86% in Germany to 44% in Latvia and 40% in Estonia. Nevertheless, there is solid opposition to the more accommodating policy embodied in the new approach to asylum in the Czech Republic, where 52% are against it versus 38% in favor, and Slovakia, where the respective figures stand at 49% versus 36% (European Commission 2019b: 27).

Another critical issue concerns support for the strengthening of the EU's external borders. Here, 68% of the respondents favor such reinforcement through the deployment of more European border and coast guards. Support for this measure is even stronger in Cyprus and Greece (both at 91%), and also in Bulgaria, where it stands at 85% (European Commission 2019b: 28).

The results of this Eurobarometer go hand in hand with the priority given to migration issues, now at the top of the European political agenda. However, the majority of the measures adopted so far, with a strong emphasis on the border dimension, highlight the deterrence dimension of EU policy towards border management (Ferreira 2019). The focus has been placed on the safeguarding of national security, as evidenced by the stress on increasing securitization of migration issues at the European level. The complex character of migration flows, and the numerous challenges presented by the need to manage them, demand the adoption of a comprehensive approach to governing migration within the EU. Migration management in the EU, particularly in the Mediterranean context, takes place within an integral and global framework comprising policies on borders, asylum, and immigration along with an external dimension that encompasses the EU's relations with its Mediterranean neighbors (Ferreira 2019: 116). Therefore, migration governance is conceived as a complex process that involves countries of origin, transit, and destination. In this sense, cooperation with those parties is a critical and central dimension and must go beyond an approach focused on border controls to include dimensions such as intelligence (for risk analysis) and diplomacy.

The notions of responsibility and solidarity are critical to the support a comprehensive model of migration governance within the EU. We argue that appealing to the solidarity of the member states should go beyond an equal sharing of responsibility in managing human mobility. The member states should refer to the principle of equity, in which each country is involved and contributes with the means it has available. Thus, the sense of proportionality should prevail over the unification of criteria (Ferreira 2019).

Concluding remarks

By the end of 2019, according to the Eurobarometer, the two most pressing issues for Europeans were immigration and climate change. At the European level, over a third of citizens (34%) ranked immigration as their prime concern and the major problem to be grappled with by the European Union. The runner-up here was climate change, polling at 24%. It should be noted that, in the hierarchy of perceived European problems, matters as important as the economy, public finances, or terrorism at best came in third. At the level of national public opinion, however, these problems tended to decline in the rank. Environment, climate, and energy issues still held the second place, at 21%, whereas immigration plummeted to fifth position, at 17% (European Commission 2019b). These trends appear to suggest a twofold perception by the Europeans: first, the crucial importance of immigration and climate change as threats to their security in its wider sense; and second, the fact that these are problems that cannot be solved nationally and must therefore be tackled at the European level. Thus, both climate change and international migrations constitute phenomena that not only have an objective impact on the human security of populations but also influence subjective perceptions concerning the threat they pose.

In the fields of migration and climate change, as mentioned previously, the European Union is developing a set of policies to address the challenges it faces. However, apart from the complexity of the European process itself, the Union today is beset by a range of major obstacles to better policymaking, ranging from internal political circumstances to the international political situation. Internally, the chief obstacle is found in the wave of populist movements and parties that, whether in government or in the opposition, object to those policies and hamper their evolution both domestically and at the European level. Internationally, the greatest obstacle is to be found in the emergence of and political support for great authoritarian or illiberal powers that attack and challenge multilateral institutions and the international liberal order, which the European Union perseveres in pursuing. One thing at least is certain: considering the sheer scope of these problems, the European Union will not be able to solve them on its own. A form of global governance is required.

Given the transnational, complex, and comprehensive nature of such threats to human security, no one should expect the answers to come from Europe alone. The response must necessarily be global, involving not only international cooperation between states but also the engagement of international organizations and NGOs and the empowerment of people themselves. What is needed, in short, is nothing less than the invention of a new kind of multilateralism.

Note

1 Several migration experts caution against using the term environmental "refugees" to underscore the forced nature of these movements (Martin 2010: 397).

References

Afionis, S. 2019. *The European Union in International Climate Change Negotiations*. London & New York: Routledge

Alkire, S. 2003. "A Conceptual Framework for Human Security." Working Paper No. 2. Centre for Research on Inequality, Human Security and Ethnicity, CRISE, Queen Elizabeth House, Oxford University

Anderson-Rogers, D. & K. Crawford. 2018. *Human Security: Theory and Action*. New York: Roman & Littlefield

Arango, J., C. Bonifazi, C. Finotelli, J. Peixoto, C. Sabino, S. Strozza, & A. Triandafyllidou. 2009. "The Making of an Immigration Model: Inflows, Impacts and Policies in Southern Europe." IDEA Working Paper No. 9. May

Burke, A., S. Fishel, A. Mitchell, S. Dalby, & D.J. Levine. 2016. "Planet Politics: A Manifesto from the End of IR." *Millennium: Journal of International Studies* 44(3): 499–523

Buzan, B., O. Weaver, & J. Wilde. 1998. *Security: A New Framework for Analysis*. Boulder, CO: Lynne Rienner Publishers

CAT. 2019a. "Pledged Action Leads to 2.9°C – Time to Boost National Climate Action." Available at https://climateactiontracker.org/publications/time-to-boost-national-climate-action/

CAT. 2019b. "EU: Fair Share." Available at https://climateactiontracker.org/countries/eu/fair-share/

CAT. 2019c. "EU: Country Summary." Available at https://climateactiontracker.org/countries/eu/

Copernicus. 2019. "European State of the Climate 2018: Summary." Available at https://climate.copernicus.eu/sites/default/files/2019-04/Brochure_Final_Interactive_1.pdf

Crutzen, P. & E. Stoermer. 2000. "The Anthropocene." *Global Change Newsletter* 41: 17

Cudworth, E. & S. Hobden. 2018. *The Emancipatory Project of Posthumanism*. Abingdon, UK & New York: Routledge

Dalby, S. 2017. "Anthropocene Formations: Environmental Security, Geopolitics, and Disaster." *Theory, Culture & Society* 34(2–3): 233–52

David, C. 2013. *La guerre et la paix. Approches et enjeux de la sécurité et de la stratégie*. Paris: Presses de Sciences Pos

Delbeke, J. & P. Vis. 2015. *EU Climate Policy Explained*. Abingdon, UK & New York: Routledge

Dryzek, J. & J. Pickering. 2018. *The Politics of the Anthropocene*. Oxford, UK: Oxford University Press

EEA. 2017. "Climate Change, Impacts and Vulnerability in Europe 2016." Report No. 1/2017. Luxembourg: Publications Office of the European Union

EEA. 2018a. "Infographic: Climate Change Impacts in Europe's Regions." Available at www.eea.europa.eu/signals/signals-2018-content-list/infographic/climate-change-impacts-in-europe/view

EEA. 2018b. "Total Greenhouse Gas Emission Trends and Projections." Available at www.eea.europa.eu/data-and-maps/indicators/greenhouse-gas-emission-trends-6/assessment-2

EHF. 2019. "The Implementation of the EU 2020 Biodiversity Strategy and Recommendations for the Post 2020 Biodiversity Strategy." Available at www.europarc.org/wp-content/uploads/2019/05/EHF-paper_Post-2020-EU-Biodiversity-Strategy_May2019.pdf

Emmers, R. 2010. "Securitization." In A. Collins (ed.), *Contemporary Security Studies*. Oxford, UK: Oxford University Press, pp. 136–51

European Commission. 2019a. "Special Eurobarometer Report: Climate Change." Available at https://ec.europa.eu/clima/sites/clima/files/support/docs/report_2019_en.pdf

European Commission. 2019b. "Public Opinion in the European Union." Available at https://ec.europa.eu/commfrontoffice/publicopinion/index.cfm/survey/getsurveydetail/instruments/standard/surveyky/2255

European Parliament. 2019. "European Policies on Climate and Energy Towards 2020, 2030 and 2050. Briefing." Available at www.europarl.europa.eu/RegData/etudes/BRIE/2019/631047/IPOL_BRI(2019)631047_EN.pdf

Evans, S. & J. Gabbatiss. 2019. "COP 25: Key Outcomes Agreed at the UN Climate Talks in Madrid." *Carbon Brief*. Available at www.carbonbrief.org/cop25-key-outcomes-agreed-at-the-un-climate-talks-in-madrid

Evans, S. & J. Timperley. 2018. "COP 24: Key Outcomes Agreed at the UN Climate Talks in Katowice." *Carbon Brief*. Available at www.carbonbrief.org/cop24-key-outcomes-agreed-at-the-un-climate-talks-in-katowice

Ferreira, S. 2016. "Orgulho e Preconceito. A resposta europeia à crise de refugiados." *Relações Internacionais* 50(June): 87–107

Ferreira, S. 2019. *Human Security and Migration in Europe's Southern Borders*. London: Palgrave Macmillan

Ferreira, S. & T. Rodrigues.2020. "El Mediterráneo: La Frontera Marítima a las Migraciones Irregulares." In I. Lirola & R. García Pérez (eds.), *Seguridad en el Mar*. Santiago: Universidad de Santiago de Compostela, pp. 114–47

Frontex. 2019. "Risk Analysis for 2019." Available at https://reliefweb.int/sites/reliefweb.int/files/resources/Risk_Analysis_for_2019_0.pdf

Frontex. 2020. "Frontex 2019 in Brief." Available at https://frontex.europa.eu/assets/Publications/General/frontex_inbrief_website_002.pdf

Fukuda-Parr, S. & C. Messineo. 2012. "Human Security: A Critical Review of the Literature." CRPD Working Paper No. 11

Geddes, A. 2003. "Still Beyond Fortress Europe? Patterns and Pathways in EU Migration Policy." In *Queens Papers on Europeanisation*. Belfast, UK: Queens University Belfast

Guiraudon, V. 2000. "European Integration and Migration Policy: Vertical Policy-making as Venue Shopping." *Journal of Common Market Studies* 38(2): 251–71

Höhne, N. & R. Tewari. 2018. "Paris Agreement Rulebook: Huge Achievement but Alone Grossly Insufficient." *New Climate Institute*. Available at https://newclimate.org/2018/12/18/paris-agreement-rulebook-huge-achievement-but-alone-grossly-insufficient/

Huysmans, J. 2000. "The European Union and the Securitization of Migration." *Journal of Common Market Studies* 38(5): 751–77

IOM. 2019. *World Migration Report 2020*. Geneva, Switzerland: IOM. Available at www.un.org/sites/un2.un.org/files/wmr_2020.pdf

IOM. 2020. "Missing Migrants Project." Available at https://missingmigrants.iom.int/region/mediterranean

IPCC. 2014. "Climate Change 2014: Impacts, Adaptation, and Vulnerability. Summary for Policymakers." Contribution of Working Group II to the Fifth Assessment Report of the Intergovernmental Panel on Climate Change. Geneva, Switzerland

IPCC. 2018. "Global Warming of 1.5°C: An IPCC Special Report on the Impacts of Global Warming of 1.5°C above Pre-industrial Levels and Related Global Greenhouse Gas Emission Pathways, in the Context of Strengthening the Global Response to the Threat of Climate Change, Sustainable Development, and Efforts to Eradicate Poverty. Summary for Policymakers." Geneva, Switzerland

Ireland, P. 1991. "Facing the True 'Fortress Europe': Immigrants and Politics in the EC." *Journal of Common Market Studies* 29(5): 457–80. doi:10.1111/j.1468-5965.1991.tb00403.x

Jiang, X., G. Peters, & C. Green. 2019. "Global Rules Mask the Mitigation Challenge Facing Developing Countries." *Earth's Future* 7(4): 428–32

Kaldor, Mary. 2011. "Human Security in Complex Operations." *PRISM* 2(2): 3–14

Kicinger, A. 2004. "International Migration as a Non-traditional Security Threat and the EU Responses to this Phenomenon." CEFMR Working Paper No. 2

Kofman, E. & R. Sales. 1992. "Towards Fortress Europe?" *Women's Studies International Forum* 15(1): 29–39

Lahav, G. & V. Guiraudon. 2007. "Actors and Venues in Immigration Control: Closing the Gap between Political Demands and Policy Outcomes." In V. Guiraudon & G. Lahav (eds.), *Immigration Policy in Europe: The Politics of Control*. Oxon, UK & New York: Routledge

Lavenex, S. & R. Kunz. 2008. "The Migration-Development Nexus in EU External Relations." *Journal of European Integration* 30(3): 439–57

Lazaridis, G. & K. Wadia (eds.). 2015. *The Securitization of Migration in the EU: Debates since 9/11*. New York: Palgrave Macmillan

Lewis, S., S. Perkins-Kirkpatrick, G. Althor, A. King, & L. Kemp. 2019. "Assessing Contributions of Major Emitters' Paris-Era Decisions to Future Temperatures Extremes." *Geophysical Research Letters* 46(7): 3936–43

Lutterbeck, D. 2006. "Policing Migration in the Mediterranean." *Mediterranean Politics* 11(1): 59–82. doi:10.1080/13629390500490411

Mabey, N., J. Gulledge, B. Finel, & K. Silverthorne. 2011. *Degrees of Risk: Defining a Risk Management Framework for Climate Security*. London, Washington, DC, & Brussels: E3G

MacFarlane, S. & Y. Khong. 2006. *Human Security and the UN: A Critical History*. Indianapolis, IN: Indiana University Press

Martin, S. 2010. "Climate Change, Migration and Governance." *Global Governance* 16: 397–414

McDonald, M. 2018. "Climate Change and Security: Towards Ecological Security?" *International Theory* 10(2): 153–80

Neuweg, I., P. Curran, & R. Byrnes. 2018. "Agreeing the Paris Rulebook: Did COP24 Deliver? Reflections from the Grantham Research Institute's Post-COP Event." *The London School of Economics and Political Science/Grantham Research Institute on Climate Change and the Environment*. Available at www.lse.ac.uk/GranthamInstitute/news/agreeing-the-paris-rulebook-did-cop24-deliver-reflections-from-the-grantham-research-institutes-post-cop-event/

Okolski, M. 2012. *European Immigrations: Trends, Structures, and Policy Implications*. Amsterdam, The Netherlands: Amsterdam University Press

Olivier, J. & J. Peters. 2018. *Trends in Global CO_2 and Total Greenhouse Gas Emissions: 2018 Report*. The Hague: PBL Netherlands Environmental Assessment Agency

Parker, C. & C. Karlsson. 2018. "EU Climate Leadership in Katowice Helped Deliver the Deal on the Paris Agreement Rulebook." *EUROPP – European Politics and Policy/The London School of Economics and Political Science*. Available at https://blogs.lse.ac.uk/europpblog/2018/12/20/eu-climate-leadership-in-katowice-helped-deliver-the-deal-on-the-paris-agreement-rulebook/

Parkin, J. 2013. "The Criminalisation of Migration in Europe. A State-of-the-Art of the Academic Literature and Research." *CEPS Paper in Liberty and Security in Europe* 61(October)

Pereira, J. & E. Viola. 2018. "Catastrophic Climate Change and Forest Tipping Points: Blind Spots in International Politics and Policy." *Global Policy* 9(4): 513–24

Pisarevskaya, A., N. Levy, P. Scholten, & J. Jansen. 2019. "Mapping Migration Studies: An Empirical Analysis of the Coming of Age of a Research Field." *Migration Studies* mnz031: 1–27. doi:10.1093/migration/mnz031

Shinoda, H. 2004. "The Concept of Human Security: Historical and Theoretical Implications." In *Conflict and Human Security: A Search for New Approaches of Peace Building*. Hiroshima: IPSHU English Research Report Series, pp. 5–22

Steffen, W., J. Rockström, K. Richardson, T. Lenton, C. Folke, D. Liverman, & H. Schellnhuber. 2018. "Trajectories of the Earth System in the Anthropocene." *Proceedings of the Natural Academy of Sciences of the United States of America* 115(33): 8252–59

Straubhaar, T. & K. Zimmermann. 1993. "Towards a European Migration Policy." *Population Research and Policy Review* 13(3): 225–41

UNDP & Climate Analytics 2016. *Pursuing the 1.5°C Limit: Benefits & Opportunities*. New York: United Nations Development Programme

Warren, R., J. Price, E. Graham, N. Forstenhaeusler, & J. VanDerWal. 2018. "The Projected Effect on Insects, Vertebrates, and Plants of Limiting Global Warming to 1.5°C Rather than 2°C." *Science* 360(6390): 791–95

WEF. 2020. "The Global Risks Report 2020." Available at http://www3.weforum.org/docs/WEF_Global_Risk_Report_2020.pdf

WMO. 2019. "The Global Climate in 2015–2019." Geneva. Available at https://library.wmo.int/index.php?lvl=notice_display&id=21522#.XZcaYlVKhhE

Wolfers, A. 1952. "'National Security' as an Ambiguous Symbol." *Political Science Quarterly* 67(4): 481–502

Wolff, S. 2015. "Migration and Refugee Governance in the Mediterranean: Europe and International Organisations at a Crossroads." *IAI Working Papers* 15(42) (October). Available at http://www3.weforum.org/docs/WEF_Global_Risk_Report_2020.pdf

WWF. 2019. "Protecting Our Ocean: Europe's Challenges to Meet the 2020 Deadlines. Report Summary." Available at http://d2ouvy59p0dg6k.cloudfront.net/downloads/protecting_our_ocean_summary.pdf

Zimmermann, K. 1995. "Tackling the European Migration Problem." *Journal of Economic Perspectives* 9(2): 45–62

# PART IV
Universalism versus relativism in protecting human rights

9

MULTIPLE MODERNITIES AND UNIVERSAL HUMAN RIGHTS

Thomas Meyer

This chapter will discuss the relationship between the concept of multiple modernities and the claim to universality inherent in human and civil rights ("basic rights") as set forth in UN declarations and treaties. As a preliminary step, let us note that the multiple modernities approach has both descriptive and normative aspects. The descriptive dimension is concerned with showing how a certain set of facts best can be understood and explained: namely, that in the current global processes of modernization we can observe significant cultural differences. In the normative dimension, something else is at stake: how responsible actors justify the paths of development that they have pioneered in their own cultural context on both the conceptual and practical levels. By "practical" I mean the internal justifications for political rule exercised over a given society. By "conceptual" I refer to justifications offered to those outside of that society for why the chosen path of development is legitimate in the framework of a global system consisting of different versions of modernization (Meyer 2018).

It is crucial to clarify one point here: to what extent does the notion of modernization contain an implicit normative claim, one that would prevent certain variants of societal development and political organization from presenting themselves as "modern" and using that claim to dismiss both internal and external critiques of their chosen path? When we talk about the normative criteria in the society in question, naturally we are referring primarily to the state's constitution and legal system as well as the role of civil society within it. In any case when a state joins the United Nations today – or for that matter any of its subsidiary organizations – it is in effect agreeing to the tacit premise that it will uphold the normative principles embedded in the UN's pacts and rules, which are at the heart of the charters and implementation controls of all such institutions. Since its founding, the UN has endeavored tirelessly to formulate a set of elementary norms that can be shared by all states, at least in principle, regardless of their specific cultural traditions and religious orientations. The initial effort to find a formula that expressed those norms was set forth in the 1948 Universal Declaration of Human Rights, which was subsequently expanded in 1966 to include a list of universal civil, political, social, and economic rights. In this much more detailed form, those rights were henceforth to be considered valid as binding statements of international law.

Finally, the fact that all UN member states hold joint debates on the goals and outcomes of their own policies implies that they assume their deliberations and actions will be based on a shared normative foundation that makes consensus and rational criticism possible. However, a very large number of states from all of the world's civilizations – ones displaying all levels of socio-economic development – have come under fire once again for ignoring or violating those rights. Because so many nations once had accepted this list of human and civil rights, it seemed as though a common normative foundation had been discovered, one that possessed timeless validity. But today this consensus appears to have been abandoned by a significant number of global actors based on claims concerning their own civilizational identities.

The controversy of the first decades

The descriptive dimension implicit in the claim to universal validity raised by the fundamental rights codified by the UN in 1948 and 1966 always has been underpinned by two important facts. One is that individuals from various civilizations and/or religious-cultural tradition around the world were involved in formulating the relevant texts. The other – most recently and impressively corroborated at the Vienna Human Rights Conference of 1993 – is that within every civilization there are civil society groups that now vociferously advocate for the universal validity of the human rights codified by the UN. Acting from within their own societies and cultural contexts, they militantly reject every attempt by their governments to relativize the validity of those rights in the name of their special cultural traditions. To cite an example, that point was given emphatic expression at the Vienna Human Rights Conference, when representatives of the Malaysian government cited identity issues – its cultural tradition of "Asian values" – as a defense against the validity of some of the fundamental rights. But subsequently a well-organized contingent from their own country criticized them sharply for that very position. On its face this story shows that the *internal homogeneity of civilizational identities presumed by many actors is highly questionable.*

More recently, an equally indisputable fact has been dragged into the campaign against the claim to universality raised by fundamental rights: namely, the clear origins of the entire semantics of the system of meanings surrounding human rights in the "Western tradition" and the derivation of its key categories from that same tradition. This fact had dominated both the institutional and non-institutional debates over the universality of human rights (Joas 2013) during the Cold War era, up to and including the early 1970s. But back then the semantic coding did not involve cultural categories; instead, it pitted the political ideologies of the opposing parties against one another. The "ideological West" was ranged against the "ideological East": that is, those from the Soviet bloc who argued in Marxist-Leninist terms plus trade unionists defending social-democratic positions versus those from the bloc led by the US, who invoked liberal democratic norms.

From the initial deliberations about the UN Human Rights Charter of 1948 up to the approval of the UN Covenants of 1966, the institutional debates about what fundamental rights are and why they are valid were pervaded by a single controversy, which concerned the relative ranking of and relationship between civil-political rights on the one hand and socio-economic rights on the other (Sieghart 1983; Tomuschat 2008; Moyn 2010). The Soviet side insisted that the majority of people would be unable to make much practical use of civil and political rights until socio-economic rights were given full real-world effect for all. The Western bloc, by contrast, insisted that civil-political rights ought to have priority; indeed, some of its representatives (the self-styled "libertarians") expressed doubts about whether economic and social rights could claim to be universal fundamental rights at all. The Western side vehemently defended the independent validity of "liberal" human rights. Representatives of the Soviet-communist bloc as well as social democratic actors from the international trade unions of that era who were engaged in the debate countered that socio-economic human rights possessed independent validity, because they affect the real lives of all people and determine to what degree individuals can actualize their civil-political rights. Besides, they pointed out, sometimes a "relativizing" of fundamental political rights might be necessary in order for the political leadership to carry out the policies that would make social rights a reality for most citizens.

But amid all the controversy, a strong third force emerged that ultimately proved decisive in the effort to upgrade human rights by incorporating them into treaties valid under international law, such as the Covenant of 1966. This was the International Labour Organization (ILO), founded in 1919. The ILO defended a social democratic line of thinking, which ultimately prevailed against the one-sided, doctrinaire arguments of the Cold War antagonists. As an offshoot of the UN, it assumed a leadership role in defining and elaborating social rights and had an influential voice in formulating the entire text. Because of its work, the Covenant represents a unique synthesis between what were then taken to be the antithetical ideologies of the political opponents East and West. It is composed of three sections. The social democratic ideas of human dignity and freedom undergird the preamble, which sets forth that idea with unrivaled clarity and welds the next two parts together. Individuals are free only if, in addition to enjoying legal protection for a space of personal self-determination (negative freedom), they have a legal claim to the material resources needed to realize the potential implicit in that freedom (positive liberty): for example, work, income security, education, health care, and so on. Part II of the Covenant lists the fundamental liberal rights, while Part I lays out their socio-economic counterparts. Both parts would have to be ratified separately. As noted earlier, the US refused to ratify Part I, arguing that it did not even recognize such a thing as fundamental social rights (although Franklin

Roosevelt had enumerated two of them in his famous "Four Freedoms" speech of 1941). In 1997–98, China signed both parts but ratified only Part I, indicating that "civil rights" would be ratified when the country's level of development permitted it. Thus, the 1966 UN Covenant terminated the crucial controversy of the ideological cold war with a fragile historical compromise.

The new challenge

Although Samuel Huntington's theory that the clash of ideologies that characterized the twentieth century will be replaced by an equally fierce clash of civilizations in the twenty-first is flawed due to his naturalistic conception of culture, he does get one thing right (Huntington 1996). The global dominance of the grand political and ideological conflicts of the Cold War and the semantics of its basic conceptual apparatus focused our political and intellectual attention almost exclusively on the systemic political and economic antithesis between capitalism on the one side and communism or socialism on the other. As a result, there was no room to give due weight to the socio-cultural dimension. In this phase of modern history, the true purpose of human rights – the creation of a society committed to human dignity – seemed to be determined so completely by the economic and social order that the cultural perspective appeared superfluous and self-liquidating. This state of affairs gradually began to change when the Soviet Union disappeared from the world stage. But that shift did not follow the script laid down by Huntington's clash of civilizations theory; instead, *a new pattern emerged, consisting of a multiplicity of cooperating civilizations*. Some observers and actors started to reformulate the question of whether the fundamental rights granted by the UN documents actually do full justice to the normative cultural circumstances prevailing in all the world's increasingly self-confident civilizations. Because of the uncompromising critique of systematic human rights violations in China and some other non-Western countries proffered by the US, which was perceived as little more than power politics in disguise, the historic UN Basic Rights compromise of 1966 grew fragile. The 1960s-era debate over whether such rights are universal, suspended ever since those years, has reemerged in a new frame. Given the current global situation, it would be highly advisable even for those who still want to take their cues from the fundamental rights spelled out in the UN documents to participate with an open mind and serious intent in the call for a renewed dialogue (Kocka 2018).

The optimal starting point for such a renewed dialogue is the debate over "multiple modernities," which has been underway ever since the latest wave of globalization began. In principle, this set of ideas assumes that both the long-term cultural hegemony of the West and classic modernization theory have come to an end. In order to build a stable basis for peace and multilateral cooperation under these new conditions, we must recognize that the great civilizations of the world are of equal rank; therefore, the challenge is to embark upon a shared effort to identify the features and norms that all of them might (and wish to) have in common. The concept of multiple modernities cannot and does not stipulate anything approaching the unalloyed cultural relativism that characterizes Huntington's view. Instead, it assumes a common core of all the different types of modernity. Eisenstadt's proposal for the definition of such a core has been widely accepted in the debates surrounding his theory. The key difference between modernism and traditionalism (here he follows Max Weber) is that the former is based on "the conception of human agency and of its place in the flow of time" (Eisenstadt 2000: 3). Modernism embraces an idea of the future as characterized by a number of alternatives realizable through *autonomous human agency* – the principle of "subjectivism." The ideas on which the social, ontological, and political order are grounded, and the legitimation of those ideas, are no longer taken for granted as "objective" or given. A new "reflexivity [has] developed around the basic ontological premises of the structures of social and political authority" (Eisenstadt 2000: 3).

Thus, from the multiple modernities approach, we learn that modern cultures do have a common core in the principle of subjectivity or self-determination, even though there may be a broad variety of related values and institutional expressions of this core. In the terminology of Richard Münch's modernization theory, it can be understood as the culturally neutral *logic of modernization* (Münch 2001), which includes very general principles of rationalism (reflexivity), secularism (separation of church and state), individualism (human agency), and universalism (all arguments address a potentially global community of interlocutors). It seems obvious that the process of implementing the same logic of modernization in the culturally variable settings of the different civilizations (the dynamics of modernization) will be conducive to different results depending on its tempo, the cultures in question, the historical and social conditions of each country in which the process of modernization plays out, and the point in time at which we observe it. Thus, Japanese, Chinese, American, Russian, Iranian, South African, French, and British modernization all will be and will remain different. Yet, it is also clear that none of the differences among them can be justified tautologically on the grounds that they are simply different. These differences must be *accessible to justification in terms of modernity*.

In that sense, a certain degree of internal pluralism in each culture with respect to these justifications is in itself part of the inexorable logic of modernization. In order to ascertain whether such a connection with the logic of modernization really exists, it makes sense, at any particular moment, to ask: is the level of modernization that has been attained so far in a given country relatively permanent, at least as judged by the relevant local actors, and is it mainly due to the cultural conditions in that country? Or is it temporary (again according to relevant authorities) and mainly due to a lack of time and/or resources? The answer to this question matters tremendously with regard to the human rights issue and suggests questions for further research.

To forestall serious confusion, we need to make it clear at this point that the model of multiple modernities by no means entails an essentialist notion of culture. The idea of a clash of civilizations and its justification by reference to static fault lines running between the basic values of the contending civilizations presupposes that cultural contexts can be treated as though they were natural phenomena incapable of any real change and internal differentiation. By contrast, the Eisenstadt/Münch model – referred to in this context – is both dynamic and open. Yet, we must go further still, treating culture under conditions of globalization (really even before that) as a *dynamic social space of discourse and competition shaped by contradictions, in which competing actors contend to interpret and pass on tradition in light of their accumulated experiences and existing social conditions*. What decides which version of tradition will be handed down is not the content of that tradition itself but instead the balance of forces among the competing elites charged with interpreting and reconstructing it. The resulting body of tradition that such coalitions of hegemonic actors succeed in getting accepted thus is always provisional. It is constantly being questioned by major or minor actors who present more or less drastic alternatives and, in various ways, try to win acceptance for their own versions. Even when it seems as though an entire society is clinging rigidly and dogmatically to certain cultural legacies, closer examination shows that its elites are involved in a constant defensive struggle against a range of conceivable alternatives offered by those with an interest in challenging prevailing schemes.

Unquestionably, when the defenders of tradition in a given cultural sphere come out on top – as is often the case – their success bespeaks a high degree of concordance between their version of tradition and the lived experience of the society, for otherwise the tensions between the latter and the claims of traditionalists would become untenable over the long run. In addition, both globalized channels of communication and changing lifeways in the society in question inevitably will cause traditions to mutate, even though this process may happen at an almost subliminal level. Here it is worth recalling the findings of political culture research between the 1950s and 1990s. They indicate that, when a significant gap arises between political culture and political institutions, the usual outcome is either institutional change that reestablishes a rough equilibrium or else a chronic crisis (Almond & Verba 1963). Even though the state or other (religious or societal) actors possessing extensive power resources can exert a degree of control over such phenomena (cultural change or stagnation), they cannot create or prevent them. It follows that, as a rule, elites will have some prospect of success in invoking traditional versions of their cultural legacy to legitimize their status only when they can count on *broad social resonance*. Obviously, this endeavor will turn out best if and when their procedures and outcomes dovetail nicely with traditionalist patterns of legitimation, especially when everyone can see that they have durably satisfied the most crucial and even some of the higher-order needs of the governed, as compared to the past and to the achievements of other countries.

The antipode of the essentialist misunderstanding of culture is the nihilist error, one that is perhaps even more problematic in its social and political repercussions. We encounter it whenever people assume that cultures are reducible to the cognitive outcomes of current political discourses. Thus – so the nihilist assumption runs – however those public debates over a culture's meaning turn out, its broad outlines are susceptible to being changed almost overnight. When one thinks of culture in this way, one loses sight of the deeper social and emotional dimensions that give it staying power. Those dimensions unceasingly are reproduced and reinforced in processes of individual socialization, the entire system of societal institutions, and the rituals and practices of everyday life. The result of the nihilist confusion is a kind of radical constructivism incapable of recognizing that real social constructivism always works with given, traditional materials. They cannot be invented ex nihilo; cultures are social facts of "longue durée" (Fernand Braudel).

As we have seen, Eisenstadt's idea that all forms of modernity share a common core underscores the principle of subjectivism or reflexivity. By those terms he means "the autonomous participation of members of society in the constitution of the social and political order, or the autonomous access of all members of the society to these orders and to their center" (Eisenstadt 2000: 5). The process of gradual modernization is shaped by the specific cultural context in question and can be measured in degrees of "more" or "less." The multiple modernities approach still would entail, among other things, the acceptance and institutionalization (in some form) of social and political pluralism and participation both at the level of debate about the common good and at the level of political decision-making. However, the core demands of modern politics might assume a variety of institutional forms. They could vary along several axes: the prevailing historical situation, the requirement that basic order be maintained, and respect for divergences in cultures and traditions.

The Western genesis

The challenge of a new dialogue on fundamental rights among several civilizations is to determine whether the justification for and the content of the concept of human dignity and the rights that protect it can *be reformulated as well in terms that originate in traditions other than those of the West*. An affirmative answer appears more probable than not. At any rate, it cannot be denied that the genesis of the notion of human rights as underlying the UN Declarations was first given expression in the West. Sometimes it is dated all the way back to antiquity, but in its modern form it was not explicitly elaborated until the early stages of the European Renaissance. In that project, two internally linked lines of argument play an especially prominent role. The first, developed by Pico Della Mirandola in 1486, is the notion of human dignity that every member of the species enjoys by nature (Burckhardt 1990). This is an argument that can be traced back as far as an important ancient Greek tradition (the stoa). The second element is the Kantian idea that all human beings have the inalienable right to lead autonomous lives, based on the essential capacity to make use of their own reason to legislate for themselves.

This represents a radical break with the previously regnant culture of Christian traditionalism (the dominant "Western" tradition for many centuries), in which "the universal" (i.e., the general essence or notion) always had both temporal and ontological priority over the particular or the individual, which was understood to be merely accidental. The political order and metaphysical-religious truths confronted individual thought and action as objective, taken-for-granted powers. The Church and the Christian theology that it controlled proclaimed and administered this "realist" metaphysics. The Renaissance, with its apotheosis of the individual, was the response to the decay of Christian doctrine and its ontological underpinnings (Burckhardt 1990; Joas 2013). By the twelfth century, medieval essentialism, in which universal essences were objectively given ante rem (in God's thoughts), in re (in the individual things), and post rem (in human thought), gradually had given way to "nominalist" ontology. The classical expression of the latter theory can be found in Kant's epistemology and practical philosophy and in the theories of the social contract between isolated individuals as the founding act of human society.

The nominalism of the post-metaphysical modern age recognizes only the particular, the individual, as a really existing entity. Hence, any attempt to establish connections among the bewildering multiplicity of individual things (or persons) can be nothing more than an uncertain construct of human cognition or will. This notion has consequences for the common life of human individuals in the state and society: no one but the individuals themselves can be the source of the claims that bind them. In this way, individuals acquire an *absolute dignity* as well as the right to legislate for themselves, both in their capacity as human beings leading their own private lives and as citizens of a state. It was this "apotheosis of the individual," according to Émile Durkheim (Lukes 1990; Joas 2013), that almost inevitably gave rise to the ideas of individual human and civil rights. The individual person, then, is the final court of appeals and the only credible source of justification for whatever allegedly valid claims might by levied upon the lives, including the common lives, of human beings. In the West, human rights laid out the conditions that have to be met in order to secure the dignity of the individual in specific cases. When it comes to the ordering of the common lives of individuals in the state, civil rights perform this same function. In short, the idea of the universality of human rights, as it arose in the West, derives its claim to universal validity from the general principles and the philosophy cited above.

No doubt, the dominant Asian philosophies up to now never shared this ontology and social philosophy (Cauqulin et al. 2013). Instead they always maintained varieties of *communalist theories* in which the individual is and remains embedded in a hierarchy of primordial communities from the cradle to the grave. In the teachings of Confucius, the social order is constituted by a factual and moral reciprocity of obligations and rights that gives the individual protection and rights that are related to the fulfillment of a complex set of obligations. The notion of a Robinson Crusoe–like individual as the basis for community, society, and ultimately for individual rights within the state is a peculiar feature of Western modernization that is not shared by the other great civilizations.

Still, once modernization begins, the ideas of an objectively valid order of things and of the commonwealth in all civilizations gradually gives way to the idea of human agency based on reflexivity. In place of self-evidently valid traditions, the notion takes hold that reasons must be given for decisions about whether and how traditions ought to be continued. And the only authorities with a justified claim to be able to make such decisions are the individuals who will be affected by them. This remains the case even when collective authorities are entrusted with the interpretation and reconstruction of the tradition. But what must remain unsettled at this point are the tempo and the radicalism with which the energizing principles of the logic of modernity will be introduced and carried through. And here, the principle of individualization proves to be the most culturally delicate and disputed one. A variety of actors and thinkers in the West, including former German Chancellor Helmut Schmidt (Schmidt et al. 1997), insist that the notions of community and individual obligations should not be excluded from the discussion of human rights.

Today, the most authoritative sources for the claims to universal validity raised by human and civil rights, the various UN Declarations and Contracts, though spearheaded by the West, appeal successfully for their endorsement to the world community beyond all civilizational boundaries. For some decades, their success in getting these rights accepted rested upon certain prerequisites, especially the negative experience with absolute dictatorships in both East and West, which gave a powerful impetus to the idea of rights and the expectations of Third World countries – desperate to rid themselves of their Western colonial "masters" (many shaped by entirely different civilizations) – that the universality of human rights might offer them leverage or "soft power" in their quest for liberation. As emphasized above, in the historical moment of the creation of the UN Human Rights Documents, the dispute between the political West and East was not about the universality of basic rights as such but about which basic rights should be included. By and large, cultural issues did not matter much, with the sole but troubling exception of Saudi Arabia's Islamism, which led that country to withhold its signature. But now it seems that the original ideological conflicts between the political East and West have resurfaced, this time transformed into a *conflict about culture and development*. With respect to the classic UN documents on human rights, Tom O'Connor concludes:

> By emphasizing the rights of individuals, the Declaration was meant as an attempt to transcend cultural bias in such a way that it became relevant to all, no matter what their upbringing. By protecting individuals, human rights do not diminish the group, but merely ensure the protection of every individual within it. And in addition, culture is not static, but constantly evolving as people come in contact with new ideas and concepts. Because some cultures do not emphasize certain rights at the moment, does not mean that will always be the case.
>
> *(O'Connor 2014)*

The evolutionary premises implicit in the above citation dovetailed nicely with the theory of modernization that was widely accepted at that time in many parts of the world, and not merely in the West. It was even the hope of such influential Third World leaders as Jawaharlal Nehru. But the times in which the modernization model of the West was widely accepted as a blueprint for the rest seem to be over. Non-Western models of modernization like that of the People's Republic of China (PRC) and others claim full recognition for their own civilizational identity and their understanding of basic rights. One of the disputed issues is again: do the civil and political rights we regard as fundamental possess an independent use-value as means of making *freedom for all* possible? Or do they acquire such a value only when the socio-economic rights are given real-world effect at the same time, and the *communal obligations* of the individual also are taken into consideration?

The divide within the West

The claims to universal validity implicitly raised by the theory of fundamental rights have proved controversial enough to provoke two splits, one of which has played out even within the politics and the political culture of the West itself while the other has divided the cultural West from parts of the cultural East (Meyer 2007, 2018).

As is made explicit in the UN Covenant, modern democracy is not equivalent to free elections; instead, it also presupposes the guarantee of the full set of individual basic rights granted by international law (Riedel et al. 2014). The philosophy of the UN Covenant (not merely its "Declaration") draws upon the twentieth-century experience that, under the conditions of negative freedom alone, the claims of democracy and of genuine human freedom cannot be satisfied at the same time. Rather, tremendous social and economic inequalities may begin to engender relations of social and economic dependency. The latter may violate the dignity of dependent individuals by undermining their life chances and social autonomy. In other words, the sphere of social action is treated by proponents of a negative-liberty approach as neutral ground in which the validity claims of universal fundamental rights are to be suspended. In addition, the exclusion of the social sphere from coverage by basic rights tends to abrogate the claims to private autonomy of those who, qua economic agents, have fallen into a state of dependency, depriving them of their power to act and putting them at the mercy of third parties in ways that universal rights should not tolerate. Furthermore, social, economic, and educational inequalities of a certain magnitude prevent those affected by them from making full use of their political or civil rights; they become in real terms politically "excluded." In short, people's actual socio-economic or cultural circumstances can influence and even shape the political process in myriad ways. Glaring social and economic inequalities always translate into severe political inequalities (Dahl 2006).

The political exclusion argument maintains that libertarianism, by permitting extreme inequalities, individual deficits in education and personal development, and relations of dependency, ends up denying equal civil and political rights to large social groups, thereby vitiating their political autonomy and the political equality required by democratic norms. As Thomas H. Marshall puts it:

> the right to freedom of speech has little real substance if, from lack of education, you have nothing to say that is worth saying, and no means of making

yourself heard if you say it. But these blatant inequalities are not due to defects in civil rights, but to lack of social rights.

(Marshall 1964: 88)

It was Marshall who developed the concepts of "social citizenship" underlying the UN's 1966 Covenant, which were meant to prevent those kinds of situations from happening. In Marshall's terminology we might say that control over the social means of securing fundamental rights needs to become just as universal as the validity of the rights themselves. Consequentially, the UN Covenant enacts five categories of basic rights and declares them to be of equal value, mutually supportive, and limiting: civil, political, cultural, social, and economic.

In this context of international law, two opposing varieties of democracy are competing in the West and other parts of the world for intellectual and political dominance: libertarian democracy and social democracy. Although both claim to be appropriate strategies for the institutional implementation of individual freedom and social justice, they contradict each other in relevant options beyond certain minimum prerequisites for liberal democratic institutions. Thus, they represent alternative ways of rendering the principles of fundamental rights relevant and meaningful in social, economic, cultural, and political life.

Libertarian democracy is, from the scholarly point of view, characterized by its acceptance of the civil and political rights alone, accompanied by rejection of the fundamental social and economic rights set forth in the UN Covenant. According to this conception, in a constitution that guarantees freedom, the political institutions of liberal democracy must be complemented by two socio-economic arrangements: a free-market economy and the free ownership of the means of production, which together are understood as the "societal constitution of liberty." The rest is left to the discretion and efforts of individual citizens pursuing their own social and economic well-being (Hayek 2001; Nozick 1974). That is in fact the origin of the notion "libertarian."

Arguments that the government should assume overall responsibility for modifying social structures, guaranteeing a sufficient level of free education and social benefits, regulating und influencing the economy with the objective of full employment, and conducting redistributive policies to achieve the basic values of freedom and justice for the less affluent are branded by libertarians as illegitimate meddling by the state in citizens' private sphere of liberty. According to advocates of libertarian democracy, then, civil rights and democratic freedom of choice in political life have equivalents in the realm of social and economic life as well, namely, freedom of ownership, private autonomy, private contracts, and the self-regulating market. Those who defend this conception of democracy do not believe that it requires a high level of societal inclusion to be underwritten by significant social and economic equality. Consequently, where libertarian democracy is instituted, it typically gives rise to rampant inequality, severe disparities of educational opportunity, and a lack of social protection, all of which promote substantial social and political exclusion.

Social democracy was the historical answer to the exclusionary consequences of libertarian democracy in Europe's core countries. Because such outcomes were seen as unacceptable, practically all European societies since the middle of the nineteenth century have developed social democracy as a political alternative. Social democracy soon attracted mass support and gradually acquired cultural dominance. The term itself was coined in the early 1920s by the German political scientist Hermann Heller, whose idea of a material/substantive rule of law instead of a merely formal rule of law anticipated both the concept of social citizenship and that of basic social and economic rights in the sense of the UN Covenant.

Nowadays, social democracy is not simply a scheme for overcoming the weaknesses and flaws of libertarian democracy; rather, it is a normative model and – at least to some extent – also a reality in a variety of European countries and the European Union as well. This model has become part of the political culture of Europe, particularly since World War II and the experience of the world economic crises of the 1920s and 1930s, both of which paved the way for that cataclysm.

The most essential component of social democracy is a rights-based, comprehensive welfare state grounded upon citizenship as the general source of social entitlements. The state offers social protection against risks that violate its citizens' basic rights; guarantees equal educational opportunities, not only for acquiring skills but also for partaking in broader cultural life; and safeguards human dignity in economic and social contexts. The social welfare state acts as a kind of shock absorber, damping down the insecurities generated by market capitalism by underwriting state-sponsored security guarantees that are independent of the market. It provides a minimum income to individuals and families while offering effective protection against sickness, poverty, and unemployment. Moreover, it provides a range of social services such as child supervision and care for the aged. The main aim of the comprehensive welfare state is to guarantee the full societal inclusion of all citizens, and thus their ability to act as free and equal democratic citizens across the board. This is exactly what the social and economic rights of the 1966 UN covenant enjoin.

To summarize, the libertarian democrats in the West, some of whom dominate political culture and political life in their countries, deny the universality of no less than half of the basic rights chartered by the UN Covenant. But currently, this problem is little discussed in the global arena.

Universality reconsidered

In the last few decades, as pointed out above, a growing number of politicians and political intellectuals from the main cultures of Asia have put forward a far more principled counterargument against the claims to universality implicit in the fundamental rights recognized by the UN. Undoubtedly, the frequent and massive attacks made by certain Western countries – with the US at the forefront – on human rights violations in non-Western societies have provoked this defensive reaction. The PRC often has borne the brunt of such attacks. The problem with pillorying these countries for rights violations is not that such attacks are generally unjustified. Rather, they are often blatantly one-sided and ignorant of circumstances and context. Moreover, they are not normally accompanied by any offer of dialogue; instead, they carry undertones of superiority or hostility. It is usually obvious that these broadsides smack of power politics, as they are intended to weaken the target of the vitriol. What is more, such criticisms often are clearly based on a moral double standard. That is especially true of the US, which manages to torture prisoners in Guantanamo Bay while harshly criticizing China for incarcerating or mistreating prisoners. The accustomed ritual frequently follows a logic that powerfully idealizes (or simply ignores) the domestic human rights situation, especially where the full granting and enforcement of political and social rights are concerned, while casting the deficiencies of the other countries it has attacked in the bleakest possible light. What worsens the situation is the fact, noted above, that the US denies the legal validity of the social and economic basic values, whereas Chinese consider those very values the pillars of their conception of human rights.

None of this should be taken to imply that human rights violations should not be subjected to trenchant critiques, only that the latter will lack credibility or efficacy unless they contain a minimum of fairness, mutuality, and realism. At any rate, this state of affairs has contributed to an unfortunate trend: The voices of non-Western political and intellectual actors who seek to "relativize" or dismiss the whole UN human rights project as an expression of Western particularism are being multiplied and amplified. But here we must draw some distinctions. It matters what kind of relativizing is being advocated in each specific case. The UN system of fundamental rights does in fact leave room for several forms of relativization. Thus, for example, in regard to the distinction between liberal and social rights, the legal principle of equal validity remains in effect, but the two concepts are distinguished in the following way: social rights impose *obligations of conduct* (implementation according to available resources), while liberal rights impose *obligations of result* (immediate and full implementation). In respect to human and liberal civil rights a distinction is also drawn between *derogable* and *non-derogable* rights, which leaves quite a bit of leeway for justified restrictions and postponements, as noted by a committee of experts in Netherlands' foreign ministry.

In 1998, that committee came to the following conclusions:

> Since abstractly phrased international human rights norms have to be applied in a variety of social, economic and cultural contexts, states have a certain degree of latitude in making policy. . . . We need a more moderate relativist standpoint which calls for tolerance of differences in the specific implementation of human rights. . . . The importance of implementing the right completely must always be weighed against other significant interests of society. . . . Universality does not mean uniformity.
> *(Advisory Council on International Affairs 1998: 14)*

After ratifying Part I of the Covenant, the PRC signed more than 20 agreements that deal with human rights. In addition, the PRC engages in long-term "human rights dialogues" with partners such as the EU and the Federal Republic of Germany. Yet, so far it has not ratified Part II of the Covenant, which emphasizes civil and political rights. Instead, the Chinese side seems to have offered three distinct arguments in the interim.

Initially, they justified their reluctance to must ratify the entire Covenant on the grounds that the country would attain greater social and political stability by prioritizing economic development. Therefore, in cases of doubt, social and economic basic rights must be given priority over civil and political basic rights. This justification seemed somewhat plausible in view of the still-widespread poverty, the long history of destabilization and repeated civil wars, and the tremendous internal diversity and complexity of such a vast empire. Implicitly, it granted full recognition to the claims to universal validity of the UN's human rights accords and spawned international dialogue concerning the exact nature of the problems China faced, the arguments the country had been presenting, and the possible scenarios under which China might ratify the full accord. On this basis it was possible to carry on a variety of human rights dialogues while keeping them consensus-oriented and reasonable.

Then came a decisive pivot away from acknowledging the universality of the UN documents. The Chinese government began to advance a claim, rooted in both culture and the imperatives of development, that it was entitled to pick and choose among human rights. This step is equivalent to establishing a human rights hierarchy, a move that is inherently neither wrong nor a subterfuge to abandon the terrain of universality that is necessary to carry on a dialogue. Both lines of argument can be understood as steps to grant the context-specific latitude called for by the Dutch committee. As we recall, the committee proposed that human rights be applied in ways consistent with each country's specific circumstances. Countries would then be expected to justify their rules of application before the UN's standing committees and the public, where they would come under scrutiny.

In recent years, a third argument has been superimposed on the first two sketched out above, without it being made clear whether the new arguments are supposed to replace the old ones completely. In "Party Document number 9" from 2012, which since has been made public, the leadership of the Communist Party of China (CPC) tells official institutions or persons with official functions to avoid, as a matter of principle, the use of terms like "universal human rights." The conception of "Chinese characteristics," which long has been applied to the Chinese variant of socialism and the country's program of modernization, now is evidently supposed to define the semantic field of human and civil rights as well. Individual authors usually refer in this context to the Confucian tradition and the concepts of *tian xia* ("all under heaven") and harmony. It is frequently argued that this traditionalist framework enables people to gain a more precise understanding about which relationships among the individual, the community, the society, and the state are best suited to Chinese conditions, and that it is in its own way an equivalent to the "Western" concepts of basic rights (Tao 2018). Above all, it is said, this frame of reference allows us to define with greater completeness and precision the mutual relations between rights and duties for every person.

Meanwhile, the Chinese constitution continues to guarantee human rights, and the PRC goes on to cosign many UN documents on human rights. However, questions arise from the official statement that norms and regulations written in the constitution must be read in the light of the so-called Four Cardinal Principles: upholding the socialist path; upholding the people's democratic dictatorship; upholding the leadership of the CPC; and upholding Mao Zedong's thought and Marxism-Leninism. Is this position still in tune with the earlier premise calling for a notion of human rights that would include social and economic rights as well as regard for the cultural, economic, and political conditions of each country? Inevitably, the question arises: how does the leadership imagine the exact relationship between universal basic rights and particularistic "Chinese values"? Do they have in mind an effort to integrate the former semantically and via interpretation into the latter, hoping to leave behind the current state of affairs in which the space of human rights has been distorted for polemical purposes and weaponized for political ends? Or do they want to turn away from the whole idea of universalism, which is supposed to transcend civilizational boundaries? It is worthwhile to mention in this context that Russian President Vladimir Putin follows a different line of argument in his public statements. While not completely denying the validity of the "Western values" of liberal democracy and human rights, he complains that they are implemented in the West in an exaggerated manner, which Russia does not intend to follow. This strategy deserves its own debate in a new dialogue on human rights.

A new dialogue?

The participants in any such multi-civilizational dialogue would have to address a couple of open questions, including the ones raised above. Obviously, a country's achievement of just a certain degree of one or both categories of rights poses a challenge for how to evaluate that accomplishment in the light of the universalistic claims discussed above. It is important to understand that the mere existence of a set of institutions neither constitutes not guarantees the realization of human rights. Moreover, the absence of the classical set of Western political institutions is not tantamount to the principled denial of human rights. The dawning awareness of multiple modernities suggests the possibility of a dialogue that might bridge the widening gap between rhetoric and reality and offer all involved parties the chance to account for the cultural connotations of their actual understanding and handling of human rights. Even if such conversations might not result in changes in the texts of valid UN documents, they would most probably build trust by allowing each interlocutor to understand everyone else's real viewpoint.

The aim of any new dialogue on human rights should not be to relativize human rights or diminish the importance of the relevant documents of the UN generally; rather it should to help establish credible links between them and the present world of multiple modernities. It could help to forge a clearer consensus regarding the absolute nature of the non-derogable human rights and the degree of latitude of the derogable rights for which a credible account can be given, one that ideally could be accepted by all. Likewise, dialogue could enhance the understanding of the ways in which fundamental rights are embedded in diverse cultural traditions. And finally, dialogue could strengthen the commitment of all participant to the fulfillment of the core rights that do not allow for much – if any – leeway for cultural variations.

References

Advisory Council on International Affairs. Ministry of Foreign Affairs of The Netherlands. 1998. *Universality of Human Rights and Cultural Diversity*. The Hague: Advisory Council on International Affairs

Almond, G. & S. Verba. 1963. *The Civic Culture: Political Attitudes and Democracy in Five Nations*. Princeton, NJ: Princeton University Press

Braudel, F. 1993. *A History of Civilizations*. New York: Penguin Books

Buergenthal, T. 2009. "The U.N. Human Rights Committee." *Max Planck Yearbook of United Nations* 5: 341–98

Burckhardt, J. 1990. *The Civilization of the Renaissance in Italy*. London: Penguin Books

Cauqulin, J., P. Lim, & B. Mayer-König (eds.). 2013. *Asian Values: An Encounter with Diversity*. London: Routledge

Dahl, R. 2006. *On Political Equality*. New Haven, CT: Yale University Press

Eisenstadt, S. 2000. "Multiple Modernities." *Daedalus* 129(1): 1–29

Hayek, F. 2001. *The Road to Serfdom*. London & New York: Routledge

Huntington, S. 1996. *The Clash of Civilizations and the Remaking of World Order*. New York, NY: Simon & Schuster

Joas, H. 2013: *The Sacredness of the Person: A Genealogy of Human Rights*. Washington, DC: Georgetown University Press

Kocka, J. 2018. "Plural Modernity and Negotiated Universals." In T. Meyer & J. de Sales Marques (eds.), *Multiple Modernities and Good Governance*. Abingdon, UK: Routledge, pp. 161–67

Lukes, S. 1990. *Emile Durkheim: His Life and Work*. Stanford, CA: Stanford University Press

Marshall, T. H. 1964. *Class, Citizenship and Social Development*. Garden City, NY: Doubleday

Meyer, T. 2007. *The Theory of Social Democracy*. Oxford: Polity Press

Meyer, T. 2018. "Multiple Modernities and Good Governance." In T. Meyer & J. de Sales Marques (eds.), *Multiple Modernities and Good Governance*. Abingdon, UK: Routledge, pp. 15–29

Moyn, S. 2010. *The Last Utopia: Human Rights in History*. Cambridge, MA & London: The Belknap Press of Harvard University Press

Münch, R. 2001. *The Ethics of Modernization*. Lanham, MD: Rowman & Littlefield

Nozick, R. 1974. *Anarchy, State and Utopia*. New York: Basic Books

O'Connor, T. 2014. "Human Rights Universal or Relative to Culture." Internet blog, February 11. Available at https://developmenteducation.ie/blog/2014/02/debating-human-rights-universal-or-relative-to-culture

Riedel, E., G. Giacca, & C. Golay. 2014. *Economic, Social, and Cultural Rights in International Law: Contemporary Issues and Challenges*. Oxford, UK: Oxford University Press

Schmidt, H. et al. 1997. "Universal Declaration of Human Responsibilities." Interaction Council. Available at https://en.wikisource.org/wiki/Declaration of Human Responsibilities

Sieghart, P. 1983. *The International Law of Human Rights*. Oxford, UK: Oxford University Press
Tao, Julia. 2018. "Harmony and Human Dignity: A Confucian Perspective." In T. Meyer & J. de Sales Marques (eds.), *Multiple Modernities and Good Governance*. Abingdon, UK: Routledge, pp. 126–41
Tomuschat, C. 2008. *Human Rights: Between Idealism and Realism*. Oxford, UK: Oxford University Press

10

HUMAN RIGHTS AND A "GARDEN" OF HUMAN COMMUNITY IN THE POST-GLOBALIZATION ERA

Eun-Jeung Lee

Notwithstanding the proclamation of a Universal Declaration of Human Rights by the UN General Assembly, it is generally agreed that a universally accepted definition of the term human rights remains elusive. At the heart of this problem lies an inability to overcome the opposition between the cultural-relativist and universalist interpretations of human rights. Dictators and authoritarian rulers who find themselves accused of human rights violations seek to counter such criticism by arguing for the existence of human rights that are based on their countries' unique and distinct cultures, refuting a universalist reading of human rights as part and parcel of their criticism of Western imperialism. The debate surrounding the cultural-relativist versus universal nature of human rights has been moving in circles ever since the Universal Declaration of Human Rights was adopted in 1948.

Irrespective of whether they derive from the universalist or relativist line of thought, most definitions of human rights include demands for the protection and realization of "human dignity" and the protection of a certain inalienable "value" inherent in all human beings simply on account of being human. Hardly anyone disagrees with these core elements of a definition of "human rights." In fact, the universalist and relativist views of human rights are opposed to each other not so much with regard to their understanding of the nature of those rights but rather with regard to the method of actually realizing them. More specifically, the difference in opinion concerns only the question of how to institutionalize "human rights protection."

It is, in fact, fully possible for the cultural-relativist and universalist perspectives on human rights to harmonize. What is needed to prove this is an approach informed by intellectual history that upholds the underlying universal nature of human rights but also reconciles it with their historical and cultural particularities. In the following, I set out to explore the potential of Johann Gottfried Herder's metaphor of human civilization as a "garden" to fit this very purpose. I want to begin with an intellectual-historical examination of three distinct categories: perceptions of human dignity, theories on natural rights, and ideas for the institutionalization of human rights protection.

Human dignity and rights viewed through the lens of intellectual history

Human dignity. During what Karl Jaspers termed the "Axial Age," a paradigm shift in human thought occurred in ancient China, Greece, and India. Previously, thinkers had been primarily concerned with the question of how to find favor with God, a transcendental being who was the source of human existence and held absolute power over life and death. That attempt to curry favor was motivated by the belief that God would be able to solve the problems people were facing. The Axial Age saw the beginning of a mode of thought that broke away from this theocentric view of the world and put humanity at its center instead. During this period, the idea that humans are worthy of respect by virtue of the mere fact of being human and that their dignity must be protected – together with a new understanding of humans as primarily social beings – took root in China, Greece, and India simultaneously.

Let us take a look at ancient thought in China, the country which in present-day debate is the most fervent advocate of a cultural-relativist stance on human rights. Of the various schools of thought that emerged from ancient China it is, without any doubt, Confucianism that has exerted the most profound influence on East Asian culture and continues to do so to this very day.

The eponym of Confucianism and most important thinker of its classical age, Confucius, sought to create a world for humankind: in other words, a world in which the Tao is alive and vibrant, allowing humans to live according to the principles of life without interference or oppression by others. The notion of serving people, not ghosts, and finding ways for humans to live humanely occupied a central place in his thought. Over and above all else, he was concerned with *ren*, the essence of being human and humane (Roetz 1992).

From Mencius, who further developed the human-centered ideas of Confucius, we can learn more about the specifics of the Confucian approach to human dignity. He says:

> Suppose there are a basketful of rice and a bowlful of soup. If I get them, I may remain alive; if I do not get them, I may well die. If they are offered contemptuously, a wayfarer will decline to accept them; if they are offered after having been trampled upon, a beggar will not demean himself by taking them.
>
> *(Mencius 2004: 6A10)*

The point here is that, no matter how close people may be to dying of starvation, they will refuse help if accepting it would undermine their dignity. By citing such examples, Mencius is teaching us that people do not want to be stripped of their dignity, and that they will accept only treatment by others that respects this dignity.

Mencius goes on to explain that it is righteous to protect one's dignity as a human being. To him, the urge to do so is common to all human beings and stronger even than the will to live and the desire to escape death. In other words, he places a higher value on human dignity than on the human survival instinct.

Mencius also regarded all humans as having been endowed with a basic inclination to preserve the dignity of their fellow human beings. In support, he offers an analogy: anyone would be ready to hasten to the rescue of a baby that looked as though it were about to crawl into a well (Mencius 2A6). All those running to save the baby in such a situation would not be motivated by a desire to enter into friendly relations with the child's parents, to appear honorable in the eyes of bystanders and friends, or to avoid the criticism they would face if they failed to rescue the child. Instead, they would act out of a feeling of sympathy for the child who seemed so close to suffering harm.

Mencius regards this capacity to feel pity as the source of the fundamental human ability to protect the dignity of others. This ability is not the result of some form of extrinsic motivation but an intrinsic part of human nature. According to Mencius, the desire of individuals to preserve their dignity and their readiness to protect that of others both have their origin in the human heart-mind, an idea which has since become a firmly established axiom of East Asian Confucian thought.

Human nature and natural rights. Mencius taught that protecting human dignity is akin to realizing human nature, and that the act of doing so is what differentiates us from savage beasts. That people must continually improve on their nature to become fully human is the very starting point of Confucian thought. According to Mencius, it is in this process of humans perfecting their nature that the moral law is created. The moral law is thus a product of the human will. This introduces the logic that laws of conduct are not external to human beings nor determined by the context of the particular conduct in question but follow from the commands set up by the individual's voluntary choice – which, in turn, is not substantially different from the logic of autonomy as a source of morality in Kantian philosophy.

This also explains why European philosophers of the late seventeenth- and early eighteenth-century Enlightenment, who were engaged in debates about natural law and natural rights, turned to Chinese Confucian thought for empirical proof to support their lines of reasoning (Lee 2003). Departing from medieval Christian thought, Enlightenment thinkers such as Gottfried Leibniz and Christian Wolff were searching for ways to prove empirically that humans were capable of judgment based on their rationality alone. The news conveyed by Jesuit missionaries dispatched to China – that Chinese society had attained a high level of morality without any reference to the notion of divine revelation, relying on nothing but moral reflection on the basis of human rationality – was enough to inspire them. At the core of modern thought in the West as it began in the Enlightenment period was the refusal to accept the given order and authority and the insistence on breaking away from existing systems of thought (foremost among them those based on theology) and instead to ground ethics on reason alone. Enlightenment thinkers were striving for a new moral philosophy in accordance not with divine command but human reason, which, they assumed, was shared by all people. It is because they have reason that humans differ from animals, engage in a social life, and grasp nature's or (God's) creation as shaped by the laws of rationality.

Enlightenment thinkers found their intellectual model in the ancient Greek philosophy of Stoicism. According to the tenets of Enlightenment thought, the exemplary natural order to be observed by ethical humans was none other than the Stoic cosmos, the latter embodying a rational and uniform law that applies to the entire universe, including humans and their society. Against this background, it should surprise no one that the early Enlightenment philosophers who were influenced by Stoic philosophy, in particular Wolff and his followers, should have detected the deeper meaning inherent in the Confucian idea that the order created by human beings enjoying moral autonomy ultimately corresponds to the normatively defined natural order. Nor is it surprising that they should have come to the conclusion that the political and moral rules of Confucian China as conveyed to them by Jesuit missionaries constituted an exemplary realization of the "natural law."

According to Wolff, the natural law was created so that humans could practice virtue and avoid vice. This, of course, presumed that humans would understand the "powers of nature" and know how to use them (Wolff 1985: 33; cf. Arndt 1975: XV). To bolster his theories, Wolff needed empirical proof that humans did indeed have such skills, and he saw evidence of this in the Chinese, who acted on the basis of their Confucian beliefs without ever having heard of Christian ethics with their reliance on the notions of divine revelation and original sin.[1] By reading the *Analects of Confucius* (Confucius 1999) and the *Zhongyong*, he discovered "ratio" and "natural law" to be mutually reconcilable.

The relationship between nature and morality in Confucian thought is, of course, not quite as straightforward and consolidated as it appeared to be to Wolff (Confucius 1999: 12.1). Nor can it be said that Confucius himself trusted human nature quite as blindly as that. To him, humans were beings who had to engage in a constant process of "overcoming" themselves in order to achieve *ren*, or humanity and humaneness. But philosophers in the early Enlightenment period found elements that matched their thinking in the Confucian classics, especially in the *Zhongyong*.[2]

In that sense, the reason Western philosophers of the early Enlightenment period were so enthusiastic about Confucianism and Confucius can be seen in the latter's belief that humans enjoy independence from divine revelation due to a unity between nature and reason. To those in pursuit of ethical illumination, Confucianism as it was understood in the Western world of the early modern period served as a source of intellectual support in the enterprise of enlightening German and European society – in other words, the process of breaking away from tradition in cultures that were still strongly marked by premodern elements. This fact, which is often mentioned in the study of the intercultural history of political ideas, has so far been overlooked in discussions on human rights. At a time when notions of natural law and natural human rights had taken root in Europe, philosophers accepted Confucian China as their ideal. To a bourgeois intelligentsia arguing for equality among all human beings and the notion of natural human rights rooted in the principles of natural law, the example of China and Confucianism became weapons assisting them in their fight against stagnant and static social structures centered around existing political powers and the aristocracy.

The institutionalization of human rights protection and cultural relativism

The intellectuals and members of the bourgeois class at the time of the French Revolution who had coalesced around early Enlightenment notions of natural law and natural human rights demanded that all human beings be treated equally. They also called for the necessary political institutions to be created that could guarantee equal rights. This is generally known to have been the starting point of the human rights discourse in world history. I do not dispute this claim as such because, at least for now, there is no basis in the historical data available to us on which to refute it.

However, it would obviously be wrong to argue that just because a good idea originated at a specific point of time from a certain class in one specific society, it should be applied only to the members of that society and class. Without exception, all social developments that have so far taken place in the history of humankind have begun in a certain location against the backdrop of specific historical conditions (Douzinas 2000: 1). That the notion of human rights protection as it had been postulated during the French Revolution became institutionalized in the international community by means of the United Nations Human Rights Charter proclaimed in 1948 is just one instance of such a process of development.

Here Edward Friedman's writings, which point out the fallacy of considering the notion of human rights to be the exclusive property of Western societies, are worth examining. In an article published in 2000, he writes:

> Some people who think of Western society as home to democracy and human rights seem to overlook the fact that the concept of "western" was created relatively recently for political ends. The concept of a democratic Western society can be seen as having been created by Cold War-era propaganda to draw a contrast with the totalitarian Eastern bloc. The mistaken concept of a democratic Western society has been widely disseminated, but is incorrectly interpreted as a demonstration of deep historical facts and quasi-permanent truths.
>
> *(Friedman 2000: 22–23)*

Similarly, there is little debate over the fact that there is no basis in intellectual history for claiming that human rights are a unique product of Western culture.

As I explained earlier, the Europeans of the early Enlightenment period were sufficiently culturally open in their thinking to rely on the examples of China and Confucian thought to prove the validity of natural law and demonstrate the fact that humans were rational beings. Due to constraints of time and space, I cannot here elaborate on the details of how, starting near the end of the eighteenth century, such early open-mindedness eventually yielded to a more Eurocentric way of thinking. Suffice it to say in relation to the institutionalization of human rights that with the European intelligentsia firmly in the grip of Eurocentrism from the middle of the eighteenth century onwards, the open-mindedness that their forebears had shown with regard to the notions of human dignity and natural human rights, particularly their eager reception of Chinese and Confucian thought, had vanished from memory (Lee 2003). The discourse on human rights accordingly had come to be perceived as something exclusively European. This narrowing of vision, in turn, paved the way for universalism and cultural relativism being conceived of as mutually exclusive in the international debate on human rights that was initiated by the adoption of the Universal Declaration of Human Rights following the end of World War II.

From the perspective of intellectual history, there is, in fact, nothing to suggest that the relation between universalism and cultural relativism with regard to the issue of human rights should be confrontational. No one denies that human life should be respected. Similarly, no one expresses reservations about the basic principle of human rights: namely, that all human beings ought to be protected in their human dignity and in their resulting worth as human beings and that they should enjoy other rights connected to this foundational insight. The disagreement is limited to the choice of methods and institutions for realizing and protecting those rights. All institutions are products of culture as much as they are agents for cultural change. This fact is often overlooked in the cultural-relativist discourse, which tends to equate any differences in the institutions for realizing and protecting human rights with basic cultural differences in the way human rights are understood.

In 1947, the American Anthropological Association expressed concern over the universalism of the International Bill of Human Rights, which was then in the process of being prepared. It criticized the declaration for being little more than a list of rights widely recognized in Western European and North American states, and for perpetuating ethnocentrism and a sense of cultural superiority (AAA 1947). The conviction that standards and values derived from the beliefs and moral codes of European culture cannot be applied to humanity as a whole has since become the theoretical foundation for the cultural pluralism, constructivism, and relativism that have informed post-colonialist debates on human rights (Goodale 2009; Charlesworth 2010; Gregg 2012; Renteln 2013).

What Western intellectuals advocating a cultural-relativist post-colonialism tend to overlook is the fact that non-Western societies and their cultures are no more likely to be immutable than Western societies and cultures, and that they are just as familiar with conflicts surrounding social diversity and political hegemony. These intellectuals are deaf to the voices of those rising against authoritarian rulers in non-Western societies. Their cultural-relativist logic ultimately comes to furnish undemocratic, authoritarian rulers in post-colonial societies with a justification for rebutting international criticism of human rights violations.

This has resulted in a strange alliance between cultural relativists of the post-colonial school of thought and authoritarian rulers justifying undemocratic acts that amount to human rights violations by invoking their countries' supposedly unique and distinctive cultures. Theorists of post-colonialism thus find themselves confronted with the problem that this kind of alliance leaves citizens of post-colonial societies with very little room to maneuver in their fight for the realization and protection of human rights.

The political instrumentalization of cultural relativism

In 1948, the United Nations passed the Universal Declaration of Human Rights. However, not all the governments of the signatory states do in fact refrain from intervening in their citizens' private lives, nor do all of them actively carry out whatever measures are necessary for their citizens to be able to exercise and understand their rights as agreed in the Declaration. Just because a state has achieved democracy does not mean it offers a full and complete protection of human rights. As Friedman has put it, democratic governments do not automatically guarantee the promotion of human rights because democracy is no more than a means of dealing with political issues. This is why we can observe the formation of human rights groups in democratic states. In fact, there is still much work to be done to protect the human rights of underprivileged persons, such as women, foreigners, specific religious or ethnic groups, prisoners, and the poor in the majority of democratic societies (Friedman 2000: 25).

There is no such thing as an international mechanism that can force all states to respect human rights. While international alliances can be used to create pressure, they ultimately must remain ineffective, given that they lack the necessary coercive power. What is more, criticism of human rights violations is often used as a political tool. All this means that governments of countries criticized for human rights abuses will counter that such criticisms seek to interfere in internal affairs by invoking the universal nature of human rights. They also attack the notion of the universal nature of human rights by, in turn, invoking cultural relativity. Such is the pattern that has been repeating itself ever since 1948.

Over the course of the Cold War, from the 1950s to the year 1990, countries of the Communist bloc countered accusations human rights violations emanating from the international community by invoking a different understanding of the notion of rights that was embedded in the political and ideological structure of the communist states. They would then, in turn, accuse the Western world of constant violations of economic and social rights. Following the defeat of Arab states in the 1967 Arab-Israeli (Six-Day) War and the 1982 Siege of Beirut, Arab countries began to assert openly that Islamic values, rather than universal human rights, were what dominated the lives of their people (Mostyn 2002: 171; Kassir & Kunzmann 2006). In the 1990s, authoritarian politicians in East Asia, such as Singapore's Lee Kuan Yew and Malaysia's Mahathir, began presenting themselves as advocates of cultural relativism (Zakaria 1994).

A considerable number of East Asian politicians, including the two just named, rely on selected sociological writings – notably ones that find the causes of economic growth in East Asian countries to be rooted in their Confucian culture – to proclaim the existence of a separate set of "Asian values" (Lee 1997; Thompson). They argue that is it wrong to apply Western cultural standards to East Asia, for Asia has its own cultural standards and community values. They do not, of course, make any mention of the fact that if one invokes cultural peculiarities shared by all Asian states to explain economic growth in East Asia, one might likewise have to refer to those same Asian values in explaining why there had been such a very long period of economic stagnation before that. This is because their interest in discussing Asian values has nothing to do with wanting to promote and further the quality of sociological research. In 1994, Kim Dae-Jung, then leader of the Korean opposition, directly refuted the arguments advanced by Lee Kuan Yew, strongly criticizing Lee for misusing the Asian cultural tradition, and the Confucian culture in particular, as tools to bolster an authoritarian political system (Kim 1994).

A number of empirical studies have addressed the validity of the relativist claim that human rights in East Asia have certain characteristics that distinguish them from the European systems (Song 2014). Their comparative analyses of the level and manner of human rights protection in 15 East Asian countries that have implemented human rights as international norms reveal that, while the scores on the human rights indices vary from one East Asian country to another, depending on whether or not the relevant countries enjoy political stability, there is no such thing as a difference in attitude towards human rights when Asia is compared to countries from other regions of the world. This goes to prove that claims about East Asian countries sharing values distinct from those of countries in other cultural spheres has no empirical basis.

In the case of Islamic cultures, most Arab countries had argued up until the 1960s that human rights were universal and therefore applicable in their territories, as well, and that such rights should not remain a Western privilege. Samir Kassir contends that up until the 1970s, many Arab countries displayed considerable cultural openness (Kassir & Kunzmann 2006). Many intellectuals in the region today are critical of the political instrumentalization of the human rights discourse on the basis of a cultural-relativist perspective.

In spite of this, arguments in favor of the traditional culture's communitarianism, coupled with a fierce criticism of the individualism supposedly inherent in the notion of universal human rights, still wield considerable influence (Lee 2019). This is not without relevance to the discourse on a supposed moral crisis in Western societies. Recently, China has become a driving force in this discourse (Lee 2018; Lee & Rüdiger 2020). A considerable number of people are open to the argument that the "China model" offers a real alternative to Western liberalism, which is said to have reached the end of its tether. These people's interest in China is radically different in character from the philosophical Chinoiserie or Sinophilia of early Enlightenment Europe. China as imagined and admired by European intellectuals of the early Enlightenment period was the embodiment of an ideal state in which all of the population enjoyed a peaceful and prosperous life under the wise and benevolent rule of a philosopher king. It was not a state that suppressed individual freedom in the name of the community.

There can be little doubt about the political intention behind the rhetoric of Asian and Arab ruling elites who pose as advocates of traditional culture in advancing arguments of cultural relativism: they seek to conceal traces of anti-democratic rule and corruption. As can be seen in the exemplary case of Lee Kuan Yew, they are the very same people who, when doing so seemed necessary, had denounced traditional culture and made Westernization their political goal (Lee 1997). To them, advocating cultural relativism in the human rights debate is nothing more than a novel strategy to preserve their power in the face of both international criticism of human rights violations and the national, internal opposition's demands for more than formal democratization. Their advocacy of traditional culture includes denouncing universal human rights as Western values, attacking those same rights as an expression of unhealthy, corrupted individualism, and accusing critics of their regime in their own countries of being sympathizers of the West.

Against the backdrop of such controversy, it was widely expected in the run-up to the World Conference on Human Rights held in Vienna in June of 1993 that Asian and Arab countries would clash with Western European countries over their differing perspectives on human rights. This was, after all, a time when those arguing for the existence of Asian values were particularly vocal and had succeeded in making quite an impact on the world stage. Contrary to expectations, however, all of the United Nations member states, including those that had experienced decolonization, unanimously adopted the Vienna Declaration, which clearly states the universality of human rights.

Declarations of human rights – a "garden" of cultural diversity for the protection of human rights

The text of the Vienna Declaration adopted in 1993 does not provide any legally binding mechanism – such as the imposition of sanctions – for dealing with states that have committed human rights violations, nor had the 1948 Universal Declaration of Human Rights done so. While it is articulate about equality, respect for human rights, and participation in cultural systems, the Vienna Declaration is silent on how such goals are to be achieved. From the perspective of a human rights activist, there would appear to be a continuous need for activism and criticism, given that human rights declarations and treaties have been in existence for several decades now but cannot be said ever to have been properly adhered to.

In spite of this, the value of human rights treaties and declarations should not be played down or underestimated. Although their value is purely symbolic, they can bring about real and positive change on the strength of such symbolic value alone. The existence of human rights declarations and international laws for the protection of human rights has provided a basis for the struggles of all those fighting to protect human rights in states, regional societies, and groups that have witnessed violations (Douzinas 2000: 144). Dissident intellectuals in Cold War–era Eastern European societies demanding respect for the human rights discussed over the course of the Helsinki process and included in the text of the Helsinki Accords may serve as a case in point.[3] In a 1999 declaration, the American Anthropological Association revised its earlier skeptical view of the universal nature of human rights as expressed in its 1947 statement, acknowledging that listing human rights in international declarations and treaties actually has proved effective in protecting them (AAA 1999).

That being said, the relationship between the universality and cultural specificity of human rights as stated in the Vienna Declaration is still the subject of controversy. While the declaration confirmed not only the universality of human rights, but also the mutual interdependence of culture and human rights, it is not entirely clear what protecting human rights in a manner that is mindful of the relevant historical, cultural, and religious background could mean in actual practice (Friedman 2000: 46).

These observations suggest that in the twenty-first century, often labeled the post-globalization era, the gulf between cultural relativism and universalism in the conception of human rights shows no signs of closing. Discourse on human rights continues to be mobilized as a mechanism of power. For want of a redefinition of the relation between cultural relativism and universalism, debates about human rights continue to go around in circles and fail to make any progress.

To overcome this state of stagnation in the human rights discourse, I suggest taking a look at Johann Herder's metaphor of a "garden," through which the eighteenth-century German Enlightenment thinker aimed to explain the relation between cultural diversity and human civilization. Herder, who is known as a representative of cultural-relativist thought, had introduced this metaphor to explain human civilization from the standpoint of progress. Having shown an interest in Chinese and Confucian thought from the 1760s onwards, when the influence of Sinophilia was still noticeable, it was Herder who came across Confucius's observations on "humanity" in the process of translating the *Zhongyong* (Herder 1797a, 1797b). He did not idealize China to the extent Leibniz or Wolff had done in the early Enlightenment period, but he did not, unlike Hegel, denigrate it either. Herder strove to understand not only the Chinese and Confucian culture but all cultures in regions outside of Europe, in and of themselves. He described this as taking a "middle course" (Herder 1774). By examining individual cultures in the process of steering that course, he hoped to understand what he termed "the garden of human civilization." To Herder, human civilization was a garden in which various kinds of cultures mixed and mingled. He was of one mind with Leibniz when it came to assessing the importance of the information on Chinese Confucianism that had been passed on to European philosophers by Jesuit missionaries dispatched to China at the end of the seventeenth century: that Europeans had come to gain a good understanding of Chinese culture through this information was to him, just as to Leibniz, no less than a God-given opportunity for the further advancement of human civilization. More generally speaking, the deeper reason behind Herder's respect for cultural diversity lay in his conviction that the latter could ultimately contribute to, and further, the advancement of human civilization. This leads me to believe that his garden metaphor can assist us in overcoming the state of stagnation in human rights discourse.

Plants that grow in a garden do not all blossom equally. Gardens are beautiful because various plants jointly create a sense of harmony. The growth of individual plants and the beauty of the garden as a whole are not two separate things. The universality and relativity of human rights need to be combined from a similar perspective. In the "garden" of human rights, the relativity of various cultures must be guaranteed if universal human rights are to be realized. This is because the protection of individual human rights is at its most effective when it takes place within the confines of clearly demarcated communities (Barry 1992; Walzer 1983; Weiner 1996; Kassir & Kunzmann 2006). At the same time, no one will dispute the fact that because human rights are bestowed on human beings from the moment they are born, no one may curtail their enjoyment of these rights nor a fortiori deprive people of them entirely. In that sense, it could be argued that every single person in this world has a responsibility to protect and promote individual human rights (Beitz 1979, 1983; Donnelly 2003; O'Neill 2008; Singer & Singer 1988). It is outright impossible even to think about choosing between cultural relativism and universalism in doing so. That is also why the Vienna Declaration confirms both the mutual interdependence of human rights and culture and the principle of their universality. How beautiful the garden of human rights of our times will be is entirely in our hands.

Notes

1 To Wolff, the Chinese had supplied the proof that he needed. They were unfamiliar with the notion of the "creator of the world" or any "testimonies of divine revelation." Therefore, "they could only rely on the powers of nature. But they were most successful in using these powers – who are part of what has been inherited from being created in the image and the likeness of God – to distinguish themselves through the fame of their virtue and wisdom" (Wolff 1985: 33).
2 They even considered the *Zhongyong* to be an authentic reproduction of the teachings of Confucius. On the book's true history, see Tu 1976: 13–21.
3 Commission on Security and Cooperation in Europe (CSCE) and Helsinki Process.

References

American Anthropological Association (AAA). 1947. "Statement on Human Rights." *American Anthropologists*, New Series 19(4): 539–43. October

American Anthropological Association (AAA). 1999. "Declaration on Anthropology and Human Rights." Available at www.aaanet.org/about/Policies/statements/Declaration-on-Anthropology-and-Human-Rights.cfm

Arndt, W. 1975. "Einleitung in Christian Wolffs Vernünftige Gedanken von dem gesellschaftlichen Leben der Menschen und Insonderheit dem gemeinen Wesen." In C. Wolff (ed.), *Gesammelte Werke*, I. Abt., Bd. 5. Hildesheim, NY: Olms. pp. V–LI

Barry, B. 1992. "The Quest for Consistency: A Special View." In B. Barry & R. Goodwin (eds.), *Free Movement: Ethical Issues in the Transnational Migration of People and Money*. University Park, PA: Pennsylvania State University Press, pp. 279–87

Beitz, C. 1979. *Political Theory and International Relations*. Princeton, NJ: Princeton University Press

Beitz, C. 1983. "Cosmopolitan Ideas and National Sentiment." *Journal of Philosophy* 80(10): 591–600

Charlesworth, H. 2010. "Human Rights and the UNESCO Memory of the World Programme." In M. Langfield, W. Logan, & M. NicCraith (eds.), *Cultural Diversity, Heritage, and Human Rights: Intersections in Theory and Practice*. New York: Routledge, pp. 21–30

Confucius. 1999. *The Analects of Confucius (Lunyu): A Philosophical Translation*. R. Ames & H. Rosemond Jr. (trans.). New York: Ballantine Books

Donnelly, J. 2003. *Universalism and Human Rights in Theory and Practice*. Ithaca, NY: Cornell University Press

Douzinas, C. 2000. *The End of Human Rights: Critical Legal Thought at the End of the Century*. Oxford, UK: Hart Publishing

Friedman, E. 2000, "Since There is No East and There is No West, How Could Either Be the Best?" In M. Jacobson & O. Bruun (eds.), *Human Rights and Asian Values: Contesting National Identities and Cultural Representations in Asia*. Richmond, UK: Curzon, pp. 21–42

Goodale, M. 2009. *Surrounding to Utopia: An Anthropology of Human Rights*. Stanford, CA: Stanford University Press

Gregg, B. 2012. *Human Rights as Social Construction*. New York: Cambridge University Press

Herder, J.G. 1774. *Auch eine Philosophie der Geschichte zur Bildung der Menschheit*. Berlin: Weidmannsche Buchhandlung

Herder, J.G. 1797a. "63. Brief zu Beförderung der Humanität." In B. Suphan (ed.), *Herders Sämtliche Werke*, Vol. 17. Berlin: Weidmannsche Buchhandlung, pp. 343–45

Herder, J.G. 1797b. "114–116, 120. Brief zu Beförderung der Humanität." In B. Suphan (ed.), *Herders Sämtliche Werke*, Vol. 18. Berlin: Weidmannsche Buchhandlung, pp. 220–55, 286–95

Kassir, S. & U. Kunzmann. 2006. *Das arabische Unglück*. Berlin & Tübingen: Schiler

Kim, D.J. 1994. "Is Culture Destiny? The Myth of Asia's Anti-democratic Values." *Foreign Affairs* 730(6): 189–94

Lee, E.-J. 1997. *Konfuzianismus und Kapitalismus. Markt und Herrschaft in Ostasien*. Münster, Germany: Westfälisches Dampfboot

Lee, E.-J. 2003. *Anti-Europa: Die Geschichte der Rezeption des Konfuzianismus und der konfuzianischen Gesellschaft in Europa seit der frühen Aufklärung*. Münster, Germany: Lit Verlag

Lee, E.-J. 2018. "Eine Wiedergeburt von Konfuzius? Die Renaissance des Konfuzianismus in Ostasien." *Leviathan* 46(1): 59–80

Lee, E.-J. 2019. "Kommunitarismus und Konfuzianismus." In W. Reese-Schäfer (ed.), *Handbuch Kommunitarismus*. Wiesbaden, Germany: Verlag für Sozialwissenschaften, pp. 450–65

Lee, E.-J. & A. Rüdiger. 2020. "China und die moderne Gleichursprünglichkeit von Demokratie und Meritokratie. Zur interkulturellen Ideengeschichte des Republikanismus in der Epoche der Aufklärung." In *Allgemeine Zeitschrift für Philosophie* (in press)

Mencius. 2004. *Menzi*. D.C. Lau (trans.). London: Penguin Books

Mostyn, T. 2002. *Censorship in Islamic Societies*. London: Saqi
O'Neill, W. 2008. "What We Owe to Refugees and IDPs: An Inquiry into the Rights of the Forcibly Displaced." In D. Hoolenbach (ed.), *Refugee Rights: Ethics, Advocacy, and Africa*. Washington, DC: Georgetown University Press, pp. 27–49
Renteln, A.D. 2013. *International Human Rights: Universalism versus relativism*. New Orleans, LA: Quid Pro Books
Roetz, H. 1992. *Die chinesische Ethik der Achsenzeit*. Frankfurt am Main, Germany: Suhrkamp
Singer, P. & R. Singer. 1988. "The Ethics of Refugee Policy." In M. Gibney (ed.), *Open Borders? Closed Societies? The Ethical and Political Issues*. Westport, CT: Greenwood, pp. 111–30
Song, Y.H. 2014. "Tongasia inkwŏn-ŭi sangdaesŏng-gwa popy'ŏnsŏng: Kyŏnghŏmjŏk yŏn'gu-ŭi kich'o" [Universalism and Relativism of Human Rights in East Asia: An Empirical Analysis]. *Segye chŏngch'I* 21(2): 165–206
Tu, W. 1976. *Centrality and Commonality*. Honolulu, HI: Hawaii University Press
Walzer, M. 1983. *Spheres of Justice*. New York: Basic Books
Weiner, M. 1996. "Bad Neighbors, Bad Neighborhoods: An Inquiry into the Causes of Refugee Flows." *International Security* 21(1): 5–42
Wolff, C. 1985. *Oratio de Sinarum philosophia practica: Rede über die praktische Philosophie der Chinesen*. Hamburg, Germany: Felix Meiner
Zakaria, F. 1994. "Culture Is Destiny: A Conversation with Lee Kuan Yew." *Foreign Affairs* 73(2): 109–26

11

THE CRISIS OF MULTILATERALISM AND THE FUTURE OF HUMAN RIGHTS

André W. M. Gerrits

This chapter discusses two related issues in international politics, both of which remain crucial aspects of the post–Cold War global liberal order: multilateralism and the international human rights regime. The dominant liberal notion of human rights, and the mostly multilateral institutions through which these rights are discussed, agreed upon, and monitored, have come under increasing challenge. The ideational and institutional aspects of the human rights regime have become sharply politicized. They are now the targets of fierce discussion and contestation, subject to deeply divergent opinions. And the lines of demarcation defining those views have become increasingly permeable and complex. The distinction between a Western-supported, liberal concept of human rights (individualist, civic) and a non-Western one (collectivist, socio-economic) is still relevant, but it has lost much of its typical and distinctive capacity. Little can be said with certainty about the future of human rights, with the possible exception that the current global power transitions will not leave the international human rights regime untouched.

Human rights are a prominent and controversial aspect of multilateralism. Multilateralism is challenged both by revisionist and status-quo powers. There is a growing sense of concern and insecurity, even among the Western states that played a key role in the development of the liberal international order, about the extent to which transnational and multilateral institutions still serve their nations' vital interests. Much has been written on the crisis of multilateralism. Three causes are commonly mentioned: power shifts from the West to other parts of the world, especially China; the rise of non-liberal great powers with authoritarian political systems and an almost dogmatic sense of their own sovereignty; and the rise of populist and nationalist political actors that openly deny the purpose and the legitimacy of multilateralism. The perceived crisis of multilateralism raises issues, not unlike those on the future of the human rights regime. What is in crisis: multilateralism and human rights generally, or their thick and exponentially expanded post-Cold

War variant, part of the global liberal order? Are alternatives to the current human rights regime possible, and are they desirable? What can be changed, and what needs to be preserved?

This chapter is written from a liberal human rights perspective. I share the conviction that individual political and civic rights are the vital core of the international human rights regime. Moreover, I do not believe that we have reached the "end-times" of (liberal) human rights (Hopgood 2013), but there is ample reason to think that current power shifts will not leave the human rights regime untouched. The dominant notion of human rights is inspired by Western liberal values. The current human rights regime has been built under the guiding influence of Western powers. If ideas follow power in international relations, the global marketplace of ideas will inevitably change, including concepts of human rights. What will these changes be? How can we preserve an essentially liberal definition of human rights under fundamentally changing geopolitical conditions?

The crisis of multilateralism

The gridlock that many international organizations, including human rights organizations, face since the mid-2000s is often interpreted as an erosion of "principled" pragmatism. Multilateralism is "hollowed out" out by institutional struggles between status quo and revisionist powers (Rüland 2018: 9) – and the latter are winning. The distinction between principled multilateralism on the one hand and "pragmatic," "diminished," or "qualified" multilateralism on the other still makes sense, but in reality multilateralism remains a strategic choice for all states. One does not need to be a hard-nosed political realist to believe that the nature of the multilateral system reflects the distribution of power between states. "International organizations . . . exist only because states have created them, and their powers apply only to the extent that states consent to them" (Hurd 2011: 10). And when global power shifts, and the global order changes, states adapt their strategies. The West is losing its material primacy and ideological dominance. This does not necessarily imply that the current liberal order will collapse, that the emerging one will be "illiberal" (Boyle 2016), or that the "jungle [will] grow back and engulf us all" (Kagan 2018: 163). In contrast to the Cold War era, no single major power in today's world rejects the global order per se. Most aspects of the international liberal order will survive, because they continue to serve the interests of a critical number of states, but some are more controversial. The international human rights regime essentially belongs to the latter category.

Take Russia, arguably the world's most active (though *not* most powerful) revisionist state. Russia's preferred form of multilateralism is informed by two closely connected imperatives: a highly developed sense of sovereign rights and a distinct ambition for global multipolarity. Russia may be a "lonely" power (Shevtsova 2010), with few allies, but it is not an isolationist one. On the contrary, Russia is present in a wide range of international institutions and organizations, albeit not, with a few exceptions, very prominently. This has consequences for Russia's foreign policy. Bobo Lo (2015: 73) talks about a "qualified" multilateralism. While Russia observes the letter of multilateralism, it often ignores the spirit. For Russia's leaders, multilateralism is not so much a foreign policy norm or principle as it is a tool, a means of "levelling the playing field" (Legvold 2009: 30). "Institutional power" (Barnett & Duval 2005) is the key variable in Russia's approach to multilateralism and international organizations. That term can be defined as the extent to which states have the capacity to influence other states in indirect ways, especially through the rules and procedures of formal and informal institutions. With the exception perhaps of its own neighborhood, Russia's institutional power is limited.

Russia understands global politics predominantly in "plutocratic" or "oligarchic" terms (Lo 2015: 41). Global politics, including multilateralism, is primarily about relations among great powers. For Russia, that is more than a statement of fact; it comes close to a normative assertion. This explains the temporal shifts in Russia's multilateralism, from an essentially defensive and compliant posture during the 1990s to a more offensive one from the mid-2000s (Bond 2015: 189). It also clarifies why Russia has a particularly strong aversion against multilateralism in the sphere of political values and other normative issues, especially when they reach into the domestic affairs of countries, and this includes, most prominently, international human rights.

Human rights and the liberal international order

Future multilateralism will entail a complex, volatile combination of normative contestation and institutional adaptation, where the lines of division will be uncertain and sometimes difficult to draw. This is the background against which we should see the development of the international human rights regime (i.e., the complex whole of dominant human rights notions, institutions, and procedures). The international human rights regime (or order) is the cumulative outcome of a decades-long history of decisions and agreements on norms, rules, and regulations on institutions, procedures, and actors in the field of human rights. The human rights regime should not be mistaken for the actual human rights situation. Ideally, they march together. Reality, however, is more complex.

The current global human rights regime is largely inspired by the Western liberal tradition. The major aspects of liberal discourse on this topic are the supremacy and the universality of individual civil and political freedoms. The dominant concept of human rights, its global reach, and its institutionalization, reflect the material and immaterial dominance of the West after World War II and, more unequivocally, during the first two decades after the Cold War. And this dominance should be understood expansively, to include norm-making, policy-formulation and institution-building, by governmental and non-governmental organizations. Still, the liberal interpretation of human rights has never been *exclusively* Western. Arguing otherwise would overstate the actual commitment of Western governments to human rights policies (human rights policies have never been without hypocrisy or double standards) while underestimating the level of agency of non-Western actors. It is vital not to overlook either the contributions of non-Western individuals who initiated the first international human rights agreements or the enormous impact that the struggle for decolonization and self-determination have had on the development of human rights. Talking about *the* West in the discussion on human rights regime is also problematic, given the sometimes strongly diverging human rights definitions and strategies between Western powers – for example, between the US and the European Union (Wouters et al. 2014). And finally, the dominant notion of liberal human rights is becoming increasingly controversial among Western audiences, too, including scholars, practitioners, and politicians.

The marketplace of global ideas is moving, with new ideas and new, powerful buyers and sellers. Post–Cold War power shifts have generated ideational changes. The unprecedented proliferation of human rights diplomacy during the 1990s, when treaties, institutions, and organizations exploded, covering an ever-expanding understanding of these rights, created its own, almost inevitable, backlash. There are multiple reasons why the human rights order is under fire today, and many are related to its very ubiquity (Hopgood et al. 2017: 19).

The state of the human rights regime

It is impossible to prove causality between the international human rights regime and the extent to which human rights are actually respected. There has always been a gap between human rights on paper and in practice, but given the unprecedented thickness of the current human rights regime, the gap seems to be widening. In the authoritative and sober words of David P. Forsythe (2018: 512), "the normative revolution in international relations that has produced a vast international law of human rights has *not*, in general, been accompanied by complete behavioral and policy revolution" (italics in the original).

There is a remarkable variety of opinions about the current and future state of human rights. Pessimism about human rights is widespread. International organizations report a powerful pushback against human rights, not only in states in transition and hybrid states, but also in both authoritarian *and* democratic countries. Even within the UN system, human rights are increasingly marginalized, as the former High Commissioner for Human Rights, Zeid Ra'ad al Hussein, openly complained when he left his position (Seiderman 2019: 7). From the mid-2000s on, non-Western states increasingly have resisted the unparalleled and practically unchallenged status of liberal human rights and the extent to which Western states were inclined to use the human rights discourse as an instrument or justification of interventionist foreign policies. But in established democracies, elements of the political leadership as well as of the general public also question the expansive liberal definition of human rights and international justice. These notions are considered elitist, and not particularly responsive to societies' own concerns and needs.

In other words, the post-Cold War proliferation of human rights seemed to have eroded rather than strengthened the legitimacy of the human rights regime. Hopgood et al. (2017b: 317–18) summarize the argument as follows:

> human rights are philosophically weak, conceptually incoherent, lack resonance with their target communities, are out of step with the times, and, most importantly, from the standpoint of a positive agenda, are a distraction of progressive energies from the task of promoting a broader basis for increasing social welfare.

Samuel Moyn (2018: xi) talks about the "self-imposed crises" of liberal human rights, largely resulting from its professed utopian nature – the global human rights regime as a liberal crusade (cf. also Hopgood 2013; Hopgood et al. 2017a; Moyn 2010, 2018). It is important to realize that the apparent global "legitimacy" of liberal human rights especially after the Cold War was never based on the persuasiveness of the idea alone but also on the unprecedented power and authority of the Western liberal states that encouraged liberal human rights.

The global human rights regime is a specific variant of multilateralism. On the one hand, it is strongly normative and intrusive, and it seriously qualifies national sovereignty; but on the other hand, states rarely prioritize human rights as an issue of supreme strategic, national interest. So why would governments be willing to commit themselves to enforcing human rights agreements, including international supervisory and scrutinizing practices, which they actually consider to be unwelcome? States may have multiple reasons to accept the extensive international human rights regime, whether from a sincere belief in the goodness of human rights, from the power of socialization, or from the fear of reputational damage or punitive measures, not to mention the potentially destabilizing domestic impact of human rights violations. But states are not likely to police themselves, and no treaty implements itself. Governmental and non-governmental international institutions are generally zealous about monitoring human rights, but much less enthusiastic about preventing human rights abuses or implementing and enforcing human rights rules. Power, of course, is a key variable. Weaker powers are more susceptible to the negative consequences of the violation or disregard of human rights than stronger powers are. It is more difficult in practice to isolate or ostracize a more powerful state than a smaller, weaker one. Moreover, even the most repressive regimes are generally not without powerful friends or allies. And finally, whatever damage naming, shaming, sanctioning, and other instruments of international human rights protection might do, it is generally considered less risky than initiating the policy reforms that the international human rights agenda would require.

The punitive capacity of international human rights institutions remains limited. The post-Cold War era showed a brief upsurge in international criminal accountability (including the tribunals for former Yugoslavia and Rwanda, and the International Criminal Court), mandated by the UN Security Council. However, the international consensus (or acquiescence) that was needed to create and maintain these institutions proved to be limited and short-lived. Major states, including the US and China, voted against the treaty of the Criminal Court, and others meanwhile have withdrawn from it. Even in the countries whose leaders were indicted by international courts for a massive violation of human rights, these institutions of justice remained controversial and unpopular. It is difficult to imagine that under the current conditions the trend to hold serious human rights violators criminally accountable at the international level, generally a rare event, will continue. Impunity may be a cause of human rights violations, as Kathryn Sikkink (2017: 207) argues, but the prospect of international accountability certainly will not stop them. Governments that aim to push back the international liberal human rights regime follow the same tactics that they employ to revise other aspects of the international multilateral system. They openly challenge existing rules, procedures, and practices, such as singling out or naming and shaming violators, holding violators publicly accountable, or applying conditionality and sanctions against them to enforce international human rights policy.

There are also reasons to be more optimistic about the future of the international human rights regime. The crux of the optimistic argument is that human rights awareness and protection (through standard-setting, compliance, and enforcement) have reached such global dimensions that they should be considered robust enough to resist political backlash (Dancy & Sikkink 2017; Petrasek 2019). Human rights have become a key normative commitment and a principal legal concept, one that is widely shared and firmly supported by a thick system of intergovernmental and non-governmental global, regional, and national institutions. No single state can safely ignore it without domestic and or international repercussions (Sikkink 2017). Most national governments seem to accept, at least publicly, the inherently normative relevance of human rights and their derivative or consequential advantages.

Optimists rightly argue that the international human rights regime has never been solely dependent on Western powers. Non-Western states and individuals have played a crucial role in the formulation of human rights norms and in the establishment of the network of institutions that are supposed to promote and protect human rights. Neither has the international human rights regime ever been exclusively liberal. The relationship between liberal internationalism and human rights has always been "contingent," as Petrasek (2019: 104) points out. While the proponents of liberal human rights emphasize that it is precisely its liberal nature that makes human rights key to domestic development and international stability, those who challenge the supremacy of the liberal human rights concept argue the opposite. They claim that the dominant liberal understanding of human rights obstructs rather than promotes development, because it is at odds with national traditions and the local prerequisites of modernization, as defined by specific historical, cultural, and political conditions. Additionally, liberal human rights arguably undermine rather than support international trust and stability due to the fact that Western powers employ them selectively, as foreign policy tools, serving interests other than human rights (key to what Petrasek refers to as the "contingent" relationship between liberal human rights and Western powers). With growing confidence – and China is the prime example – non-Western states present their own definition of human rights as superior to the liberal variant. However, as much as states may subordinate liberal human rights to other concerns, and although they may present their own definition of human rights as the new standard, they rarely reject the liberal human rights concept completely. Individual human rights remain an integral part of the global political discourse. Optimists argue that the expansion of the human rights regime is a sign of its strength, and not of its perceived illegitimacy, as more pessimistic observers assert. Treaties continue to be negotiated. Organizations attempt to expand their agendas. States rarely withdraw from human rights agreements and organizations (Petrasek 2019). More issues increasingly are presented in terms of human rights, including the struggle against poverty, against environmental degradation, or for justice and equality. Thus, human rights discourse is more extensive and more diversified than ever before.

Full confidence in the future of the international human rights regime reads as a variant of the optimistic interpretation of the world liberal order: human rights norms are so deeply institutionalized in domestic and international law and politics that their continuation is possible, even under a significant realignment of power relations (Reus-Smit 2017: 11). Sikkink (2017: 134) refers to the "stickiness" of international organizations: "Human rights institutions give continuity to human rights norms and policies that last beyond the power of those that set them up." It is the power of institutions, she argues, rather than what I would call the power of ideas (and the coalition of forces that enabled their global spread), that sustains the continued relevance of human rights. In this view, institutions are supposed to be able to mitigate and accommodate cultural differences and to neutralize their disintegrative effects (Reus-Smit 2017). This is an attractive but, in the case of human rights, perhaps not a particularly persuasive argument. Human rights institutions, as Sikkink (2017: 233) acknowledges, "are mainly tools and arenas." They can be used constructively or harmfully. Institutions that are captured by human right violators actually can help to legitimize repressive state behavior. In comparison with other functionalist international organizations, the power of accommodation (to reach consensus on diverging views) and of implementation by human rights institutions is limited. The effectiveness of the human rights regime largely depends on the extent to which governments wish or feel the necessity to comply. And the price for non-compliance is now lower than it has been for decades.

A new human rights regime?

The current international human rights system is not a mere instrument of neoliberal imperialism, and neither is it irrelevant to the actual state of human rights, as the radical criticism of liberal human rights would have it (Hopgood 2013; Moyn 2018). The development of human rights has been characterized as a long history of "buildups, eruptions, backlashes, and backsliding" (Sikkink 2017: 135). Against the framework of this pattern of expansion and regression, the unique features of the post–Cold War international human rights regime become clearly noticeable, as do the signs of "backlashes and backsliding" that we are currently witnessing. The international human rights regime will change, but to what extent remains difficult to predict. "The future of human rights depends on agency in context," as Forsythe (2018: 7) argues; "nothing is set in stone." The liberal international order has never been a *global* order, with the partial exception of the first post–Cold War decades. And those were exceptional times, a unique confluence of circumstances: the unprecedented material and ideational prominence of the US (the "unipolar moment"), the weakness of its potential competitors (Russia after the collapse of the Soviet Union and China during the initial decades of reform), and the lack of material and ideological/ideational alternatives to Western-style liberal democratic and economic orthodoxies. This constellation of factors created the global liberal order and the current international rights regime. But it is history now, and it is not likely to return.

Key revisionist states feel powerful and confident enough to challenge the dominant liberal interpretation of human rights, and to present and defend their own alternative understanding of these rights. They do so domestically, but also for an international audience. Non-Western, including authoritarian, states will continue to attempt to decrease Western dominance over the institutions of the liberal international order. China, especially, has adopted an activist and offensive international human rights approach. In the UN Human Rights Council, of which it currently is the largest contributing member, China pushes and gathers support for its own state-centered and developmentalist perception of human rights. This is a clearly offensive strategy, one that reflects the dualist nature of China's human rights conceptualization: human rights are both a source of regime threat and of state legitimacy, domestically and internationally (see also Chen 2019). Human rights as regime threat (i.e., the liberal notion of human rights), needs to be pushed back; human rights as the right of development, China's interpretation of human rights, should be pursued and promoted as the new global standard. China presents its own model of human rights as both superior to the liberal one and universally relevant. That strategy is not without success, as the country's diplomatic achievements in multilateral human rights bodies indicate. It exemplifies an attractive combination of indifference to the universal and intrusive claims of liberal human rights and of determination to propose an alternative concept. That alternative is persuasive, if only because it is "[much] closer to the classical foundation of international law than the permissive interpretations championed by the US throughout the post-Cold War period" (Boyle 2016: 49–50). Generally, non-liberal powers seem more interested in changing than in eliminating the international human rights regime. They will continue to promote their own interpretations of human rights, but they will do so with a considerably stronger voice. And to the extent that they speak in unison, they will push for a human rights regime that fits their preferred international order more generally (i.e., less normative, less liberal, less universalist, and less intrusive).

The future of human rights: three key issues

I will briefly discuss three issues that are key to the future of human rights: the role of the state, the effort to "regionalize" human rights, and the need to bring those rights closer to the lives of ordinary people.

The first major challenge is about human rights and state sovereignty. It is open to debate whether the infrastructure of norms, rules, agreements, treaties, and organizations surrounding human rights that was built up during the second half of the twentieth century actually has advanced the human rights situation. But if there is a certain causality, as there probably is, it is because of state policies. The state is the crucial variable in the development of international human rights. Human rights originate in struggles against the state. The national state is the ultimate guarantor and it is the principal violator of those rights. Too much state is a problem; too little state, and the anarchy, conflict, and insecurity that can ensue from that condition, may pose even more of one.

Practically all states prioritize sovereignty and the right of non-interference over transnational human rights concerns. But if human rights can only be realistically fought for and won within the context of the sovereign state, the recognition of sovereignty should be a key aspect of the global human rights struggle. The relationship between national sovereignty and human rights should not be seen as inevitably dichotomous but as complementary. And if the national state remains the key institution of the human rights regime, then advocates for such rights should focus more on the national than the international level. Further capacity-building at the global stage, expanding the international human rights regime with new norms and new institutions, will not be particularly effective. We need to strengthen counterweights at the national level. Global human rights advocacy should primarily aim to facilitate local civil society participation. The human rights regime needs to be localized and democratized.

Democratization of efforts to defend human rights needs transparency and extra-governmental involvement. The possibilities of independent, non-governmental participation depend on the nature of the domestic political system. In the liberal perception this implies *democratic* governance. But if only democracy promises human rights, the future of human rights is bleak. Are there alternatives? The United Nations Economics and Social Commission for Asia and the Pacific (UNESCAP 2009) identified eight major features of *good* governance: participation, rule of law, transparency, responsiveness, consensus orientation, equity and inclusiveness, effectiveness and efficiency, and accountability. If good governance promotes development, is it also good for human rights? Not necessarily, of course, but then neither is democracy. The provision of public goods and orderly society are typical aspects of the official Chinese discourse on good governance and human rights. In the perception of the Chinese authorities, good governance is a condition for human rights, if not the most important human right as such. In the liberal interpretation, by contrast, human rights are a central aspect of good governance. This difference is fundamental, and it will not be easily bridged, but it may be the starting point of a productive dialogue.

The second key issue concerns universally and regionally versus locally driven human rights ideas and practices. Debate on whether human rights should be defined in universal or local terms is as old as the international human rights regime itself. It has become considerably more relevant with the expansion of the human rights agenda after the Cold War. At that time, an extended variant of liberal human rights became the norm. How relevant will universal notions of human rights remain in a global environment where power and ideas will be more evenly divided? It is the same old question, but more acute: can we continue to combine generally shared ideas about human rights with locally driven and contingent values and practices without falling into the trap of relativism? The issue has different aspects, two of which deserve our attention: institutional regionalization and localization. Regionalization has two different meanings, an institutional and a normative one. It not only refers to regional cooperation among states and other institutions in the sphere of human rights (which is not related to any part of the world in particular), but also concerns deviations from the liberal "norm." In the latter sense, regionalization and localization are closely related. They are deemed especially appropriate for parts of the world where the liberal human rights regime is relatively weak and where the norms and practices that are considered adverse to liberal human rights are particularly prominent: namely, in the Asia-Pacific, African, and Arab regions.

Regionalism was introduced into the human rights regime as a means of implementation. The idea was that the application of universal rights would be more effectively done by regional institutions (Hurrel 1999). From a liberal perspective regionalization and localization are both attractive *and* risky (see Heyns & Killander 2013 for an overview of the expansion of regional human rights systems). The most widely discussed case of regionalization, the "values" that are apparently unique and common to all Asian nations, always has been controversial. Are these values a legitimate alternative for globally acknowledged norms or a means for self-serving Asian elites to evade the international agreements to which they have formally committed themselves? The discussion continues, encouraged by China's offensive human rights policies.

Regionalizing the human rights regime could be effective, because it coincides with more extensive regionalization efforts. Regionalization can soften the traditional emphasis on state sovereignty. It can be more responsive to regional human rights advocacy, and it can appeal to perceived common cultural and political traditions, thereby adding legitimacy to the overall human rights effort. This potential has been realized to some degree only. The European human rights infrastructure, which includes two international courts with the authority and the jurisdiction to issue mandatory rules on states, remains a rare example of an effective regional human rights regime.

Regionalization is also risky, and unfortunately it seems especially so with regard to human rights. Regionalization efforts typically are dominated by great powers. Like great powers (and colonial ones) historically, Russia and increasingly also China tend to distinguish between two domains in international relations:

the global system and their own environment. They perceive their geopolitical neighborhood as a zone of political, if not legal, exception, where they claim special entitlements. These claims for a sphere of influence add to an emerging diffused international order, in which regional powers such as India, Brazil, Saudi Arabia, Iran, Turkey, and South Africa will play an increasingly prominent and autonomous role, in a more hierarchically structured setting. "The emerging international system is not marked by the absence of order," as Michael Boyle (2016: 41) quips, "but rather by more of it." And although the type of regional order may be negotiated among states rather than imposed by the regional hegemon (as the troublesome development of the Eurasian Economic Union shows), this does not necessarily help the human rights regime.

Regionalization of human right norms and practices can have a "solidarizing" impact on participating states. This may be supportive of the human rights effort in a region where states tend to respect human rights domestically (e.g., the larger part of Europe), but it may have a constraining impact in those parts of the world where authoritarianism reigns supreme (Latin America, Africa, and Asia during much of the Cold War, and the Middle East) and regimes share the ambition to defend their self-perceived interest against meddlesome outsiders. The relatively poor record of regional human rights efforts thus far tends to confirm these qualifying observations. Regionalism has not led to a formal divergence of human rights norms (there is not more consensus on Asian values than three decades ago, when the discussion started), nor has it contributed to the actual enforcement of human rights, irrespective of the specific nature of these rights. Not much has changed about the actual relevance of regionalization. As Forsythe reminds us, a robust regional system for the protecting human rights can only be based on a strong domestic commitment by the governments involved (Forsythe 2018: 206, 208).

Regionalization is a supra-state political effort; localization concerns the relevance of human rights for the daily lives of people. In the discussion on *global* human rights it is easy to lose sight of the actual impact of human rights. In 1997 Michael Ignatieff remarked that "[w]e are scarcely aware of the extent to which our moral imagination has been transformed since 1945 by the growth of a language and practice of moral universalism, expressed above all in a shared human rights culture" (Ignatieff 1997: 8). Two decades later, on a mission to "observe ethics in action," his inferences were considerably more sober. He again commends the post-1945 "rights revolution" as a key moment in the long history of creating the shared notion of human equality. "The privileges that once attached to race, gender, and religion may not be gone," he adds, "but their moral authority is contested everywhere" (Ignatieff 2017: 200). The sources of our shared moral awareness and authority are not abstract and universal, he notes; they are local: "We were struck, everywhere we went, by the primacy of the local. . . . Democratic sovereignty and the moral universalism of human rights are on a collision course everywhere" (Ignatieff 2017: 207). This is a remarkably pessimistic conclusion, too pessimistic perhaps. But it does indicate again that the understanding of human rights in exclusively universal or legal terms has little impact. Authority needs diversity. Diversity is culture. "[T]he universalism of rights is not a property of their implementation. It is a property of their origins," as Darren O'Byrne (2016: 110) remarks. "*Human rights is the generic language that we use to give force to our demands; it is not the content of that language, the words*" (italics in the original).

Global human rights discourse needs to move away from the abstract, the ideological, the theoretical. The morality of human rights should be linked with ordinary virtues and local challenges: the environment, health care, the rule of law, and good governance. Although human rights are not the "Doppelgänger" of neoliberalism, as Moyn (2018: xi) argues, a more balanced relationship between civic and socio-economic rights will enhance the normative power and the practical meaning of the discourse. Absolute poverty and deep insecurity are incompatible with any interpretation of human rights, including the liberal one. If Moyn (2018: 8) is correct in arguing that human rights tend to conform to the political economy of the age, there is ample reason to expect change. China's insistence on development as a principal human right is a powerful indication of changing preferences from the non-Western world.

In conclusion: the relevance of pragmatism

If ideas follow power in global politics, the international human rights regime will change. It is changing already. How should the proponents of liberal human rights respond to these challenges?

For states, organizations, and individuals that remain committed to the norms and institutions of liberal human rights, the way ahead will involve a complex combination of competition and compromise.

The challenge is twofold. First, they will need to engage in a much tougher (because more even) competition in regard to human rights concepts, institutions, and procedures. New forms and institutions of multilateralism already are being developed, driven by regional, functional and political imperatives. They will replace or be added to current (global) institutions. Human rights will follow. States and international organizations have to redefine their strategies, making them more effective and responsive to these changing circumstances.

Critical to ensuring that liberal democratic values are advanced globally is making certain that they are upheld at home. If democratic states do not have their own houses in order, their foreign policies will continue to lose the legitimacy to defend key aspects of the liberal notion of human rights and to engage in effective competition with non-liberal challengers. In other words, much of the work needs to be done domestically.

Second, in relations with non-democratic states and other challengers of liberal human rights, states and international organizations must show solidarity with like-minded entities and follow a mix of competition, compartmentalization, and cooperation with opponents. It will not be enough to collectively defend and promote the notion of human rights that matter for our own values. Human rights discourse is not a timeless and universal language but a product of its time. And the fact that it worked at some times does not necessarily mean it will work at other times as well. It is precisely for reasons of efficacy that liberal powers need to compromise on a future human rights regime and find ways to develop institutions that simultaneously configure authority and organize diversity. Liberal states need to ask, what is possible to keep, and what will certainly change? What are the risks and what are the opportunities of a new global rights regime?

The liberal human rights regime demands pragmatism – a combination of competition and compromise. And pragmatism applies to both the ideational and the practical aspects of human rights policies. It requires that we focus on a smaller set of fundamental rights, adopting an approach that is less intrusive and less legalistic. I agree with Geoff Dancy (2016: 514), who contends that "pragmatism is less the heart of a stunning indictment against current human rights practices and more a useful framework for developing those practices." In short, the challenge is to adapt the human rights regime to a new world of multiple modernities. Andrew Hurrel (1999: 281) puts it persuasively:

> The international community has a legitimate role in ensuring that governmental power is not abused, in setting human rights standards and in reviewing compliance with those standards. But if external involvement is extended beyond this into the detailed ways in which policies are chosen and implemented, then central liberal principles of representation, of accountability, of pluralism and the respect for diversity will be undermined.

Unfortunately, prudence is a word not often used in the human rights discussions.

References

Barnett, M. & R. Duvall. 2005. "Power in International Politics." *International Organization* 59(1): 39–75

Bond, I. 2015. "Russia in International Organizations: The Shift from Defence to Offence." In D. Cadier & M. Light (eds.), *Russia's Foreign Policy: Ideas, Domestic Politics and External Relations.* Houndmills & Basingstoke, UK: Palgrave Macmillan, pp. 189–203

Boyle, M. J. 2016. "The Coming Illiberal Order." *Survival* 58(2): 35–66

Dancy, G. 2016. "Human Rights Pragmatism: Belief, Inquiry, and Action." *European Journal of International* Relations 22(3): 512–35

Dancy, G. & K. Sikkink. 2017. "Human Rights Data, Processes, and Outcomes: How Recent Research Points to a Better Future." In S. Hopgood, J. Snyder, & L. Vinjamuri (eds.), *Human Rights Futures.* New York: Cambridge University Press, pp. 24–59

Forsythe, D. P. 2018. "Human Rights." In T. G. Weiss & R. Wilkinson (eds.), *International Organization and Global Governance.* London & New York: Routledge, pp. 511–22

Heyns, C. & M. Killander. 2013. "Universality and the Growth of Regional Systems." In D. Shelton (ed.), *The Oxford* Handbook *of International Human Rights Law.* Oxford, UK: Oxford University Press, pp. 670–97. Online Publication. doi:1093/law/9780199640133. 003.0029

Hopgood, S. 2013. *The Endtimes of Human Rights.* Ithaca, NY: Cornell University Press

Hopgood, S., J. Snyder, & L. Vinjamuri. 2017a. *Introduction: Human Rights Past, Present, and Future*. New York: Cambridge University Press, pp. 1–23

Hopgood, S, J. Snyder, & L. Vinjamuri. 2017b. *Conclusion: Human Rights Futures*. New York: Cambridge University Press, pp. 311–29.

Hurd, I. 2011. *International Organizations: Politics, Law, Practice*. Cambridge, UK: Cambridge University Press

Hurrel, A. 1999. "Power, Principles and Prudence: Protecting Human Rights in a Deeply Divided World." In T. Dunne & N.J. Wheeler (eds.), *Human Rights in Global Politics*. New York: Cambridge University Press, pp. 277–302

Ignatieff, M. 1997. *The Warrior's Honor: Ethnic War and the Modern Conscience*. New York: Metropolitan

Ignatieff, M. 2017. *The Ordinary Virtues: Moral Order in a Divided World*. Cambridge, MA: Harvard University Press

Kagan, R. 2018. *The Jungle Grows Back: America and Our Imperiled World*. New York: Alfred A. Knopf

Legvold, R. 2009. "The Role of Multilateralism in Russian Foreign Policy Approaches." In E. W. Rowe & S. Torjesen (eds.), *The Multilateral Dimension in Russian Foreign Policy*. New York: Routledge, pp. 21–45

Lo, B. 2015. *Russia and the New World Disorder*. London & Washington, DC: Chatham House/Brookings Institution Press

Moyn, S. 2010. *The Last Utopia: Human Rights in History*. Cambridge, MA: Harvard University Press

Moyn, S. 2018. *Not Enough: Human Rights in an Unequal World*. Cambridge, MA: Harvard University Press

O'Byrne, D.J. 2016. *Human Rights in a Globalizing World*. London: Palgrave Macmillan

Petrasek, D. 2019. "Not Dead Yet: Human Rights in an Illiberal World Order." *International Journal* 74(1): 103–18

Reus-Smit, C. 2017. "Cultural Diversity and International Order." *International Organization* 71: 851–85

Rüland, J. 2018. "'Principled Multilateralism' versus 'Diminished Multilateralism': Some General Reflections." In C. Echle, P. Rueppel, M. Sarmah, & Y. Lay Hwee (eds.), *Multilateralism in a Changing World Order*. Singapore: Konrad Adenauer Stiftung, pp. 1–12

Seiderman, I. 2019. "The UN High Commissioner for Human Rights in the Age of Global Backlash." *Netherlands Quarterly of Human Rights* 37(1): 5–13

Shevtsova, L. 2010. *Lonely Power: Why Russia Has Failed to Become the West and the West is Weary of Russia*. Washington, DC: Carnegie Endowment for International Peace

Sikkink, K. 2017. *Evidence for Hope: Making Human Rights Work for the 21st Century*. Princeton, NJ & Oxford, UK: Princeton University Press

UNESCAP. 2009. *What is Good Governance?* Available at www.unescap.org/sites/default/files/good-governance.pdf

Wouters, J., L. Beke, A. Chané, D. D'Hollander, & K. Raube (eds.). 2014. *A Comparative Study of EU and US Approaches to Human Rights in External Relations*. Brussels: Policy Department Directorate-General for External Policies. doi:10.2861/69726

PART V
Towards a new multilateralism: deepening the conceptual dimension

12

MULTILATERALISM VIA INTER-PRACTICALITY

Institutions and relations

Qin Yaqing

I discussed elsewhere (Qin 2019) two types of multilateralism for cooperation and coordination in international and transnational governance: institutional multilateralism and relational multilateralism. Two passages, by Robert Keohane and by Kishore Mahbubani and Jeffery Sng, reflect in large measure how these approaches actually function.

Keohane places emphasis on the role of international institutions to bring about cooperation in anarchy when he argues that

> "the emergence of cooperation among egoists" . . . is possible, even in the absence of common government, but that the extent of such cooperation will depend on the existence of international institutions, or international regimes, with particular characteristics.
>
> *(Keohane 1984: 13)*

Kishore Mahbubani and Jeffery Sng, on the other hand, seem to prefer informal and even personal relationships for successful cooperation. Playing golfing together, wining and dining, and small gift-giving – such ASEAN activities promote cooperation through enhanced human relations. They discuss the ASEAN way as follows:

> Kishore has often said – only half in jest – that Southeast Asia is at peace because of a four-letter word. This four-letter word is golf. Kishore resolved many thorny issues with his ASEAN colleagues after a happy round of golf that generated friendship and camaraderie. Former Foreign Minister of Singapore Wong Kan Seng agreed that "Golf was an important factor. It helped to break down barriers and promote camaraderie. We even had an ASEAN golf game at a weekend when we attended the annual UN General Assembly." He added: "The annual ASEAN dinner in the UN was a show of unity.

Ministers' wives would come and shake people's hands – that was not seen in other regional organizations. There were memorable but simple gifts as well. Orchids would be given at the end of receptions. A lot of people would turn up, including the UN secretary-general. In short, the whole world could see at first hand at the UN ASEAN's model of peaceful cooperation."

(Mahbubani & Sng 2017: 51–52)

It is interesting to note that although these quotations share a lot in terms of objectives and principles, a most important part of which is cooperation for governance in international and global affairs, the former relies primarily on institutional practices while the latter pays much more attention to human relations. I argued that there exist various forms of multilateralism or simply multiple multilateralisms because different practices in different cultural communities as well as the different background knowledges therein over history have made such a multiplicity inevitable.

The world consists of many worlds (Tickner & Waever 2009; Tickner & Blaney 2012), composed of multiple cultural communities and therefore multiple practices (Qin 2019). At the same time, the world is also one: peoples have similar goals and ideal aspirations, of which peace, prosperity, and progress are most representative and may constitute what Thomas Meyer terms the "common core" (Meyer 2018a). Globalization has further made the world into a global village. To realize our common goals, it is important to enable various practices embedded in diverse cultural communities to empower one another in a positive way. Identifying the differences in their respective practices provides a necessary condition for their mutual learning for continuous improvement. Likewise, realizing common human goals necessitates positive mutuality and interactive complementarity of various practices among different cultural communities and around the globe. I term this "inter-practicality."

In the following sections, I will discuss practicality in general, distinguish between two types of practicality – intra-practicality and inter-practicality – and argue that multilateralism as practice may be facilitated in different regions through different practices. A comparative study of regional multilateralism needs to find such differences and encourage inter-practicality for positive mutuality (Telò 2019).

Practicality and localness of background knowledge

Multilateralism is recognized as the most appropriate approach to international and transnational governance through practice. Almost all theories on multilateralism, whether they discuss the United Nations, the European Union, or the Association of East Asian Nations (ASEAN), are based on human practices in international society. The human practice of multilateralism goes before any theorizing that tries to represent it.

It is therefore quite reasonable that practice enjoys ontological priority (Schatzki et al. 2001; Adler & Pouliot 2011). Practice theory has gained attention in international relations as its significance is excavated and construed. It is practice that produces background knowledge intersubjectively shared in a community of practice, which not only shapes common features of the community, but also provides its members with a similar pattern of doing things at the macro level. As John Searle remarks, background knowledge is the pre-intentional capacity that makes the intentional capacity possible (Searle 1995). Simply put, background knowledge is the invisible hand that orients people towards certain actions, and the logic of practicality demonstrates that practice is the prime mover of human action.

Emanuel Adler and Vincent Pouliot (2011) have described several defining features of a practice. A practice is first of all a performance; it is patterned, exhibiting regularities over time and space; it is more or less competent in a socially meaningful and recognizable way; and it weaves together the discursive and the material. Although Lechner and Frost (2018) believe that such a description confuses what they term "simple action" and "practice-dependent action," the definition that practices are competent performances and that practices depend on background knowledge reflects the general meaning that is widely accepted.

A most significant argument of practice theory is that background knowledge shapes the thinking and doing of members of a community of practice. Wittgenstein famously argues that language is primarily a practice, the meanings of which are not defined in abstraction but in use (Wittgenstein 1968). By doing so, he pays attention to the language employed by local people whose mother tongue it is. As Pouliot contends:

> most of what people do, in world politics as in any other social field, does not derive from conscious deliberation or thoughtful reflection. . . . Instead, practices are the result of inarticulate, practical knowledge that makes what is to be done appear "self-evident" or commonsensical.
>
> *(Pouliot 2008: 258)*

Furthermore, Pouliot particularly employs Scott's term "*métis,*" referring to "a rudimentary kind of knowledge that can be acquired only by practice and that all but defies being communicated in written or oral form apart from actual practice" (Pouliot 2008: 270).

Such a definition, together with what Searle and Bourdieu discuss about practice, assumes in the first place that the "inarticulate, practical" background knowledge is local, starting from the everyday practice of a local group of people and accumulating over time in and through practice by those people. In this sense, any logic of practicality presupposes the localness of practice and practical or background knowledge. This characteristic of localness also means that practice is always situated in a particular context. It is exactly what Wittgenstein means by "in use." Any practice is understandable only by grasping the context within which it is performed. Ways of cooperation in the tribute international system, for example, differed from those in the Westphalian system because they were situated in different cultural, social, and political contexts (Ringmar 2012). This point is particularly emphasized in and discussed by "practice internalism" (Lechner & Frost 2018), which I will consider in more detail below.

The localness of background knowledge, by default, assumes that there are many communities of practice and therefore that practice may well vary across these communities. I elsewhere argued that practices are multiple, and that cultural communities are most representative of communities of practice (Qin 2018). This argument is based on three interrelated propositions. First, practice is what a collective or a group of people perform according to shared and intersubjectively intelligible background knowledge, which they tend to take for granted. The often-cited example is a diplomatic community whose members practice diplomacy according to the background knowledge accumulated over time, in and through the practices they perform every day. Second, civilization-based cultural communities are the prototype of communities of practice, because a cultural community is formed and developed through practice over millennia and the background knowledge is more consolidated than in other communities of practice, such as the diplomatic community. Indeed, culture is defined in terms of shared background knowledge. It is not difficult to discern the patterned behavior of a cultural community at the macro level and the rules and norms formed in practice by which appropriate behavior is defined and recognized. Third, there are multiple communities of practice, notably, as well as more relevantly, in terms of international relations, those based on civilizations or cultural communities as I have termed them. Due to different cultural backgrounds, members of these cultural communities practice in some different ways. Even when they are pursuing the same goal, such as peace and prosperity, they may demonstrate different behavior to realize that goal. Good governance, for example, is a common goal of humans, but how to reach it may be understood and practiced in different ways, mainly because the cultural backgrounds vary.

Multilateralism is practice. Practice is always in the plural due to the coexistence of various cultural communities in the world. Thus, multilateralism tends to demonstrate the various ways it is practiced in different communities. It is only natural that, when international governance is concerned, European multilateralism shows a more institutional and legalistic orientation, while East Asian multilateralism demonstrates a more relational tendency. Multilateral cooperation takes various forms because the practitioners in various cultural communities may well practice it following what their background knowledge tells them implicitly, working as an invisible hand. The practice approach in this respect is useful indeed for the study of multilateralism in our world composed of multiple worlds, and its most inspiring aspect is the implication that there are multiple communities of practice, which assumes the localness of their background knowledge.

Intra-practicality: endogenous intersubjectivity and continuity

Practice theory focuses primarily on what I called "intra-community" activities, or simply "intra-practicality." Common practice generates shared background knowledge and over a period of years enables rules, norms, and conventions to emerge out of practice that work implicitly to make a community cohere and that orients members towards a similar way of thinking and doing. It is a meaningful approach to the study of international relations because it touches upon a most fundamental aspect of social behavior – that is, background knowledge, the implicit and inarticulate knowledge that comes from and through practice – and takes it as the prime mover of human action. What people do and how they do it depends much more on background knowledge than rational reasoning.

Perhaps it is the localness of background knowledge that orients people's attention to intra-practicality, for practice theory, no matter whether it follows more the ideas of Wittgenstein and Oakeshott or those of Bourdieu and Searle, focuses largely on the practice inside a community and tries to determine how a certain pattern of activity has been formed and developed and what background knowledge is at work. This focus enables analysts of the practice approach to go deep into the localness of background knowledge and to trace how such knowledge gradually has become the daily life of the community members and oriented their behavior and activity. In short, the practice approach so far has discussed in detail and in depth how practice by members of a community produces background knowledge, which in turn shapes the pattern of practice and makes a community what it is.

The study of the security community as a community of practice is one of the foci for the practice agenda. Usually, such studies start with the intra-activity of a group of nation-states that form a security community. A pioneer study in this respect, *Security Communities*, edited by Emanuel Adler and Michael Barnett, is designed around intra-community activities so that chapters are organized around each of the communities the authors discuss, such as the West European non-war community, the Organization for Security and Co-operation in Europe, the Association of East Asian Nations, and so forth (Adler & Barnett 1998). The detailed analyses explore the origins, developments, objectives, principles, and activities of those security communities or quasi-security communities, while external factors are at best treated as stimuli to the community development. There is little mutuality across those communities discussed in that edited volume. Each stands alone.

A more practice-focused study of the security community is Pouliot's article, "The Logic of Practicality: A Theory of Practice of Security Communities" (Pouliot 2008). The article criticizes earlier studies such as the Adler and Barnett anthology for their heavy reliance on representational knowledge, and argues that a security community is a community of practice where background knowledge rather than representational knowledge plays the most important role for the pacific nature of a security community. As Pouliot argues, "Security communities thrive on a practical *modus operandi* that has a different logic than its objectified *opus operatum*" (Pouliot 2008: 278). In this, personal and collective history, or (to use Bourdieu's term) "habitus," play a more important role in peace-proneness than instrumental calculation.

More recent practice-oriented studies have followed this mode of analysis, focusing more on intra-activities of a community of practice, even though the communities discussed are more professionally than geographically oriented. The collection edited by Emanuel Adler and Vincent Pouliot, *International Practices* (2011), deliberates on practices in various special fields such as international law, deterrence, banking, and so forth, but the method of intra-practicality is similarly employed. Pouliot's most recent work, *International Pecking Orders: The Politics and Practice of Multilateral Diplomacy* (2016), analyzes the formation and development of the diplomatic hierarchy in the multilateral setting, following even more the logic of intra-practicality. Its key concepts, including situations, dispositions, relations, and positions, all work in the internal process of multilateral diplomacy.

The intra-practicality approach follows the development of a community of practice, focusing on how background knowledge has developed and accumulated over history within this community, no matter whether it is geo-culturally or professionally defined. Essentially, it is the study of the evolution of a community that is assumed to stand as an isolated system without much external interference and influence. In other words, practice theory pays adequate attention to the community's internal development while neglecting another important aspect of social life, that is, interactive practice among and across communities. Insofar as practice theory views a community of practice as a system of self-development, it may enable a tendency towards self-enclosure.

The study of the European regional cooperation provides a telling example. To a great extent, regional cooperation and integration in Europe has established a model for cross-national or supranational cooperation in the world. It is only quite recently that Europe suffered two cataclysmic wars, human-made disasters that claimed millions of lives. The efforts following World War II for peace and cooperation through multilateralism have been tremendous and successful. It is almost impossible today to imagine that major warfare would break out in the continent and the multilateral framework of a regional cooperation would be demolished. Despite the recent rise of populism and nationalism in Europe as well as the Brexit, the European way of governance through multilateralism will continue. One of the most valuable experiences is that multilateralism based on international or supranational institutions, rather than war and conquest, is the most reasonable and acceptable pathway to cooperation in the globalization era.

The experiences of the European practice for cooperation are indeed worth studying. A mere scan of the rich literature on this topic reveals that most contributions examine the experiences of European efforts based on European practices. From the history of European integration to the structure of the European Union, from the socialization of European community members to the constitutions of rules and norms in the region, and from the legal system to the foreign policy, almost every aspect of the European multilateral, supranational governance has been thoroughly explored and analyzed. Although external factors, such as the US influence and the Soviet/Russian impact, also have been investigated, they are after all external factors, affecting but not determining the practice of the community itself.

Undeniably, the intra-practicality approach constitutes a very useful way of approaching the practice of a particular community, because background knowledge, the key word for practice theory, is produced and consolidated locally within the community. However, while intra-community practice is very much emphasized, inter-community practice is perhaps unconsciously taken as a constant or even neglected. Valuable though it is, the intra-practicality approach is inadequate, especially in a period of globalization. As I have argued, there are multiple communities of practice across which multiple ways of practice coexist. None develops in isolation. Furthermore, globalization is what has brought them together. Mutuality is thus inevitable. It is, therefore, perhaps equally important to see how these various practices interact, how they learn from one another, and what results the mutuality among them can produce. This raises the question of inter-practicality.

Inter-practicality: mutuality and change

Inter-practicality is the mutual empowerment of different practices in terms of their positive elements towards achieving a common goal. While insisting on the ontological significance of practice in social life and recognizing the coexistence of multiple cultural communities and therefore different ways of practice, inter-practicality posits that mutuality of various practices is inevitable in a globalizing era, and therefore that communication among various communities of practice is not only necessary but also probable, leading to positive and productive results. Multilateralism, as the most appropriate approach to international and transnational governance to date, is expressed and performed through different forms of practice. How can we realize diversity in unity and facilitate the mutual empowerment of different practices to achieve common goals? In other words, how can we enable the various practices of multilateralism to work together for better and more effective governance and cooperation? That is the key question raised in this chapter.

Practicality consists of two dimensions, intra-practicality and inter-practicality. When the practice approach in international relations focuses on the former and neglects the latter, it fails to achieve an adequate understanding of practicality. In fact, inter-practicality is going on every day in the world. It generates mutual influence and empowerment across communities of practice and is even more likely to bring about changes in background knowledge.

Inter-practicality refers to communication among the practices of various communities. Unlike intra-practicality, it points to communication among practices between communities that are obviously different in regard to their background knowledge. By the same token, it also differs from (though is related to) interregional or interpersonal communication, mainly because of its emphasis on communication and interaction in and through practice. The dimension of practice through *participation* is what matters most here. Members of different communities communicate and learn from each other as *participants* in each other's practice. They understand how other communities practice not as observers but as participants, and try to see if such practices can be practiced in their own contexts, having lived in both the background knowledge of the other-community and the self-community. They may adopt, adapt, and decline practices of other communities and at the same time modify or change their own practice or even transform its background knowledge. To some extent, intra-practicality explains more habits and habitual behavior, while inter-practicality explains more transformative change.

Inter-practicality rests on the following premises: the coexistence of multiple practices; practice internalism; practice as an open process; and the centrality of human agency. Let us examine each of these in turn.

Coexistence of multiple practices

The logic of inter-practicality presupposes the coexistence of multiple communities of practice. Meyer (2018b), in his discussion of multiple modernities, criticizes two extreme arguments: Fukuyama's prophecy that the liberal-democratic model of modernity represents the end of history (Fukuyama 1992), and Huntington's model, positing inevitable clashes among civilizations (Huntington 1996). While the former predicts an eventual homogeneity of the global society, the latter foresees a fragmented and conflict-ridden world. Meyer favors Eisenstadt's multiple-modernity framework. That framework recognizes the coexistence of multiple ways of modernizing due to the different cultural contexts in which modernization is carried out, even though the common goal for all is the same, that is, modernization.

Recognizing the coexistence of multiple modernities due to multiple cultural contexts entails recognizing the coexistence of multiple cultural communities and practices. Huntington and Eisenstadt both acknowledge such coexistence, though Huntington's interpretation of its possible consequences is misleading. The prerequisite for the clash of civilizations is the simultaneous existence of various civilizations, and so it is for the multiple modernities approach, which believes that cultural contexts largely explain the multiple ways towards modernization. Even Fukuyama's uniform model recognizes that there are multiple models at least nowadays, though they eventually would converge to one and end on a uniform path (Fukuyama 1992). The coexistence of and therefore inevitable interaction among various communities of practice is a generally acknowledged fact in our world, especially in the era of globalization. To some extent, therefore, inter-practicality is a key principle for modernity in a globalized world.

It is important to affirm the coexistence of multiple practices in our world. Lechner and Frost criticize the international practice theory for following Bourdieu's externalism, which presumes that "an invariant realm of knowledge overarching all practices must be postulated to make sense of any particular practice" (Lechner & Frost 2018: 27–28). In reality no such overarching knowledge exists, enabling people to understand practice in a particular community from a mere observer's viewpoint. The reality of the coexistence of multiple communities of practice means that practice-dependent action varies and that different communities may practice in different ways even if their objective or goal is the same. This agrees with Meyer's assessment that

> almost every society, regardless of which civilization it belongs to, wishes to be modern – at least in some respects. But because the desire to modernize finds expression within quite different cultural contexts, it may turn out that modern societies will never converge on a single model. Instead, they will remain culturally distinct as far ahead as the eye can see.
>
> *(Meyer 2018a: 5)*

Practice internalism

The question then is how to understand practice in a largely unfamiliar other-community, without which inter-practicality cannot be realized. In this respect, the approach of "practice internalism" is inspiring. In other words, inter-practicality requires personal participation in the actual practices of the other-community of practice. It is the mutual understanding of the practice of two different communities of practice, such as the EU and ASEAN, through being a participatory member in each other's practice of multilateralism. According to Lechner and Frost, a philosophical definition of practice in line with Hegel, Oakeshott, and particularly Wittgenstein is "social activity constituted by rules" (Lechner & Frost 2018: 11). The authors criticize the practice approach to the study of international relations as well as the main intellectual sources it draws upon, notably Bourdieu's practice theory, saying that it is basically an externalist way of understanding practice. "Externalism" tries to understand practice from outside and to use a pre-set theoretical framework to analyze and interpret practice, or everyday doing by members of a community. It is the wrong way, because an outsider, without the "we-feeling" and shared understanding of the participants, can never really understand the meaning of practice in a particular community.

To understand practices, we need internalism, or the shared, intersubjective understanding of the participants as a group "who have learned to perform actions within the framework of their own practice" (Lechner & Frost 2018: 12). In other words, if one is to understand the practice of a community, one needs to be a member of that community because the understanding can be acquired only by an insider who lives as other members live and does as other participants do. Though what Lechner and Frost label "internalism" has its own problems, their reasoning is commendable. The most important and relevant implication of their argument is the definition of practice as "an entire system of rules and norms" in the social sense (Lechner & Frost 2018: 15), constituting a framework of intersubjectively comprehensible and shared meanings. It is impossible to understand and interpret practice merely by singling out a particular practice or a concrete rule and analyzing it with a ready-made theoretical paradigm. Practice must be understood as a whole. To accomplish that, one needs to be a participant and do as members of the community do, so that one can grasp the inarticulate and tacit background knowledge that constitutes the prime mover of action of the community members at the macro level.

Turning to practice internalism, we need to know that practical knowledge varies across practices and communities of practice. To study and understand a practice thoroughly, we need to think and do from the "vantage point of practice participants" (Lechner & Frost 2018: 28). In other words, concrete practices can only be understood in the whole social context within which they take place, for understanding practice presupposes a meaningful context as a whole.

Practice as an open process

Furthermore, practice is an open process. It is not only what members of a community do but also what they do in relation to what members of other communities do. Practical knowledge is shaped and informed by the practices of community members and at the same time by inter-practicality among different communities. The process is open because it is one of learning, adopting, adapting, changing, and declining. Spreading international norms, for example, is in fact a process of inter-practicality. For example, ASEAN accepted the norm of mutual security and turned down the norm of humanitarian interference because the former fit well into its own practice while the latter did not (Acharya 2001). The process, however, is still open, because it may be subject to modification sometime in the future due to continued inter-practicality.

Furthermore, practice as an open process also means that practice itself is changeable. This argument implies that background knowledge is changeable, as well. It differs obviously from mainstream practice theory, which takes background knowledge as largely invariant. The two levels, practice and background knowledge, are closely related and mutually affected. Practice theory, by taking practice as ontologically significant, tends more to see background knowledge as something super-steady, or even static (Schatzki et al. 2001). The argument of the logic of habit (Hopf 2010) is still more conspicuous in this respect, holding that human behavior is highly predictable because most of it depends on habit. As such, uncertainty and rationality matter little. This generalization is true to some extent and it may explain continuity. But it cannot explain change.

Change in practice and even in the background knowledge of a community of practice not only is possible, but it occurs quite often. What brings about change can be traced to the internal factors within a community. The European Union exemplifies a great shift in human history, from a place where most serious wars broke out to a security community where war is basically unlikely and unthinkable. There are of course numerous causal factors at work, but serious reflection by Europeans themselves, especially after experiencing the greatest conflicts in human history and their efforts to change this particular practice, has played a most important role. It is in this sense more the internal driving force that had brought about the change. Moreover, what has changed is not only the practice of warfare, but also the background knowledge that highlighted the glories of military strife and conquest.

In the process of modernity, however, it seems that significant changes have been brought about, quite often, through inter-practicality. The story of China's modernization is a case in point (Li 2003). When China met the West in the nineteenth century, two different types of practices, each with its civilization-based, time-honored background knowledge, began to interact. This inter-practicality caused tremendous shock in the traditional Chinese society and polity. In the political arena, the empirical court was overthrown and there appeared for the first time a "republic." In intellectual affairs, there were dynamic debates among those favoring "wholesale Westernization," those supporting "Chinese learning as the base and Western learning for application," and those advocating "keeping a balance between Chinese and Western learning." Finally, in the social realm, the millennium-long traditions of polygyny and foot-binding imposed on women were gone. These changes took place largely due to inter-practicality between the traditional Chinese society and the outside world. They were not only changes in everyday practice but also a profound transformation of the background knowledge.

Human agency as the key factor

Because practice is an open process, inter-practicality may produce positive or negative consequences and changes. The clash-of-civilizations argument paints a pessimistic picture, but it is not completely wrong-headed. Once practices of various communities enter into interaction, which globalization has made inevitable, differences may well lead to conflict. Once such conflict is related to fundamental ideational practices, such as religious and ideological practices, Huntington's prophecy may come true. In today's world as well as in history, many conflicts are related to religious or ideological difference and such conflicts are extremely difficult to resolve because they concern matters of belief. Beliefs tend to be non-negotiable.

At the same time, it is also clear that inter-practicality leads to cooperation and human progress. Eisenstadt's multiple-modernity model is an optimistic theory, indicating that various cultural communities are able to communicate in and through practice positively and constructively once their differences are recognized, respected, and even valued. Fukuyama's argument also is optimistic in a sense, but it is unrealistic. It is impossible for various cultural communities to take the same path and for the world to reach the homogeneity he imagines. It never will be possible in this multiplex environment. Even though the goals and objectives are shared, the ways to realize them are practiced differently.

How can we enable inter-practicality to produce positive results that promote cooperation rather than to cause negative consequences? The key factor is human agency. Practice theory tends to pay less attention to human reflection as well as the human ability to reflect, for (as noted previously) what people do is the result of the inarticulate know-how that makes "what is to be done appear 'self-evident' and commonsensical" (Pouliot 2008: 257). The argument of the logic of habit has gone even further to deny the role of agency in human affairs in general and in international relations in particular. As Ted Hopf contends, "Where the logic of habit predominates, international relations have less agency, less rationality, and less uncertainty than other logics would lead us to expect" (Hopf 2010: 540). For example, security and cooperation dilemmas, by the logic of habit, are in fact not dilemmas at all. Rather, they are "straightforward habitual routines of enmity and amity" (Hopf 2010: 540).

This denial of human agency in practice-oriented theory owes much to its differentiation between background knowledge and representational knowledge as two isolated opposites and its exclusion of the latter out of the discourse of practice and practicality. I have argued elsewhere that representation is practice. Theory, for example, belongs undoubtedly to representational knowledge. For Wittgenstein and especially Austin (2002), speaking is doing. In this line of thinking, representing also is doing. If activities such as workers making machines and diplomats performing diplomatic duties are practices, the activities of scholars generating theory also must count as practices. Theory is representational knowledge and producing theory involves reflection. If we agree that theory generating is practice, then practice entails reflection.

Inter-practicality, therefore, cannot be carried out without thinking people. But it is not a mere superficial understanding of what the other-community is practicing. Tourism is usually an example of this type of superficiality. Inter-practicality requires, as practice internalism believes, a holistic understanding of the practice in an other-community through personal participation, speaking the language of its members and thinking the way its members think. Working on a PhD degree in a foreign academic community provides a good example here, for it requires a deep understanding of the whole set of rules, norms, and principles that sustain the academic construction in that community.

In this process of inter-practicality, people are the most important, for it is people who perform inter-practicality – trying to understand as participants, to use the language as if it were their mother tongue, and to think and reflect as locals do. In this process human agency is particularly important, for it is necessarily required to see, to compare, and to judge, for instance, what will lead to cooperation and what will cause conflict. To a large extent, the question raised at the beginning of this section (i.e., how to promote positive results and avoid negative consequences in inter-practicality) can be answered by how people as participants in the process understand, interpret, reflect, and evaluate. It is therefore human agency that shapes the orientation of inter-practicality. It is also human agency that enables inter-practicality to produce better and more effective governance in global affairs.

New multilateralism: of institutions and relations

Inter-practicality is a useful approach for comparative regionalism and interregionalism with a clear focus on the mutuality of various practices across regional communities and for the purpose of mutual complementation and empowerment.

In a previous study (Qin 2019), I followed the intra-practicality approach, comparing the practices of the EU and ASEAN so as to find the anchoring or pivot practice in each community for cooperation. As the quotations at the beginning of this chapter indicate, though both communities aim at building up multilateralism to encourage cooperation for regional peace, prosperity, and progress, the anchoring practice for the EU is very much institutionalized or contract-binding cooperation, while that for ASEAN is more relation-oriented or friendship-driven cooperation. Simply put, the EU practices more institutional multilateralism and the ASEAN practices more relational multilateralism. This is definitely not to suggest that there are no institutional efforts in the ASEAN and no bonds of friendship in the EU, only that their anchoring practices, that is, the practice that makes other practices in the community possible, differ.

This chapter, as a follow-up to my earlier contribution, moves further to discuss how positive practices in various communities can complement each other so that multilateralism for governance will be enhanced through mutual empowerment. It is also helpful to see how those positive practices and the reasonable elements of the background knowledge behind them in different communities of practice can come to blend in a synthesis for the benefit of all. That is exactly what inter-practicality means and tries to achieve.

It is inspiring to see how the EU's institutional multilateralism and ASEAN's relational multilateralism can work together through inter-practicality. Despite the vicissitudes of the process of the European regional integration, the EU has achieved great success in terms of its set goals of peace and cooperation in the region. Its practice in region-wide cooperation and integration has produced enormous influence in the world, too. ASEAN, another successful example, began by learning from the European model, and its goals were very similar to those of the European regional integration, such as peace and development. Also, despite the ups and downs in its decades-long course of development since the 1960s, ASEAN has shown great resilience and become a "miracle" in building multilateralism and regional cooperation. In short, institutional multilateralism seems to be more legally binding, whereas relational multilateralism is more resilient.

From the examples of the EU and ASEAN, we can draw some interesting generalizations. First, the models of institutional and relational multilateralism coexist. Both approaches to multilateralism are practices in reality because both are imbued with certain universally applicable values. It means that for multilateralism to work effectively, institutions and relations should be simultaneously at work. "Interest" is perhaps a key word for institutional multilateralism, which is expected to bring benefits to all parties to the multilateralism. The interest calculation is assumed and based on individual rationality. It is also true of all other models of multilateralism. When we turn to the relational model, "trust" is the key word, for good relationships rest on trust rather than contract. The relational model is human and value-laden. However, even for primarily institutional multilateralisms, trust cannot be absent. Interest and trust are both indispensable to the workings of any and all multilateralisms. Reliance exclusively on one at the cost of the other will lead nowhere.

Second, cultures and practices matter. Why is relational multilateralism more conspicuous in ASEAN, while institutional multilateralism remains more attractive in the EU? I argue, with Meyer, that it is the cultural and social contexts that matter as background knowledge. Because of the significance of cultures and practices, adoption of relational multilateralism or institutional multilateralism is not a mere choice; it is a practice embedded and nurtured in culture and society. In other words, both have their roots in social practices as well as in their respective background knowledge. In a more individualistic society, for example, formal institutions have been emphasized because long practices have cultivated and justified such a model. In contrast, a more relation-oriented society may have a long tradition of different practices that have nurtured a relational way of multilateral cooperation. Consequently, multilateralism, whether predominantly institutional or predominantly relational, is quite often more the result of social practice than rational choice. Therefore, each deserves respect.

Third, inter-practicality aims to bridge the two models, enabling them to realize a mutually empowering effect. Often, institutional multilateralism is considered the right way to multilateral cooperation and transnational governance. It is based on reason, interest, and even the selfish nature of human beings. To some extent that is true. At the same time, any cooperation cannot exist and develop without human relations. What Kishore Mahbubani and Jeffery Sng say in the passage quoted at the start of this chapter indicates that "friendship and camaraderie," or good relations, are also crucial for cooperation, which is obviously an important element in the so-called ASEAN way (Acharya 2001). The fact that institutional multilateralism and relational multilateralism coexist at the same time and in different socio-cultural settings means that there is a reason for each.

The above discussion has demonstrated some important features in multilateralism. For multilateralism in use there are (perhaps at least) two basic models: namely, the institutional and the relational. The former works through providing contracts that work on the rationality of individual actors, making them sensibly follow established rules and norms, while the latter works through managing human relations, leading to a more harmonious relational context for cooperation. The two approaches have different conceptions and assumptions on how multilateralism is effectively practiced. The core of the former is rationality, or the rational choice of the economic actor, and that of the latter is relationality, or embedded relationships based on trust among social persons. They coexist. Institutions are not absent in relational multilateralism, or vice versa. Though each has its distinctive features, they are complementary rather than contradictory, and can be mutually reinforcing. Furthermore, which multilateralism approach to be taken is both a choice and a practice. It is a choice because actors may opt for an institutional or relational model of multilateralism by calculating costs and benefits. But it is perhaps more a social practice because which one is used depends very much on the long-standing practice of a community in a certain socio-cultural setting. It is reasonable to argue that communitarian societies tend more to use relational multilateralism, and individualistic societies emphasize more the institutional approach. But any workable multilateralism contains elements of both, no matter where it is practiced.

The question thus is how to combine the positive elements of the two so that a more effective and resilient multilateralism for cooperation can be generated and can work. Taking an approach of analytical eclecticism (Sil & Katzenstein 2010) and particularly applying the Chinese *zhongyong* dialectics,[1] I argue that the two can be synthesized so that a more effective multilateralism will be developed. Moreover, they coexist and work together to inform the practice of multilateralism. Thus it is possible to combine their important aspects, and also to reflect more the reality and real problems of multilateralism. I therefore hypothesize that an appropriate combination of institutional and relational multilateralism with due measure and degree is likely to facilitate rather than impede cooperation and governance.

The key to a synthetic approach is how institutions and relations are intertwined in actual governance, reinforcing each other under certain conditions. It is clear that each model has its advantages and disadvantages. Institutions, for example, are effective where they are supported and enforced by power, where they specify clearly the terms, and where individual actors tend to abide. International institutions can lower transactional costs, increase transparency and inhibit, at least to some extent, cheating in cooperation (Keohane 1984). They can also generate sets of rules and norms for members to follow. It is not an exaggeration to say that rule-based multilateralism has been and will continue to be the most reasonable and relevant form of multilateral governance.

However, institutional multilateralism has its weaknesses. For example, it places particular emphasis on legal and formal institutions and by doing so may neglect the role of human emotion in cooperation and governance. Any successful cooperation in human society, whether domestic or international, entails both reason and emotion. Institutions, designed and established to maintain social order for better human conditions, may lead to a dilemma where increasing the role of rationality automatically reduces the role of emotion. Society is human in the final analysis, and abstract rationality embodied in institutions and written in contracts cannot work alone without considering the factor of human emotion. It may even lead to the collapse of a community if institutional rules are too rigid without considering the complexity and flexibility of human emotion, for a well-governed society is one full of human feelings.

Relational multilateralism can create a favorable environment through management and harmonization of relations, wherein multilateral cooperation is based upon mutual trust and is therefore sustainable and lasting. According to the Chinese savant Mencius, harmonious relations are the best condition for realizing both common goals and individual objectives. Any society, domestic or international, cannot work without human factors and human considerations. It is exactly here that relational multilateralism is able to compensate for the weaknesses of institutional multilateralism or add a human face to institutional rules and regulations. Friendship has always been a key to good governance.

Relational multilateralism, however, may place too much emphasis on relationships, which may even enable actors to make every effort to bypass and violate rules or exploit loopholes in existing rules. Cheating may be justified in the name of promoting friendship. It has been found that Confucianism tends to overstress the importance of morality and humanity to the extent that it neglects the use of explicit rules and regulations to define rights and obligations of various sectors in society. It is here that institution-building is crucial to be added for addressing the possible collapse of multilateral cooperation.

An ideal combination is that both models complement each other in a positive and beneficial way. I chose to use the quotation from Kishore Mahbubani and Jeffery Sng at the beginning of this chapter not only because it describes the most distinct feature of relational multilateralism, but also, perhaps more interestingly, because it depicts an ideal picture of blending institutional and relational approaches in a multilateral setting. The United Nations, as a typical example of institutional multilateralism, was founded to be a rules-based international body for governance in world affairs. It is exactly in this highly institutional setting that ASEAN golf games are held and annual ASEAN dinners receive guests and friends, including the UN secretary-general. Such "relational" activities help "break down barriers and promote camaraderie." It is the ASEAN way of peaceful cooperation.

Conclusion

The quotation by Kishore Mahbubani and Jeffery Sng draws an interesting picture of inter-practicality, that is, inter-practicality of institutions and relations. The United Nations is a most comprehensive intergovernmental, multilateral organization, highly institutionalized and primarily rule based. Weekend golfing, annual dinners, hand-shaking, hospitality by ministers' wives, gift-presenting, and orchid-giving – all these activities are informal, aiming to generate friendship and promote harmonious relations. When these practices are performed in a highly institutionalized setting, they are most revealing and inspiring. This may represent a benign blending of institutions and relations.

Institutions and relations, blended in a positive way, can generate better multilateralism. It is reasonable to say that institutions work better and more effectively when friendly relations are managed and maintained among staff members, and harmonious relations are promoted when institutions are full of vim and vigor. They are mutually reinforcing. That, at least, is the ideal, but it is not impossible.

The realization of that state of affairs, however, does not occur spontaneously. When the former foreign minister of Singapore said that such activities were "not seen in other regional organizations," he perhaps pointed out a fact: relation-building practices are not contained in their background knowledge and therefore are not in their menu of practices. It is the question of "understanding the other" examined by Mario Telò in his discussion of intercultural dialogue (Telò 2018). This brings back the important role played by "practice internalism": only by co-living as a participant in the practice of an other-community, taking an insider's viewpoint, and understanding the whole set of rules and norms that come from the background knowledge therein can we capture "the common understanding which participants in a common practice share and which enables them to make sense and interact within their practice" (Lechner & Frost 2018: 34). On that basis we can find appropriate ways for inter-practicality to generate positive, mutually empowering effects for peaceful cooperation and multilateral governance in global affairs.

Note

1 The Chinese *zhongyong* dialectic takes a "both-and" approach, believing that any two poles or forces in the natural and the social world are complementary rather than contradictory to each other, depending each other for articulation and life. The interaction of the two is a process of harmonization. As such, it denies the "either-or" way of thinking and assumes harmony as the original state of all relationships. See Cheng (2006).

References

Acharya, A. 2001. *Constructing a Security Community in Southeast Asia: ASEAN and the Problem of Regional Order*. London: Routledge

Adler, E. & M. Barnett (eds.). 1998. *Security Communities*. Cambridge, UK: Cambridge University Press

Adler, E. & V. Pouliot (eds.). 2011. *International Practices*. Cambridge, UK: Cambridge University Press

Austin, J. L. 2002. *How to Do Things with Words*. Beijing & Cambridge, UK: Foreign Language Teaching and Research Press & Cambridge University Press

Cheng, Chung-ying. 2006. "Toward Constructing a Dialectics of Harmonization: Harmony and Conflict in Chinese Philosophy." *Journal of Chinese Philosophy* 33(1): 25–59

Fukuyama, F. 1992. *The End of History and the Last Man*. New York: Free Press

Hopf, T. 2010. "The Logic of Habit in International Relations." *European Journal of International Relations* 16(4): 539–61

Huntington, S. 1996. *The Clash of Civilizations and the Remaking of the World Order*. New York: Simon and Schuster

Keohane, R. O. 1984. *After Hegemony: Cooperation and Discord in World Political Economy*. Princeton, NJ: Princeton University Press

Lechner, S. & M. Frost. 2018. *Practice Theory and International Relations*. Cambridge, UK: Cambridge University Press

Li, Z. 2003. *Zhongguo Jindai Sixiangshi Lun* [An Intellectual History of Modern China]. Tianjin, China: Tianjin Social Science Press

Mahbubani, K. & J. Sng. 2017. *The ASEAN Miracle: A Catalyst for Peace*. Singapore: Ridge Books

Meyer, T. 2018a. "Introduction." In T. Meyer & J. de Sales Marques (eds.), *Multiple Modernities and Good Governance*. London & New York: Routledge, pp. 1–11

Meyer, T. 2018b. "Multiple Modernities and Good Governance." In T. Meyer & J. de Sales Marques (eds.), *Multiple Modernities and Good Governance*. London & New York: Routledge, pp. 15–28

Pouliot, V. 2008. "The Logic of Practicality: A Theory of Practice of Security Communities." *International Organization* 62(2): 257–88

Pouliot, V. 2016. *International Pecking Orders: The Politics and Practice of Multilateral Diplomacy*. Cambridge, UK: Cambridge University Press

Qin, Y. 2018. *A Relational Theory of World Politics*. Cambridge, UK: Cambridge University Press

Qin, Y. 2019. "Transnational Governance and Multiple Multilateralism." In T. Meyer, J. de Sales Marques, & M. Telò (eds.), *Regionalism and Multilateralism: Politics, Economics, Culture*. Abingdon, UK, & New York: Routledge, pp. 48–65

Ringmar, Erik. 2012. "Performing International Systems: Two East-Asian Alternatives to the Westphalian Order." *International Organization* 66(1): 1–25

Schatzki, T. R., K. K. Cetina, & E. von Savigny (eds.). 2001. *The Practice Turn in Contemporary Theory*. London & New York: Routledge

Searle, J. R. (1995). *The Construction of Social Reality*. New York: The Free Press

Sil, R. & P. Katzenstein. 2010. *Beyond Paradigms: Analytical Eclecticism in the Study of World Politics*. Basingstoke, Hampshire, UK, & New York: Palgrave Macmillan

Telò, M. 2018. "The Past and Present of Europe's Intercultural Dialogue: Beyond a Normative Power Approach to Two-way Cooperation." In T. Meyer & J. de Sales Marques (eds.), *Multiple Modernities and Good Governance*. London & New York: Routledge, pp. 101–17

Telò, M. 2019. "Multiple Modernities in a Multipolar and Multiregional World: Some Conditions for an Interregional Dialogue." In T. Meyer, J. de Sales Marques, & M. Telò (eds.), *Cultures, Nationalism and Populism: New Challenges to Multilateralism*. London & New York: Routledge, pp. 112–32

Tickner, A. B. & D. L. Blaney (eds.). 2012. *Thinking International Relations Differently*. London & New York: Routledge

Tickner, A. B. & O. Waever (eds.). 2009. *International Relations Scholarship Around the World*. London & New York: Routledge

Wittgenstein, L. 1968. *Philosophical Investigations*. 3rd ed. D. P. Pears & B. F. McGuinness (trans.). London: Routledge

INDEX

Note: Page numbers in *italics* indicate a figure and page numbers in **bold** indicate a table on the corresponding page.

9/11 attacks 82, 143
11th Five-Year Plan (China Plan) 60, 62–3
12th Five-Year Plan (China Plan) 60, 63
15th Conference of the Parties (COP15) 32, 38, *50*
21 Conference of the Parties (COP21) 84, 85
26th Conference of the Parties (COP26) 32
1948 Universal Declaration of Human Rights 154, 170, 17546, 178
1962 Trade Expansion Act 102
2005 UNESCO Convention on the Protection and Promotion of the Diversity of Cultural Expressions 90, 113, 115
2019 US-China trade restrictions *98*
2030 Agenda for Sustainable Development (United Nations) 7, 25–6, 29–30, 35, 44

absolute dignity 160
acid rain 59
Adler, E. 201, 203–4
Advisory Council on International Affairs, The Hague, Netherlands 165
African Union 85
aggressive religious fundamentalism 6
agricultural civilization 41
air quality 56, 58–9; measurement 57; regulation 58; standards **60**; targets 61
Alkire, S. 135
Alternative for Germany (AfD) 119
American Anthropological Association (AAA) 175, 179

Amin, S. 74
Analects of Confucius (Confucius) 173
annual deaths in military combat *125*
ASEM (Asia-Europe meeting) 81, 87
Asian values 154, 177
Asia-Pacific Economic Cooperation (APEC) 81
Asia-Pacific Economic Cooperation Free Trade Agreement (APEC-FTA) 82
Association of Southeast Asian Nations (ASEAN) 82, 200
Austin, J. L. 210
Axial Age 171

Barnett, M. 203
Basic Rights, social and political 10, 156
Belt and Road Initiative (BRI) 82
Bernstein, S. 38
bias: technocratic 9, 120; transcend cultural 161
Biden, J. 71
bilateralism 10, 47, 72, 76, 80–2, 92, 99, 103
biodiversity 26, 47–50
Blair, T. 73
Bolsonaro, J. 122
Borrell, J. 103–4
Brazil 56
British-India railway system 108
broad social resonance 158
Buddhism 42
Bush, G. W. 82
Buzan, B. 133

calcium sulfite (CaSO$_3$) 65
Canada 8, 19, 48–9, 72, 77–9, 83–4, 88
carbon emissions 22–3, *23*
Chevènement J.-P. 74
China Council for International Cooperation on Environment and Development (CCICED) 42
China Dialogue (Shanahan) 50
China Quarterly (Ely and Geall) 44
Chinese FDI *100*
citizenship 164; *see also* social citizenship
civilian power 88
civilization 3–7, 11–12, 21, 25–30, 79, 90, 138, 154, 156–7, 159–62, 167, 202, 206–9; agricultural 41; culture and 12, 41, 157; ecological 7, 26–8, *27*, 33–4; global ecological 32–51; human 11, 41, 170, 179–80; industrial 41; primitive 41
civil rights 153–4, 160–6
civil society, influence of 91
Clayton, P. 46
climate change 7–8, 47–50; EU citizens' attitudes on 139; EU citizens' perceptions of 139; EU's response to crisis 139–42; impacts on Europe 138–9; security 136–8
Climate Policy (Jiang) 42
Clinton, B. 82
coal 24, 42, 56, 58–61, 65–6, 141–2
coal-fired power 58–9
Cobb, J. 46
coexistence of multiple practices 206–7
Cold War 11, 73, 91, 121–2, 134–5, 154–6, 176, 184–7, 192–3
colonial rule in India 108
Commission on Human Security (United Nations) 36, 79, 136
common but differentiated responsibility and respective capabilities (CBDR-EC) 37–8
Common Foreign and Security Policy (CFSP; EU) 82, 103
common global concern 6
communalist theories 160
communal obligations 162
Communist Manifesto, The (Marx and Engels) 74
Communist Party of China (CPC) 39–41, 43, 166–7
community of common destiny (CCD) 34, 39–43, 46
community security 135
competition 65

Comprehensive Agreement on Investment (CAI) 8, 104
Comprehensive and Progressive Agreement for Trans-Pacific Partnership (CPTPP) 80
Comprehensive Economic and Trade Agreement (EU and Canada) (CETA) 79, 83–4
Confessions (Augustine of Hippo) 108
Confucius 160, 171, 173, 179, 180n2
Confucianism 42
continuous emissions monitoring systems (CEMS) 61–4
Corbyn, J. 74
Cotonou Agreements 84–6, 88, 108, 112
Council of Ministers of the EU 140, 165
Court of Justice of the European Union (CJEU) 84
COVID-19/coronavirus pandemic 1, 2, 8, 32, 49, 95, 96, 104–5
crisis: of multilateralism 183–95; socio-economic 1
critical historical junctures 91
cultural exceptions 90
cultural nationalism 6
cultural relativism: human rights 174–6; political instrumentalization of 176–8
culture: and civilization 12, 41, 157; global trade and 88–90; industrial *v.* traditional 42; political 4, 7, 40, 51, 101, 158, 162–4; Western 174

Daoism 42
David, C. 133
de facto cultural relativism 6
democracy: libertarian 163; social 164
Deng Xiaoping 40
Deudney, D. 71
differentiated universalism 90
Ding, C. 8
dirty coal 24
divide within the West 162–4
Durkheim, E. 160

East India Company 108
ecological civilization (EC) 7, 26–8, *27*, 33–4; Chinese concepts of 39–43, *40*; institutionalization of 40; international community 43–6; international promotion of 42; multilateral environmental governance 47–50; potential implications of 39
ecological progress 43
economic attainment 18
economic development 18

economic expansion 18
economic interdependence 1
economic nationalism 95
Economic Partnership Agreement (EPA) 85
economic prosperity 26
economic security 135
economic-security nexus 87
economic transformation 28–9
economies, mature/developed 21
Eisenstadt, S. 4–5, 157–9, 206, 209
Ely, A. 44, 47
emerging economies 17–18
emissions trading scheme (ETS) 140
end of history 4, 206
End of History and the Last Man, The (Fukuyama) 73
endogenous intersubjectivity 202–5
energy consumption 20–2, *22*, 25, 140
Engels, F. 74
environmental politics 33
environmental protection 7–8, 43; *see also* climate change
Environmental Protection Bureau (EPB) 62
environmental security 135
Erdoğan, R. T. 119, 122
Esprit des Lois, De L' (Montesquieu) 73
essentially state-centric security 134
EU-China Bilateral Investment Treaty (BIT) 103; *see also* Comprehensive Agreement on Investment (CAI)
EU-China economic and trade relations 95–105; China-WTO 103; geopolitical commission 103–4; geopolitical trade policy 103–4; hard times of world economy 96–9; overview 99–101; triplexity in making 104–5; US-China trade war 101–2
European Commission 88, 102–4, 139–42, 144–6
European Council xvi, xx
European Economic Community (EEC) 96, 99
European Parliament 81, 84–5, 88, 112, 141
European Union (EU): migration regime 144–5; partners in trade of goods *99*; trade policy 82–8, **83**

Fawcett, L. 8, 81, 87
Ferreira, S. 10
Flores, R. G. 9
flue-gas desulfurization (FGD) 59–61, 63
food security 135
Ford Motor Company 89
foreign direct investment (FDI) 96, *97*, 99, 109

foreign investment restrictions and regulations *98*
Forsythe, D. P. 186, 190, 193
Fortress Europe 143
Freedom Party of Austria (FPO) 119
Free Trade Area (FTA) 72, 82, 90, 96
Free Trade Area of the Americas (FTAA) 81
free-trade liberalism 72–3
Friedman, E. 174
Frost, M. 201, 206–7
fuel choices 65–6
Fukuyama, F. 4, 73

Gamble, A. 1
Gare, A. 45
Geall, S. 44, 47
General Agreement on Tariffs and Trade (GATT) 71, 76
geographic indications 83
geopolitical commission 103–4
geopolitical trade policy 103–4
Gerrits, A. W. M. 11
global ecological civilization 32–51; Chinese concepts 39–43; global environmental governance institutions 34–9; international community 43–6; in multilateral environmental governance 47–50; overview 32–4
global economic policy uncertainty *98*
global environmental governance institutions 34–9
global Gini index 124, *125*
global governance system 9–10, 120–2, 126
global multilateralism, classic 80
global political system 120, 122, 126
global trade 71–91; arguments against free trade 73–4; change in 71–2; comprehensive approach to 107–15; cultural implications 72–5; culture and 88–90; EU trade policy 82–8; hard times of 96–9; multilateral trade 75–6; non-financial interaction 109–11; obstacles to reforming the WTO 77–80; political implications 72–5; reviving by reforming the WTO 76–7; reviving through bilateralism 80–2; reviving through interregionalism 80–2; rules-based trade 74–5; slowdown in *96*; social justice 107–15; suggestions 112–15; unrestricted free trade 72–3; worldwide trade 75–6
Goron C. 7, 38, 40, 45
grandfathering 60
greenhouse gas (GHG) 132, 136

green industrial revolution 38
Green Is Gold (UN Environment Programme; UNEP) 44

health security 135
Heller, H. 164
Herder, J. G. 11
Heurtebise, S. J.-Y. 45
High-Level Economic and Trade Dialogue (HED) 100
Hirschman, A. 73
Hoffmann, M. 38
Hogan, P. 104
Hopf, T. 209
Hopgood, S. 187
human: agency 209–10; civilization 11, 41; community 170–80; dignity 170, 171–4; nature 172; rationality 172; security 135–6; survival demands 6
Human Development Index (HDI) 20, 23–4, **24**, 124, *124*
human rights 5, 10–12, 170–80; cultural diversity for the protection of 178–80; cultural relativism 174–6; declarations of 178–80; future of 183–95; institutionalization of 174–6; intellectual history 171–4; liberal international order and 185–6; new regime 189–90; overview 170–1; state of regime 186–9; *see also* Vienna Conference on Human Rights 1993
Huntington, S. 4–5, 79, 156–7, 206, 209
Hurrel, A. 195
hybrid interregionalism 80

ideological West 155
ideology/ideological 4–5, 51, 176, 184, 209; conflicts 156, 161; of domination 4; human rights and 190, 194; ideological competition 19; political 154–5
Ikenberry, J. 71
India 17, 19–24, 56–66
industrial civilization 41
industrial culture 42
industrialization 20, 22–3, 25, 27, 45–7
Industrial Revolution 25
inequality 9, 124
institutionalization 9, 35–6, 40; *see also* global environmental governance institutions; *specific institutions*
institutionalized inequality 128
institutionalized universalism 6
interconnection treaty 83
Intergovernmental Panel on Climate Change (IPCC) 32, 36, 136

Intergovernmental Science-Policy Platform on Biodiversity and Ecosystem Services (IPBES) 32, 36–8, 52n4
internal migration 142
international authority *123*
international cooperation practices 33
International Covenant of Human Rights 1966 10, 155–6, 162–6
international human rights regime 11, 183–92, 194
International Labour Organization (ILO) 79, 83, 85, 88, 155
international migration 142
International Monetary Fund (IMF) 3, 123
International Telecommunications Unit (ITU) 113
international trade 8–9; *see also* global trade
Internat Telecommunic Union *see* International Telecommunications Unit (ITU)
inter-practicality 199–215
interregionalism 8, 80–2, 95, 210
investor-state dispute settlements (ISDS) 79
Iraq 6
Islamic State 6

Jaspers, K. 171
Jiang, K. 42

Kant, I. 72, 74–5, 105, 107, 160
Karlsson, C. 140
Katzenstein 6, 79, 91, 213
Keohane, R. 35, 199, 213

Lafer, C. 9
Lassalle, F. 74
Lechner, S. 201, 206–7
Lee, E.-J. 11
legitimacy 9, 11, 189, 190; belief in 127–2; deficits 3, 9, 84, 112, 120; democratic 88; of the human rights 187, 192, 194; issue of 91; of multilateralism 183
legitimation 4, 9, 120, 126–9, 130, 157–8
Leibniz, G. 172
Le Pen, M. 122
liberal international order 185–6
libertarian democracy 163
liquefied petroleum gas (LPG) 59
Lo, Bobo 185
logic of modernization (Munch) 157
London Smog 57
long-standing air quality 58
longue durée 159
low-carbon consumption policy 30
low-income countries 22

Macau Forum 7
Mahbubani, K. 199
Mamström, C. 101
Mao Zedong 39
Marinelli, M. 41
Marshall, T. H. 162–3
Marx, K. 74, 105
mature/developed economies 21
megadiverse developing countries 34, 47, 51n1–51n2
Melanchthon, P. 74
Mencius 171–2
mercantilism 73
MERCOSUR (market of the southern cone) 8, 80, 82, 85, 88–9, 112
Meyer, T. 10, 86, 200, 206–7
migration 142–3
migratory dynamics 143–4
Mill, J. S. 75
Ministry of Ecology and Environment (MEE) 39
Mirandola, P. D. 159
modern/modernity 3–5, 35, 107–8, 153; democracy 162; forms of 5, 157; liberal-democratic model of **206**; Western **6**; *see also* multiple modernities
modernism 5
modernization: variety of paths towards 3–6; Western 6, 160
Montesquieu, C. 72–3
Morrison, R. 46
Moyn, S. 187, 194
multilateral cooperation 2
multilateral environmental agreements (MEA) 35
multilateral environmental governance 32–4, 47–50; *see also* global ecological civilization
multilateral forum 1, 119
multilateralism: crisis of 183–95; international human rights regime 11, 183; intra-practicality 202–10; localness of background knowledge 200–2; institutional 79, 199, 211–14; overview 199–200; practicality 200–2; qualified 184–5; via inter-practicality 199–215
multilateralism in crisis 119–30; of global governance system 120–2; overview 119–20; as a problem of legitimation 126–9; reason 122–6; relational 199, 211ion
multilateral networks 1
multilateral organization 1, 214
multilateral peacekeeping 9–10
multilateral regimes 1, 51
multilateral trade 8, 75–6, 80

multiple modernities 3–4, 10–11, 113, 127, 153–68, 195, 206; challenge 156–9; controversy 154–6; divide within the West 162–4; overview 153–4; universal human rights 153–68; universality reconsidered 164–7; Western genesis 159–62
Munch, R. 157–8

Napoleonic Wars 108
Nationally Determined Contributions (NDC), climate change regime 7–8, 48–9, 51, **60**, 137
national security 134
National Security Strategy (US NSS) 121
natural gas 59
natural rights 172
Nehru, J. 161
neoliberalism 75
new multilateralism 2–3, 12, 80, 90, 210–14
non-financial interaction, trade as 109–11
non-governmental organization (NGO) 10, 49, 84, 122, 129, 136, 185, 187, 191
North American Free Trade Agreement (NAFTA) 72, 79

obligations: of conduct 165; of result 165
O'Byrne, D. 194
O'Connor, T. 161
Orban, V. 119, 122
Organization for Economic Co-operation and Development (OECD) 17
outward foreign direct investment (OFDI) *100*

Pan, J. 7
Paris Climate Agreement 23, 132, 137; *see also* 21 Conference of the Parties (COP21)
Parker, C. 140
peaceful trade 108
People's Republic of China (PRC) 162, 164–5, 167
Pereira, J. C. 10
personal security 135
Petrasek, D. 188
Philosophical Foundations of Ecological Civilization, The (Gare) 45
political instrumentalization 176–8
political liberalism 75
political security 135
political-security factors 91
political violence, organized 136
population growth 19, *20*
post-globalization era 170–80

post-hegemonic era 82, 87
Pouliot, V. 201, 204
power sector regulation 56–66; competition 65; enforcement 61–4; fuel choice 65–6; monitoring 61–4; overview 56–8; power generation 56, 59; standard setting 58–61
practice: as an open process 208–9; internalism 207–8
practice-dependent action 201
primitive civilization 41
principled pragmatism 184
pro-multilateralism factors 1
protectionism, trade 2, 8, 74
Putin, V. 119, 122

Qin, Y. 12, 80, 86

Regional Comprehensive Economic Partnership (RCEP) 80, 82, 86–7
Ricardo, D. 72, 110
Rio Earth Summit 35–6
Roosevelt, F.D. 121, 156
Rutte, M. 104

Schmidt, H. 161
Schwartz, W. A. 46
Searle, J. 201, 203
security 133–5, 142–3; climate change 136–8; community 135; concept of 134; economic 135; environmental 135; essentially state-centric 134; in the field of international relations 134; food 135; health 135; human 135–6; national 134; personal 135; political 135; threats 78
Security Communities 203
self-enforcement payment feedback system 63
self-imposed crises 187
Sen, A. 5
Shanahan, M. 50
Sikkink, K. 188–9
Singapore decision (EU Court of Justice) 84, 88, 91
small and medium-sized enterprises (SME) 84
Smith, A. 72
Sng, J. 199, 212, 214
social citizenship 163–4
social democracy 163–4
socio-economic crisis/rights 1, 162
state-owned enterprises (SOE) 102
Strategic Partnership Agreement 85
subjective factors 91

sumak kawsay 33
sustainable development (SD): concept of 45; global norm of 42
Sustainable Development Goals (SDG) 17–30, 35; change in the global landscape 20–5; ecological civilization 26–8; emerging world pattern 17–20, *18*; institutionalization of the concept of *36*; Sinicization of 34; transformative process 28–30; vision for a sustainable future 25–6
Syria 6

technocratic bias 9, 120
Teixeira, N. S. 10
Telò, M. 8, 214
Tharoor, S. 108
Tian, S. 41, 46
trade: liberalization 71; rules-based 74–5; *see also* global trade
traditional culture, China 42
traditionalism 5
transatlantic alliance 102–3
Transatlantic Trade and Investment Partnership (TTIP) 79, 110
transcend cultural bias 161
Trans-Pacific Partnership (TPP) 72, 79, 81, 110
tri-party complexity 96, 104–5
triplexity *see* tri-party complexity
Trump, D. 10, 71–2, 74–5, 78–87, 101–3, 119, 121–2
Twitter 57

ul Haq, Mahbub 135
ultra-low-emissions (ULE) 58, 61
UN Agenda for Sustainable Development 25–6, 35
UNCITRAL (UN Arbitration Rules) 79
UN Commission on International Trade Law 79
UN conventions on human rights 79
UN Environment Programme (UNEP) 44
UN Framework Convention on Climate Change (UNFCCC) 30, 32, 36–8, 47, 140
UN Human Rights Council 190
United Nations (UN) 1, 35, 111–12, 120; Agenda 25–6; Covenants on Basic Rights 10, 155, 162–5; Declarations 6, 153, 159, 161; Rio Earth Summit 35–6
United Nations 2030 Agenda 7
United Nations Convention on Biodiversity (CBD) 32, 36–8

United Nations, Department of Economic and Social Affairs, Population Division (2019) 30n1

United Nations Economics and Social Commission for Asia and the Pacific (UNESCAP) 191

United Nations Human Rights Charter 135, 155, 174

United States (US) 1–4, 8–10, 29, 37–8, 46–8, 60, 62–5, 71–2, 77–81, 101–5, 107–11, 121–2, 155–6, 190, 204; administration 47; CO2 emissions in 23; economy 19, 21, 25; energy consumption 22; EU-China trade relations 96, *98*, 101; global political system 121; human development level 24; interregional negotiations 81; multilateral trading 75; trade liberalization 71, 82; trade policy of 82, 86; WTO 77

UN Secretary-General's Climate Summit 49

UN Security Council (UNSC) 128, 187

universal human rights 153, 166, 176–8, 180, 193–4

Universal Declaration of Human Rights 154, 170, 175, 176, 178

universalism: cultural relativism and 11, 175, 179–80; differentiated 90; of human rights 179, 193–4; nationalism and 41

universality, of rights 10, 11, 153–4, 160–1, 164–6, 178, 179–80, 185

urbanization 20, 22–3, 27, 42, 45

US Administration's National Security Strategy 121

US-China trade war 9, 96, 98, 101–4, 110–11

US Environmental Protection Agency (EPA) 57, 62

US-Mexico-Canada Agreement (USMCA) 72

US National Security Act of 1947 134

Vienna Conference on Human Rights 1993 154, 178–9

Von der Leyen, U. 103–4

Weale, A. 33

Weibo 57

What Is Ecological Civilization (Clayton and Schwartz) 46

Wittgenstein, L. 201, 203, 207, 210

Wolfers, A. 133

Wolff, C. 172–3

World Bank 3, 19

World Economic Forum (WEF) 47, 132

World Health Organization (WHO) 2

world market shares **76**

world trade growth *97*

World Trade Organization (WTO) 6, 71–2, 75–82, 102–3, 111–13, 120

World War II 71, 120, 123, 175, 185, 204

Xi Jinping 41, 43, 47–8, 82, 105, 121

Zhang, X. 8

Zum ewigen Frieden (Kant) 107

Zürn, M. 9